Undressing Lesbian Sex

A new series of books from Cassell's Sexual Politics list, Women on Women provides a forum for lesbian, bisexual and heterosexual women to explore and debate contemporary issues and to develop strategies for the advancement of feminist culture and politics into the next century.

COMMISSIONING:

Roz Hopkins
Liz Gibbs
Christina Ruse

Undressing Lesbian Sex

Elaine Creith

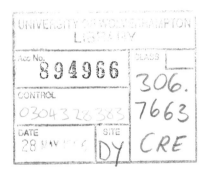

For a catalogue of related titles in our Sexual Politics/Global Issues list please write to us at the address below:

Cassell plc
Wellington House
125 Strand
London
WC2R 0BB

215 Park Avenue South
New York
NY 10003

First published 1996

British Library Cataloguing-in-Publication Data
A catalogue record for this book is available from the British Library.

ISBN: 0 304 328383 (hardback)
    0 304 328499 (paperback)

Typeset by York House Typographic

Printed and bound in Great Britain by Biddles Limited, Guildford and King's Lynn

contents

*a*cknowledgements

I would like to thank the many people whose contributions have helped make this book possible. Included in Chapter 4 are data from two surveys in which I have been involved, and my thanks go to the women who took the time to answer questionnaires either on their sex lives or their drinking habits. The sex survey, originally conceived by Deborah James, was produced in collaboration with SIGMA research, who generously provided input at all stages of the process from design to analysis. The members involved were Peter Davies, Ford Hixon, Michael Stephens, Peter Weatherburn and Andrew Hunt. In addition, contributions made by Rosa Benalto, Diane Richardson and Mary McIntosh in a planning meeting were vital to the strengths of the project. The data were analysed initially by Andrew Hunt, who sadly died on Christmas Day 1992. The detailed statistics are a testimony to his life and work. Peter Weatherburn completed any outstanding computations. For his patience and persistence he has my deepest affection and gratitude. I would also like to thank Jean Waugh for taking the time to advise on the results.

Throughout writing, conversations have primed my thoughts and widened my perspective. Thanks in particular to Valerie Mason-John, Carol Ann Uszkurat, Margaret Melrose, Dr Celia Skinner and Dr Jayne Kavanagh. Thanks also to Beth Follini for the generous loan of her MA dissertation. To those who read the text during its writing, I am grateful for their faith, encouragement and insightful comments. Lynne Segal has not only patiently tolerated yet another delay to my PhD but offered advice and support throughout. Lesley Pattenson, Mary Archer, Miriam Mackie, Wendy Machin, Kerry Hunt and Deborah James have been nothing short of invaluable.

Special thanks go to the team at Cassell who have made this text possible, despite its long overdue deadline: Christina Ruse, Steve Cook and, especially, Roz Hopkins, not only for her patience and reassurance but for her never-failing sense of humour. Writing a book is a lonely and at times frustrating task – it is also a privilege, for many reasons. And the one most apparent to me is the wealth of support I have had around me. I do not have the space to thank all my friends, but no one is forgotten. My family, Jim, Dave, Alex, Jo and Kate have offered encouragement and love across distances far and near. Ann and Bill Wilson have provided practical support. Ian Golten has performed the most remarkable computer troubleshooting while at all times reminding me of his love and friendship. Gillian, Chris, Jane, Mary and Amy have over the past two years provided a supportive and entertaining home life. Marian Judge has always been just a phone call away.

At several points in the book, I break with conventions of writing, and I'm about to do so again with my style of dedication. Having been given so much by the following people in their own unique ways, a solitary name would be an injustice to my support network. Therefore I dedicate this book to the following people: To Naomi Sharpe and Kerry Hunt, who epitomize the warmest and most generous definitions of friendship imaginable. To Jane Cooper, for listening and for being there. To my father, Jimmy Creith, for his never-ending supply of pencils, and my mother, Isabel Creith, for absolutely everything: who has never faltered when I have stumbled, and in whose love and pride for me I have never had to doubt. To Miriam Mackie, for her love, her support and constancy. To Wendy Machin, for being in my life for over a quarter of a century, for promising to stay for the rest, for holding me when it hurts and when it doesn't. And for Deborah James, because of who she is and because she will always have my love. For her in particular I borrow and begin with these words:

> I have come to believe over and over again that what is most important to me must be spoken, made verbal and shared, even at the risk of having it bruised or misunderstood. (Lorde, 1980, p. 11)

introduction

A book on some aspect of lesbianism was inevitable at some point in my life, although I had not anticipated it would be written at the same time as a demanding teaching schedule and with a PhD in progress. As if this were not in itself enough of a challenge, I had moved my attention from the area of lesbian health to focus more specifically on sex and sexuality. Having been aware of my own desires from a young age, my route to becoming a 'lesbian' was one of romance as opposed to an act of conscious resistance. It was to be some time before my passion extended to politics. Moved as I have been by the touch of another woman, the intensity of her desire and the knowing look in her eyes the morning after the night before, I have lived long enough to have been both loved and left, the lover and the leaver. Familiar with pleasure but no stranger to pain. And so having decided to write, I went back to where I first found meaning – desire, romantic fantasy and, eventually, sex.

However, looking back, everything that had once appeared so simple now seemed little more than a carefully constructed conspiracy to oppress large proportions of the population, based on gender, race, ethnicity and other dimensions along which difference is defined. A means of maintaining not only the social structures and traditional sex roles by which women were oppressed (as were men in the narrow confines of masculinity), but the continued subjection of lesbians and gays, and a shoring up of western capitalism. The issues involved were usually complex, often contradictory and always controversial.

I was intrigued, I was in 'love', and once this concept itself was not beyond scrutiny – I was in trouble! How could something as physical as sex be so theoretical? How could the language of love, secrets of seduction and declarations of desire be trapped in such complicated texts? For better or for worse, sex had become my preoccupation. Whatever fantasies

I had entertained about the research required, the reality was inevitably somewhat different. In a society which is becoming increasingly sexualized there is a great deal written about sex. Much less is written on the subject of lesbian sex specifically, although the literature generally available on wider aspects of lesbian and gay culture has proliferated rapidly. Psychology, the discipline which had for a long time consumed so much of my interest and energy, had generated many questions but fewer acceptable answers. When it came down to it, psychology could not live up to its reputation. Sex, not for the first time in my life, was to lead me into territories less familiar. Turning to areas including sociology, cultural studies and political science made for a better account. For while women have a long history of same-sex liaisons, the meanings of these connections have changed, determined by the point in history and the cultural context in which they occurred. The sex about which I write is informed by the past, a distillation of the present, and will inevitably change in the future.

Immersed as I had been for so long in the book, a welcome break arrived in the form of the Lesbian and Gay Pride march and festival in June 1995. For years now, I have gone on these marches, and despite my growing reservations about the balance of the political message and the partying pleasure principle, I'm glad I went. Dragged from my distraction, I was reassured, revitalized and reminded as to why I had embarked on the project. The sequence of events brought many of the issues over which I laboured alive – Pride, while a public statement, became my own private performance. The theme, 'Visibly Lesbian', controversial in its adoption, reflecting the still unresolved misogyny in our community, was displayed proudly be many marching dykes. Everywhere I looked women were holding hands, kissing and hugging – in the park and in the women's tent, some were more intimately intertwined. The sex toy stalls, with their predictably swollen crowds, did not attract me. Whatever products they displayed had long ceased to be a novelty to me – I had worked and reworked the debates surrounding these symbols of sex and their potential meanings.

The one-minute silence organized in memory of all those lost in the battle against AIDS, unsuccessful in its first attempt, was successfully repeated later due to the persistence, direct action and activism which have come to characterize our communities. And as with such silences, much could be heard – cutting across gay/lesbian, black/white, queer/straight. And there were straight people there, in numbers which prompted a comment from a compère on the main stage, which I had never heard issued before. It was a reminder, in addition to the one 'we' got, for those for whom it was not 'their day' to put money in the collecting buckets. This was much-needed revenue to pay for the event and allow for future celebrations. The community had already paid, and would continue to do so in ways beyond those necessary to meet the immediate fiscal debt. For as long as we lacked the rights of full sexual citizenship, differences of sexual identity and their consequences would prevail. And while it was becoming increasingly apparent that the prescriptions of identity were problematic, this awareness could not distract from the vital functions such identities continued to serve, both personally or politically. Closing with Labbi Siffre's 'Something Inside So Strong', a song written originally in protest at apartheid, was a powerful reminder that oppression of sexuality is but one human difference by which people are repressed, subjugated and denied civil rights. No amount of redirecting the route of the Pride march will stop us; no matter how many parks the authorities refuse us entry to – we are not going to go away. Expressions of institutionalized homophobia and prejudice make me angry, but they do not stop me loving – they never will.

Careful as I have been in the writing of this book, wary of words and their power, I cannot complacently assume that what is written is what is read. Even the most conscientiously constructed texts are subject to readings and interpretations other than those intended by the author. Throughout the book I adopt not only the personal pronoun 'I' but the collective 'we'. This is not because I am attempting to speak for others, but as a strategy to nurture a sense of community. In addition, 'communities' is used throughout in the plural, to signify the diversity within; that our subculture, in effect, consists of many different cultures. Just as I do not own or identify with all the approaches and experiences outlined in the text, I do not expect the reader to do so either. There are times in our communities when it is apparent that we share no other common ground than that marked out by sexual preference, and even this is not enough to guarantee cohesion. In a parent culture – the society into which we were born – that operates on heterosexual assumptions, colluding with anti-lesbian and -gay prejudices, and which rarely acknowledges individuals, let alone the lesbian and gay community, my use of we/us/communities, is a deliberate act of empowerment and defiance.

Undressing Lesbian Sex is not an instruction manual or explicit erotica. It is an overview of the forces and ideologies through which we come to think, feel, experience and talk about 'sex'. Comprehensive but not exhaustive. Drawing on academic theories, scientific research and the media of popular culture in the forms of literature, television and film, I have left lesbian sex exposed. With sex as the emphasis, recurring themes are discussed from different perspectives. Sex, as I hope to demonstrate, involves many positions.

Chapter 1, 'Factual Foreplay', provides a selective account of the history of the counter-culture, including the role of sexology (sexual science), feminism and the rise of lesbian and gay sexual/identity politics. The lesbian 'sex wars', including the pornography debates, are discussed, as is the impact of the law (British) upon sexual practice. It concludes at the contemporary cultural moment, with the queer movement. Chapter 2, 'Representation: Primetime Fictions and Real Life Stories', takes a look at how lesbian sex(uality) is represented in fiction, television and film. And while 'love' and 'romance' play a part, they are but two necessary frameworks through which we mediate meaning. The latter part of the chapter focuses on real-life events, and how they are related to our disclosure and discussions around sex and sexuality. Included in this section is an alternative approach to the concept of lesbian safer sex, looking at the impact of sexual abuse upon women and the community in general.

Chapter 3, 'Language: Louder Than Words', examines the role of language in both the parent and counter-culture. Discussion of how we label our partners, why we talk and don't talk in the words we have available, and the limitations of our explicitly sexual vernacular, is accompanied by examples of how lesbians define 'lesbian sex'. Chapter 4, 'A Lesbian's Vital Statistics', details findings from the various sex surveys specifically on or including lesbian women. Special attention is paid to data drawn from a survey of lesbians who attended the Pride festival in London in 1992. Also in this chapter is a discussion of the practice of safer sex, in the age of HIV and AIDS. The chapter concludes with an analysis of the effect of sex surveys in relation to the growing industry of self-help books and the therapy movement generally.

Last but not least, Chapters 5 and 6, 'Butch and Femme 1 and 2', detail the multifaceted butch/femme debate. The biological, the psychological and the cultural all come under close scrutiny. As do the functions which femme and butch serve as a romantic language, an erotic code and a sexual style. Wider meanings of gender, drag, transgender and transsexuality are also documented. A poignant ending in an age not only of sexual uncertainties, but one where we cling desperately to our labels lest we lose our grip and they fall into the space of what academics variously describe as late or post modernity. The contemporary cultural moment where fixed identity is threatened by fluid multiple meanings. Where gender itself, not just sexual practice, is a recognized site of instability.

factual foreplay

This is a book on lesbian sex for the 1990s and in an era encouraging of open communication, I'm going to state my intentions and then you can decide whether or not this meets with your expectations and desires, so we both know where we stand. Consider this a type of 'informative' foreplay which will leave you wanting more. This chapter is a review of lesbian and gay history and sexual politics; it is selective, a flirtation with a vast amount of detail, providing an account of the past and how it informs our thinking today.

Unfortunately a compact social history and sexual politics is not provided in our do-it-yourself lesbian starter kits. And why should it be – what has this got to do with my sex life, you may ask? In fact, the starter kit contained little beyond instructions for a regulation look, a vegetarian cookbook and a cat. It gave little information as to what to do with a girl after we kissed her, and provided little preparatory socialization for the way the rest of society would respond to that kiss. Many of the events of which I write will remind some of a history too powerful to be forgotten, explain to others what was happening when they were too young to notice, and describe to others events before their birth – a history recreated in books, media images and in the words of our older lovers and friends. Our history as women, as lesbians, should not be the sole property of the academy (universities) – secrets held in ivory towers, available only to library ticket holders. All too often, the events and debates that affect our communities are the property of academic departments. Knowledge is held captive in texts by an exclusive language which serves only to perpetuate existing divisions in a society based on class, race and education.

What follows can loosely be referred to as sexual politics – a politics of sexuality, moving beyond and yet related to the politics of governmental structures and their far-reaching rules – a politics of our gender, ethnicity and identity, what we do and who we do it with. Sexuality, like race, ethnicity, gender, disability and a range of socio-economic variables, is identified in society as a means of social division. As a result, lesbians occupy a lower status in the sexual hierarchy or class system. Homosexuality is seen as inferior to heterosexuality. We as individuals are relegated to second-class sexual citizenship. For many, such a dislocation merely builds on already marginalized positions, as in the case of race and ethnicity, as sexuality is overlaid onto more visible signifiers used to oppress difference – resulting in the experience of multiple oppression.

The hierarchical organization of sexual practice does not stop with the creation of a heterosexual/homosexual binarism in which heterosexuality is considered superior. Practices like sado-masochism are located even lower down the hierarchy. Many in our counter-culture are intolerant of such preferences and SM practitioners find themselves not only alienated from the ruling sexual order, but also marginalized from those already occupying peripheral positions in the sexual society.

When you reach for your lover in bed the immediate meaning is deeply personal and private. On another level, its meaning is read in a context by a wider society. Sex and sexuality, therefore, can never be apolitical. It is not my intention to take the fun and pleasure out of our lives – awareness of sexual politics does not have to be a passion killer; for some, awareness of political correctness provides a list of rules to be broken, fuelling desire. While having sex, I do not think politically; in fact, in true hedonistic style with probably a slight 'Mills and Boon' contamination, I am less conscious of thinking than of feeling. Yet without a doubt, my love, passion and desire for her can all be viewed politically, in a political context. What 'makes' us lesbian, how we have sex, Pride marches and the age of consent for gay men – all have political implications for us, and like those more embarrassing moments during sex, they have a nasty habit of appearing when we least expect them. And before we really get down to it, I think it's important that we talk about all these issues.

The birth of the lesbian and the construction of her girlfriend

Lesbians (and homosexuals) have not always existed as a category. While same-sex erotic behaviours undisputedly have a long history, by comparison the history of the lesbian identity is relatively short. It was only at the turn of the century that lesbians and homosexuals became defined according to their practices.[1] These labels, deployed in the works of early sexologists (sexual scientists), allowed for the stigmatization of individuals, reflecting the religious and medical ideologies that were codified into social norms. Thus the scientific identification of a specific type of sexual deviant gave birth to the first in a long line of lesbians and homosexuals, in effect laying the foundations upon which the community as we recognize it today was built.

Of course, typical of patriarchal society, male homosexuals, as opposed to female homosexuals, were the centre of scientific enquiry and social speculation. Amidst the general acceptance of women's inferiority, lesbians got the dubious privilege of specific sexological scrutiny from turn-of-the-century sexologists like Havelock Ellis. In his phallocentric (male-centred) quest, he identified two types of lesbian: the invert and the pervert. The inverts were those who were 'born that way', a product of irrevocable biological mismanagement, and were usually of the 'masculine' variety. Perverts were just as deviant, but were usually corrupted by the aforementioned invert on the hunt. Ellis, who was married to a lesbian, went on to suggest that all lesbian sex involved penis substitutes, believing that we couldn't get it together without one. Leaving aside his prehistoric patent of the dildo, such thinking around the biological and the social, in the guise of the invert and the pervert, epitomizes current debate as to the cause of our erotic preference. This is reflected not only in the enquiry of both scientists and parents ('what did we do wrong?'/'well it sure as hell didn't come from my side of the family'), but in our own communities – producing a range of answers on which we ourselves do not agree.

Beliefs that we were born this way, that we have no choice but to be lesbian, that our sexuality is caused by something inside us, can collectively be referred to as essentialist – the idea that our sexuality is predetermined in some way, and is therefore devoid of social or historical influence.

Notions which challenge such biological/psychological explanations, while emphasizing the role of social context, can loosely be termed social constructionist. According to such theories, sexuality is not a biological/psychic given but a social construction, reflecting ideas produced in a specific time and place. (This does not mean that we easily reconstruct ourselves.) Some constructionist theories give the individual as little choice as the essentialists, the difference being that the determining influence is external, not internal.

Some of us believe we are born lesbian, while others believe that our sexuality is more fluid and flexible, and hence at any point we can become lesbian. Such polarized frameworks are related to the homosexual–heterosexual dichotomy or sexual binarism, the tendency to see things as either/or. A blatant omission of such duality is bisexuality, which such sexual segregation fails to explain.

It appears to be a basic human need that we understand ourselves and our environment, as it allows us to function more efficiently. That our sexuality is a target for such enquiry, however, is potentially less a product of cognition (thought processes) than of a culture obsessed with gender difference and sexual binarism. Many of us (irrespective of orientation) at some time wonder why we are attracted to certain people, especially when prompted to do so by the discomfort of relationship breakdown. To question why we are lesbian seems a characteristic of the 'coming out process'. If a sexual hierarchy or caste system did not exist, however, it is unlikely that we would feel the need for such a focus. Heterosexuals do not feel the same pressure to examine the nature of their desires. It is in the context of a society which invests so much energy in identifying and trying to explain 'minority sexual behaviours' that we learn how to think and perceive. In a culture where sexuality was not used to divide and oppress, where orientation or preference was not an issue, our experience would be different. But we live in a society which tells us our feeling and attractions are wrong and therefore it is inevitable we may question 'what makes us lesbian'? We look for an explanation, because everyone else does.

You may be less concerned with how you got that way and more interested in who you're going to date tonight. Born that way? Made that way? Who cares? The implications of such arguments are thus: If we were born this way, we have a congenital problem which may or may not be amenable to change by medical intervention. They are still a long way off from finding the gay gene, if they ever do – and for what? Do prospective parents really want the opportunity to abort a lesbian/gay foetus? Certain areas of our brain may 'look' different – does this really predispose us to be sexually attracted to the girl next door? The appeal of essentialist arguments lies in 'we can't help it so stop victimizing us'. Constructionist arguments allow us to read our sexuality as more flexible, and our lesbianism as a positive lifestyle or political choice. By making such a decision, however, we pay the price. Our failure to conform to accepted sexual norms results in stigmatization and alienation. We suffer – but it's our choice. Constructionist arguments allow for greater analysis of the political implications of sexuality. Sexual minorities in any social system are stigmatized to ensure the conformity of the masses – sexuality is constructed as a form of social control.[2]

Straight ... to the Sexual Revolution

The filters through which we see, feel and think about our world are shaped by the language we use. For example, essentialists refer to a sexual 'orientation', constructionists, a 'preference'. Thus when we talk of the sexual revolution, it conjures up images of rebels and radicals; we think of the overthrow of an existing order and replacement with a new and potentially enlightened one. In the 1960s, the morality and inhibitions left over from the Victorian era were challenged. Although this was not the first 'sexual revolution', the oral history of the 1960s generation ensured the survival of a most recent past. Fashions of the 1960s may be experiencing a renaissance in the 1990s, but the revival has a definite un-Sixties restraint to it. Image and music are acceptable imports, but the ideas are out of context and popular notions of 1960s sex seem dangerously unappealing. The 'permissive' decade did encourage activities like swinging (partner swapping), group sex and acceptability of a woman's right to screw around. As is common of social revolutions, it influenced younger generations more. For those who wanted it, the climate had changed – the status of sex was elevated and pleasure prioritized, not only his but hers as well. So she gets to come too, but what if she wants to come with another woman? How revolutionary are we talking here? The revolution catered for the masses, an extension of the heterosexual imperative – fucking, sucking and swapping were all encouraged as long as your partner/s were the opposite sex and you never forgot the first golden rule of sex: real sex is synonymous with heterosexuality.

The Kinsey studies[3] of the 1950s had demonstrated the diversity of sexual behaviour that was then on the menu. In the 1960s Masters and Johnson[4] (building upon Kinsey's work) made the sexological discovery confirming what most women knew already – that orgasms were located in the clitoris, not the vagina. While science celebrated its anatomical breakthrough, 'presumably its discovery was as much a surprise to its owners as the discovery of America was to its indigenous occupants.'[5] Although some more astute writers like Ann Koedt[6] did realize the implications of the clitoral orgasm from the point of view of masturbation and lesbian sex, the implications were not explored in the popular do-it-yourself texts of the time, or by the leading sexological experts like

Masters and Johnson. In their terms, it was clear that women had to learn to orgasm from intercourse, the 'traction' of thrusting stimulating the clitoris. What was new, in emphasis, was the importance attached to women's sexual satisfaction. Sexologists were erecting a new sexual standard. Research was revealing new problems – and researchers marketed new treatments. His coming too soon became 'premature ejaculation'; her vaginal tension preventing penetration was now 'vaginismus'. When the heterosexual procreative pleasure machine ground to a halt, willing assistants instructed on where to lubricate and how to change the screw.

When it came to lesbian sex, the best-selling manuals of the day did not encourage it. This was not always from some moral platform, but on the grounds that it was not as good as real heterosexual sex (permissible as sexual play or as a warm-up exercise for action with the boys, but discouraged as a lifestyle choice). The rise of sexology had allowed the emergence of the sexual expert, and a proliferation of the sex text. We could excite ourselves, solve those little problems, and check that we were doing it right. Those lesbians avidly scanning the index for the 'L' word – or failing that, the ever-familiar compromise of the 'H' word – would have been sadly disappointed. In one of these delightful little numbers by Dr David Reuben[7] in a book called – check this out girls – *Everything You Wanted To Know About Sex (But Were Afraid To Ask)*, lesbians are covered in several pages. Here's a man who has obviously never had lesbian sex – didn't he realize foreplay takes at least five chapters? If he can cover lesbian sex in a couple of pages he's hardly going to tell me everything I wanted to know. Playing on all existing stereotypes, but neglecting the gender difference emphasized by so many social scientists, he failed to differentiate between gay and lesbian sexual behaviour. Like the (gay) boys, according to the doctor, we are 'just as' promiscuous and sex is just as unsatisfying, although we win hands down on romance. His explanation, couched in the jargon of mathematics and anatomical science, was indicative of little more than ignorance and bigotry:

 Like their male counterparts, lesbians are handicapped by having only half the pieces of the anatomical jigsaw puzzle. Just as one penis plus one penis equals nothing, one vagina plus another vagina still equals zero. ... basically all homosexuals are alike – looking for love where there can be no love and looking for sexual satisfaction where there can be no lasting satisfaction.[8]

Much as I dislike academic elitism, would you trust a doctor whose basic maths was this bad? Surely one vagina plus one vagina equals two vaginas? As such a 'knowledgeable' man, did he do as many men do and simply forget about the clitoris – even the extra-long ones (he suggested) we're supposed to have? And as for the comment on love ... how can a self-professed expert on some of the most basic and seemingly essential tenets of human behaviour ignore such a wealth of affection as exists in our communities?

On feminism, fornication and the lavender menace

The women's liberation movement in the 1960s emerged at a time of general social upheaval and activism. Black power, student uprisings and anti-war lobbies in North America impacted upon British society, and the re-emergence[9] of feminism on both sides of the Atlantic was characteristic of the era of social protest. The goals of feminism were broad and far-reaching. An elimination of gendered inequality and the empowerment of women were the basic philosophies. In addition, reflecting the social context of the time, many women viewed sexual liberation as being as important as other objectives. In an era of sexual freedom, women wanted the same rights as men. For many women, sexual agency was as central as any other accepted goal – 'part of my attraction to feminism involved the right to be a sexual person.'[10]

However, feminists soon began to question the gains of a sexual revolution that did not change things very much, and was beginning to seem like all talk and no action. Sure, we gained some sexual liberation within the constraints of male ideas of sex and pleasure, and the earth may have moved with a little anatomical awareness, but little else did. The energy the movement put into revolutionary fucking was soon reinvested in the ongoing goals of women's safety from male aggression, reproductive rights around abortion and contraception, and the far-reaching implications of gender roles and unequal power relations.

While writing of 'feminism' it is important to acknowledge that reference to a unitary movement is somewhat misleading. Although united by global philosophies of women's liberation, feminism is an umbrella term for a range of different theoretical perspectives. These divergent theories relate to the fragmentation of the women's movement as a whole. Of interest in a book of this nature is how 'feminism' generally influenced women's sexuality in terms of social attitudes, sexual behaviours, the challenge to sextyping and role socialization, and the realities of sexual danger.

A particular perspective which is essential to any discourse on lesbian sex is that of radical, revolutionary or lesbian feminism. Essential to this particular brand of feminism are the concepts 'heteropatriarchy' and 'compulsory heterosexuality'[11] – the idea that patriarchal society is maintained by compulsory heterosexuality. Women, it is argued, will never gain equality while they are in subordinate sexual positions to men, a positioning resulting from the inherent inequalities of institutionalized heterosexuality. By accepting that heterosexual liaisons are inevitable, we as women are colluding with our own oppression. The only way to challenge the heteropatriarchal order is to stop 'sleeping with the enemy'. The so-called sexual revolution was merely a large-scale recruitment drive, the missionary position symbolizing our position in the hierarchy – underneath men.

The women's movement lacked a consensus as to the primary cause of oppression – patriarchy, capitalism or heteropatriarchy – and hostility amongst feminists began to fragment the movement as rifts appeared from the 1970s onwards. In the early days of the women's movement, lesbians or the 'lavender menace' had been discouraged from being too visible for fear of alienating the wider movement and the society being targeted for change. However, as radical feminism gained momentum, heterosexual feminists were made to feel like the second-rate citizens, it being their sexuality which was betraying true feminist principles. Radical feminists advocated the adoption of 'political lesbianism', whereby women withdrew their energies from men and focused them on the sisterhood and the developing lesbian nation. This was the only way to bring heteropatriarchy to its knees (so to speak). Feminism was the theory, lesbianism became the practice. Any woman could be a lesbian. Thus with the emergence of radical feminism, the much earlier, wider goal of maximizing sexual potential shifted to fifty ways to leave your (male) lover.

The idea of the political lesbian popularized at this time, was prescribed by the Leeds Revolutionary Feminists: 'Our definition of a political lesbian is a woman identified woman who does not fuck men. It does not mean compulsory sexual activity with women.' Women could become lesbians but did not have to do what sexologists said they did. By adopting the term 'political lesbian', the radical feminists moved the identity of lesbian women beyond that dictated by sexual activity, as any woman who wished to identify politically as lesbian was lesbian – just so long as she did not fuck with men. To many working-class and black dykes/lesbians, outside the movement, all this sounded like teaching your grandmother to suck pussy – or not, as the case may be . . .

For many lesbians, in describing lesbianism as a form of direct-action politics and setting guidelines for sex which negated their realities, political lesbianism was not the answer. To some, holding a woman, loving her in every way possible, dressing and acting to excite her, were not actions to obliterate heteropatriarchy or even *consciously political* acts – they were acts of love, lust and desire. Adoption of the lesbian identity for political reasons went hand in hand with acceptance of prescriptive notions of acceptable sex. Politically correct sex did not in any way mimic heterosexual sex; there was more to the act than orgasm, and desire was not to start with or be contaminated in any way by objectification of your lover, that is, to see her as a sexual object, to respond on the level of pure physical attraction. Monogamy was also discouraged on the grounds that 'personal ownership' was an attribute of the heteropatriarchal institution of marriage and that lesbians should not try to possess other women in the same way.

The principle was not the same as the 'free love' era of the 'permissive Sixties'. If the sexual revolution of the 1960s was a recruitment drive for heteropatriarchy, radical feminists tried to even the score with political lesbianism. Even before the emergence of radical feminism, lesbianism had been equated with feminism by those eager to denigrate the movement, fearful of the threat posed by a collective force of women. It was deployed as a term of abuse to deter women from challenging the male order, not as a celebratory title for the collective energy of the sisterhood. It is a familiar tactic which remains in circulation two decades later. As a result of radical feminism some women did become lesbians – some, but by no means all. Neither were all lesbians feminists – feminism during this time became predominantly a white middle-class movement and its 'membership' reflected this. Like many social movements, the omissions were not so much deliberate, more a consequence of prioritizing gender over other factors upon which stratification is based: race, ethnicity, class, disability. However, in some instances the exclusion was not unintentional, as women experienced a hostile exile – certainly from radical feminists – for relating through butch/femme roles or indulging in SM sex. This became increasingly common in the sexual struggles within the lesbian communities in the 1980s, commonly known as the sex wars.

Another revolution and a lesbian sex war

The 'sex wars' reached fever pitch in the late 1980s with the growth of the lesbian sex industry and the proliferation of lesbian sex texts. The United States played host to several sexperts including JoAnn Loulan, Susie 'sexpert' Bright and Pat Califia – all advocating uninhibited, adventurous and seemingly value-free sex. The books of Bright and Loulan, entertaining and informative, provided positive affirmation, West Coast-style. Whatever you were doing, you were doing right – and in Califia's assertive approach to SM, instructions were available on how to do it safely. Loulan, with her psychobabble, Bright with her in-your-face and on-your-backs attitude, and Califia, the pussy-piercing public image of SM sex, have not been without their critics. Condemnation stemmed not only from women's ego defences as sexual anxieties surfaced (breaking down the closet door was hard enough, but now the bedroom?), but because of what they were advocating. Strap-ons, lesbian erotica, and playing with the dynamics of power, pain and pleasure transgressed not only the social norms dictated by the righteous in society, but also the boundaries of political correctness.

Some of the more well-published voices in this debate are radical feminists – who see the aforementioned activities as imports from heteropatriarchy, the main effect being to ensure its survival. Radical feminists oppose the use of sex toys, role-play, sado-masochistic sex and pornography. They argue that sex toys are a symbol of male domination, butch/femme are emulations of heteropatriarchal inequality, sado-masochists are would-be Nazis, and porn the plaything of the heteropatriarchal devil. In a review of JoAnn Loulan's *Lesbian Sex*,[13] radical feminists warn of the dangers of this 'hetero' identified text, moving from Loulan being a heterophile because her therapeutic training was based on 'marriage counselling', to practically calling her heterosexual because she is a biological mother. According to these writers, neither Pat Califia nor JoAnn Loulan are 'real lesbians'. It would seem that biological motherhood, professional training based on heterosexual paradigms, and particular sexual practices, can result in your lesbian credentials being revoked.

As the 1980s progressed, some communities underwent the transformation of a lesbian sexual revolution more than a decade after the notorious Swinging Sixties. The timing could possibly be explained in terms of a community coming of age and reaching sexual maturity, the irony here being that a glance at some of the works of more 'risky' writers like Nestle remind us that the issues of 'contemporary controversy' are far from new. The main difference was that in bygone eras you could not buy your strap-on at a shop on Valencia (in San Francisco) or in the East End of London. The sex industry as we know it today did not exist. As sexual repression began once more to raise its head in an era where gay men were altering behaviour patterns in response to HIV and AIDS, sexual communication was encouraged, and – bang – the lesbian sex revolution occurred in the midst of all the chaos.

The sex texts were already around, reassuring, encouraging and daring. Loulan labelled problems and provided solutions in typical West Coast style, 101 ways to keep your inner child amused while your grown-up wants to get it on! Loulan's approach, engaging and amusing, demonstrated that if this was a revolution it was going to be fun and for those more difficult moments a twelve-step programme should do the trick! As DIY books go, Loulan has a recipe for success both for the older reader and the less discerning inner child. With the growth of such literature and the development of a lesbian sexual consciousness, albeit hindered by a socialized sexual shyness, lesbian sex was boldly put on the agenda, which then, of course, was wrapped in a brown paper bag. What constituted actual lesbian sex became a question in itself, as did whether or not we needed to discuss it at all. Our revolution had turned into a war between those who advocated sexual liberation, the 'sexual radicals' for whom anything went, and the radical lesbian feminists who argued against the adoption of certain sexual activities, favouring the adherence to prescriptive notions of lesbian sex, and a commitment to the notion of 'the personal is political', (just as long as they were the politics of radical feminism). Those who tried to subvert the politically correct into a game of authoritarian 'correction' were seen as a threat to the lesbian nation.

The commercialization of the lesbian sex industry was not so much a by-product of the lesbian sex revolution as the fertile ground in which the revolutionary seeds were being planted. With the development of the lesbian and gay identity, and the emergence of the gay ghettos in large urban areas, the 'scene' developed as we created our own pubs and clubs, pleasure domes of safety and reality validation. Commercialization did not stop there as a range of pink services emerged and the sex industry was no exception. The expansion of consumer culture allowed people a certain freedom of choice as well as encouraging a type of individualism more characteristic of Thatcherism. The extension of the pink economy is testimony to a counter-culture: a visible population with needs and desires. The products made by the heterosexual and gay men's industry were inadequate – so lesbians created their own. In an atmosphere of accusations of misguided energy, the 'misguided' continued to purchase and play.

The commodification of lesbian sex has created our own sex industry in which the silicone dildo is only the tip of the iceberg. We now have our own porn industry, sex worker Annie Sprinkle claiming that 'nineties lesbians are definitely in the vanguard of the new porn.'[14] The role of lesbian pornography remains equally as contentious as pornography generally, adding to the irreconcilable differences which were to rupture feminist unity in the 1980s. At this time, pornography was seen by anti-pornography activists as being the prime cause of women's oppression, its 'humiliating and degrading' representations seen as perpetuating sexual harassment and sexual violence. Women worked in the industry in service of men. While pornography continued to exist, Andrea Dworkin and many others insisted, women could never be free from sexual danger. Activists in North America proposed legislative changes to enable women to fight back against the negative consequences of the industry.[15] Their attempts have so far been largely unsuccessful, despite alliances made with the right, who co-opted the feminist agenda for their own purposes. The persuasive influence of North American anti-porn activists took hold in Britain. Proposed anti-porn legislation, based on the American model, was also unsuccessful.[16]

At a glance, it is easy to see why the explicit sexual representation characteristic of pornography is a prime target for feminists striving to end gender inequalities and the constant threat of sexual danger. Across the movement, many feminists would agree as to the sexist, if not humiliating and degrading nature of pornographic imagery and text. However, this broad consensus goes no further, as opinion is divided over both the role and effects of pornography in patriarchal culture. The split between anti-pornography feminists and anti-anti-pornography feminists resulted from such debates. The anti-pornography feminists argued that while the sex industry remains in place, women will be forever seen as an expendable commodity. The continual degradation and exploitation of women in this fashion prevents the wider goals of feminism ever being achieved. For as long as women are exploited and degraded, equality will be unobtainable and the realities of sexual danger sustained. Their arguments are supported by an extensive body of scientific evidence,[17] which shows that pornography is harmful, not only encouraging sexual violence and the exploitation of women, but dangerously desensitizing the viewer to the reality of such abuses.

However, social scientists, like feminists, cannot agree on this issue. The evidence is far from conclusive, for while it is convincing, there is an equitable amount of research which contradicts it, suggesting the effects of pornography are benign.[18] And any review of the research must be conducted with an appreciation of the limitations of psychological research methods and the potential political uses to which the findings may be put. While anti-pornography arguments have credence, they must be viewed in the wider context of a patriarchal, capitalist society where women are not only striving for equality but for sexual empowerment. An outright ban on sexual representation would not address the complexity of women's oppression, concomitant sexual danger, or the nature of women's desires. Equating pornography with all that is negative in women's lives is an over-simplification. Some women enjoy commercially produced porn. For others, many of its familiar themes form part of a private fantasy life. Porn, like fantasy, can offer escapism and taboo without running the risks of reality. A counter-argument is that there is a very real risk of fantasy running over into reality, manifesting itself in violence against women and in the behaviour of women re-enacting male styles of sexual power play.

Up to this point I have been discussing pornography without providing a definition, to demonstrate that you the reader will have applied your own understanding of the term. I did not specify whether the sexual representation was photographic, filmic or literary. Definitions vary, ranging from: any sexually explicit material designed to titillate (as typical of the liberal position), any portrayal of sexuality outside the context of the procreating heterosexual married couple (as typical of the moral right, who also oppose any sex education that applies to anything beyond the aforementioned narrow constraints of acceptability) and the various feminist definitions reflecting the diametric oppositions of the debate. To talk of the pornographic is to refer to the illicit and taboo. What constitutes pornography to some may not be read in the same way by others. For example, homoeroticism is frequently labelled porn and censored as a result, even when designed as a medium for health education. Writings labelled 'erotica' by publishers are branded pornographic by some readers – for example, Sheba's texts, *Serious Pleasure* and *Restricted Country*.[19]

So what can be said about the pornography/erotica distinction? Erotica is supposedly devoid of the gendered inequalities on which a lot of porn rests. It is supposedly more artistic, a property of high culture as opposed to low. Cherry Smyth succinctly sums up popularist notions of difference by describing porn as masturbatory and erotica as celebratory.[20] In everyday language, erotica also lacks the emotive connotations so readily associated with the word pornography.

It seems ironic that a judicial system responsible for controlling the sex industry lacks water-tight definitions of what constitutes porn. It is understandable, however, not only because of the difficulties in defining something so subjective, and the intricacies of a capitalist culture, but because lack of clarity is functional, allowing for the over-application of vague legal concepts to representations produced by sexual minorities. In 1984, when charges were brought against staff working at London's Gay's the Word bookshop, stock was seized under the archaic Customs Consolidation Act (1896) on the grounds that the material was indecent and obscene. The charges against the nine individuals were dropped – the texts were not so much 'obscene' as simply lesbian or gay. Some of the books seized were already available in the UK and were used in higher education courses. So apparent is the double standard that lesbian and gay books are targeted while het-designed soft porn is accessible to anyone who can reach the shelf!

So where does lesbian pornography leave us? By lesbian porn I mean porn depicting lesbian sexuality for a lesbian market, made by lesbians, as opposed to that made by men for the male gaze and men's arousal. Are lesbian pornographers merely continuing to exploit women in their adoption of heteropatriarchal capitalist practice? Or are they responding to a commercial need of a counter-culture starved of its own sexual reality? Watching/reading pornographic fantasy does not necessarily mean we take up the position of the male 'subject' viewing the female 'object'. The boundaries of subject–object are fluid; we can be either and both at once. On the one hand, by enjoying porn we could be accused of acting in a male-identified, anti-feminist, pro-patriarchal way. On the other, we are claiming our right to represent our desires, demonstrating a pro-active sexual agency.

The 1980s has seen lesbian-made porn movies, texts and magazines. *On Our Backs* in North America and *Quim* in Britain are two such magazines. Available through specialist bookshops, they carry stories, information and graphic images for the budding sexual connoisseur. *Quim* has since gone out of print, although another magazine called *Common Denominator* has appeared in its place. Can those of us who can find or afford such literature, read it without losing our feminist credentials?

Researchers are always keen to inform us that lesbians have more in common with heterosexual women than gay men, on many variables including sexual behaviour. Do women really want porn? Or are pulp romances the socially accepted feminine equivalent? Does the desire to view some form of sexual representation make us male identified, or sexually revolutionized assertive women? The goal of safety and equality is not incompatible with our sexual exploration. The debates over pornography and the lesbian sex wars reveal some interesting contradictions. For example, some anti-porn activists insist on showing the exact material they are trying to get banned from circulation. A consequence of the sex wars was a rise in consumer demand for sexual material. Meanwhile, pro-porn activists maintain that pornography does not promote violence or degradation, yet claim that lesbian pornography promotes education and empowerment. The politics of the porn debates are complex and writers on both sides are well informed, passionate and persuasive.

Gay Liberation; lesbians and gay men do it together ...

While the 1960s are commonly coupled in the popular imagination with 'free love', the 1970s are often associated with what is loosely referred to as gay liberation, a period in which we became out, loud and proud. As in North America, the 1950s and 60s had been characterized by the emergence of homophile organizations, revolutionary in their existence, timid in their approach (by today's standards).

These organizations aimed to improve the situation of lesbians and gays in the straight world, while providing a sense of belonging and support. In North America, The Daughters of Bilitis organization discouraged role-playing – living as butch and femme – because it was seen as detrimental to our cause. By the late 1960s the lesbian and gay communities on both sides of the Atlantic, inspired by the social movements of civil rights and student unrest, were ready for a change. The change began late one summer evening at the Stonewall bar in New York. To the clientele, familiar with police raids and harassment, that night was a push too far, and a riot began which lasted over two days. The resistance was seen as the dawn of a new era – a new politicized movement based on a more visible cultural identity. A force the New York Police Department could neither contain nor control.

In the UK it was a movement we literally imported, as the London version of the Gay Liberation Front (GLF), formed in 1970, was the work of two young men returning from a trip to America. Gay liberation as an organized movement was short-lived, as it was subject to the type of faction-forming characteristic of most political groups. The membership, typically white, male and middle class, were ambitious and innovative – existing organizations like the Campaign for Homosexual Equality feared its radical tactics of leafleting the streets, on the grounds that it would alienate the mainstream, preventing further legislative reform. GLF's manifesto documented its goals and demands, including 'honour, identity, and liberation'.[21] Amongst its other demands was the freedom to hold hands and kiss in public. Despite its apparent radical nature at the time, the press seemed to offer tacit acceptance in the absence of any mainstream public response. Lacking the energy and inspiration afforded the American experience by Stonewall, and plagued by horizontal hostility as lesbians withdrew due to endemic sexism, the movement burned out by 1973, with its London office closing. The Gay Liberation Front may not have instigated the revolutionary change implied by its name, but the transition triggered by its formation, if not its manifesto, was irreversible. As the 1970s progressed, more people came out – though not to the extent hoped for by GLF, who advocated it as a strategy for change of the status quo and prevailing gender norms.

Ironically, while paying lip service to sexism and adopting the strategies of the feminist movement, GLF did little for 'lesbian liberation'. The movement lost momentum not only because we lacked the energy and excitement of Stonewall, but also because of the redirection of lesbian energy into feminism. Sexual identity proved inadequate cement to keep lesbians and gay men working together when so many experiences and goals differed. In addition, GLF not only lacked support from the public but from many in our own communities, shy of its visibility and militancy. The first Pride march in 1972 numbered 2000, dramatic for its time, but timid in comparison to estimates of 150,000 in 1994. GLF may not have created a sexual utopia, or burned the closets for firewood, but it added momentum to an unstoppable surge of lesbian and gay activism.

Lesbian outlaw – outside the law

It is said that during the reign of Queen Victoria she refused to have lesbianism included in the criminal codes (in other words, made illegal) because she did not believe women would engage in such behaviours. This is how the popular myth goes, but set in the historical context of a tradition where 'bed warmers' were employed to warm a lady's bed and keep her company through the night, could there be an alternative explanation? Lesbianism is still omitted from the criminal codes of Britain – it is not illegal to be lesbian (although this is not the case worldwide). Male homosexuality was criminalized in 1885; prior to this the sodomy laws introduced in the 1500s were used. Legislation by the then monarch, Henry VIII, brought sodomy under state law as opposed to that of the church. Although this act was used against homosexuals, they were not an identifiable group; anyone could be executed for committing this heinous crime. For a man notorious for killing his wives as a solution to infertility and for creating new religious sects for self-gain, his hypocrisy is as typical as that of many modern legislators. There is little documentation of the persecution of widows, spinsters and witches around the same time, when mere social withdrawal from men could result in death.

In 1885 the 'Labouchère Amendment' (Section 11, the Gross Indecency charge) was introduced into the Criminal Law Amendment Act making homosexual (male) acts, either public or private, illegal and punishable by imprisonment with or without hard labour. .This Act was also intended to legislate against prostitution – an oppressive measure directed at working-class women, part of which raised the age of consent from thirteen years to sixteen years. The 1898 Vagrancy Act also tightened legislation on prostitution and homosexual soliciting. As already mentioned, during this time the 'advances' of sexology had created the homosexual and lesbian identities: both were stigmatized but only men were criminalized, as they posed more of a threat to patriarchal order. It was only with women's increasing education and economic opportunity that it became apparent that women could become a force for instability.

The fact that we were not outlawed protected us from prosecution – not persecution. Although less visible at the beginning of the twentieth century than gay men, we were still subject to the same stigma. Since gay liberation, we have fought against legislative measures directed at gay men, not out of some kind of 'penal' envy, but because of the realities of second-class sexual citizenship (and that's before we get on to women's subordination) – the statutory disparity of civil liberties, attendant with a lesbian/gay identity. Working on initiatives with gay men is not always easy in communities where the gendered inequalities parallel those in the parent culture. Such unions are not contra-indicative to the wider ideologies of feminism, although they may appear so on close examination of specific doctrines, e.g. separatism. When laws discriminate against gay men, lesbian communities – even those living in segregation – feel the repercussions. Homophobia, sexism and heterosexism function as inter-dependent oppressive systems, operating against both gender and sexual orientation.

In 1928, in the decade when women would become enfranchised, and Radclyffe Hall's book, *The Well of Loneliness*, was to be banned on the grounds of obscenity, an attempt was made to criminalize lesbianism by bringing it under the Labouchère Amendment as 'Acts of Gross Indecency by Females'. The attempt failed, not through any desire to protect the rights of deviants, but to prevent the perversion spreading – containment would do until they could find a cure! Some of the speeches against its introduction were in effect early constructionist arguments based on notions of some type of erotic contagion, as men in the House of Lords obviously feared the widespread adoption of lesbianism: 'You are going to tell the whole world that there is such an offence, to bring it to the notice of women who have never heard of it, never thought of it, never dreamed of it. I think that is a very great mischief.'[22] With true British imperialist arrogance, Lord Desart thought legislation would influence the obviously easily corruptible global sexual hierarchy. (I wonder how many politicians wish David Wiltshire had been given the same caution![23]) Lord Birken-head followed in similar vein with 'I would be bold enough to say that of every thousand women, taken as a whole, 999 have never even heard a whisper of these practices.'[24] Even in the absence of data for this period, we're talking not so much 'gross acts of indecency' as 'gross acts of under-estimation', as I'm sure his successors would admit, having been con-fronted by several representatives of this 'noxious and horrible suspi-cion'[25] abseiling down to greet them in 1988.[26]

In 1967 when homosexuality was decriminalized for gay men over twenty-one, as long as what they did was done in private, there was no mention of lesbianism in the new legislation. Although the Act seemed to suggest greater freedom in private, the emphasis of the public–private divide resulted in harsher policing of the public. The Wolfenden Report on which the reform was based had been completed ten years previously, but the government was slow to implement it, first because of the pending election and then by further pontificating that society had to be ready for the social change. One of the early attempts to implement it was sup-ported by a very young MP, Margaret Thatcher – however, as was to become apparent, this was her one and only flirtation with the notion of fairer treatment. Lesbianism was mentioned in the Wolfenden Report, but only in the context of demonstrating that this (as well as adultery) was just as damaging to family life, and therefore to isolate one unnatural vice (in the form of homosexuality) was unjust. The age of consent at which individuals are allowed to have sex, since 1885, has been sixteen for heterosexuals, and was twenty-one for gay men until changes to the 1994 Criminal Justice Bill lowered this to eighteen. The rationale behind the age of consent is supposedly one of protection, to protect the young from sex. The law states that those under the age of sixteen or eighteen, depending on your fancy, are not allowed to have sex, and this law is for their own good. The continuing disparity of the consent laws gives a clear message: homosexuality is dangerous.

Although without an age of consent or a gross indecency clause, not all lesbian sex is beyond the arm of the law. The case I'm thinking of, however, gives new meaning to the debate of what constitutes lesbian sex, as the right of definition should first and foremost lie with the women or girls involved. In November 1991, seventeen-year-old Jennifer Saunders was charged with indecently assaulting two girls, aged fifteen and sixteen, by pretending to be a man and engaging in sexual relations. In court, both the girls claimed they would not have had sex had they known Jennifer was a woman. In her defence, she maintained they knew and that she was 'passing'[27] at their request, to hide the fact that they were lesbians.

At issue here was not the age of consent but consent itself. While sentencing her to six years in prison, in summing up Judge Crabtree said:

> I suppose that both girls would rather have been raped by some young man ... I assume you must have some sort of bisexual feelings and I suspect that you have contested the case in the hope of getting some ghastly fame from it. I feel you may be a menace to young girls.[28]

There speaks a man who has never been raped. There speaks a man who has no idea of the pain of being scorned, ridiculed and pathologized by a media with no respect for privacy. There speaks a man who has no concept of 'presumed innocent until proven guilty'. What greater crime is there than a member of the judicial system who cannot even entertain the notion that individuals may contest the charges on the grounds that they are innocent? There speaks a judge in the same judicial system which lets male rapists go free on the grounds that a wife's pregnancy makes it understandable that a stepfather should abuse his daughter, or that a girl can recover from rape by a fifteen-year-old boy if he pays for a holiday. He further commented that in an era of openness around lesbianism and bisexuality, he wanted the sentence to make people 'count the cost'[29] of their behaviour: in the absence of anti-lesbian legislation he resorted to playing on women's fears. The judiciary made an example of Jennifer Saunders.

Smyth documents how LABIA (Lesbians Answer Back in Anger)[30] were the only women's group to demonstrate on Jennifer Saunders' behalf, and questions whether or not this was because of the use of the dildo, or because of her passing. Both these acts did provoke a lot of reactive distancing from lesbians, as many felt the need to distinguish between their lesbianism and that of Jennifer Saunders. Butch and femme was one thing, but passing as a man? It is equally, if not more likely, that many women did not protest because of the nature of the offence in question, that of sexual assault. That both 'the perpetrator' and 'victims' were women evoked a lot of confusion which left many reluctant to act. The issues which the case raised were not only the usual ones related to rape, coercion and sexual violence, but also that these are potential realities in the lesbian community (though not necessarily in this case).

What is unusual about the Jennifer Saunders prosecution is that it was not just her lesbian relationships that were brought into the public eye, but her sexual activity. Here we not only had a lesbian, but one brandishing a dildo! I wonder why the male-dominated media are not frightened by the prospect of such effective passing. If all androgynous lesbians did this without detection, what would that say about male prowess? Is this what the judge was so afraid of – was this the real reason why a deterrent seemed so necessary and why the sentence was longer than those passed on most convicted rapists?

The tabloid press did not question what types of pressures young lesbians may feel in order to attempt passing, and it certainly did not consider such gender bending as an erotic preference or act of queerism. In terms of pressures, the answers lie not in psychiatry (although I'm sure it would willingly provide some) but in a society where homophobia and heterosexism still remain rampant. Saunders may have felt it necessary to appropriate a male gender, or equally (as plausible) her lovers may have wanted to disguise their socially reviled lesbianism. The media were not concerned with these issues; they satiated popular hunger with yet another sensationalist horror story, by resorting to their favourite commodity – sex. Consensual lesbian sex would have been juicy enough, but to imitate a man and claim his right to penetration! The media treated Jennifer Saunders like a Havelock Ellis caricature; a congenital dangerous predator – a menace indeed, a lavender one! The media had capitalized on a story and created its own lesbian fantasy – whatever did occur between the young women involved, Saunders later claimed, it did not involve a dildo (although in court she did not deny penetrating with an object). After a successful appeal, having completed nine months of her sentence, she was released in June 1992. The appeal judge queried Crabtree's comment on 'counting the cost', not on the grounds that it was a blatant example of homophobic bigotry, but in terms of whether it would be an effective deterrent. The mainstream press did not greet Saunders' release with the enthusiasm with which it documented her conviction – Jennifer's coming out was not news.

A spanner in the works

Sado-masochism (SM), the presumed 'wicked witch' of lesbian sex, is not only alive and kicking but also piercing. SM involves sex scenes where a top/sadist acts from a position of power, while the bottom/masochist behaves in a subservient fashion. The dynamic is consensual and is pleasurable to all parties involved. 'Vanilla' sex, by contrast, covers all other acts of lesbian sex considered more mainstream. However, I would argue that classifying sexual activity into two polarized categories leads not only to the formation of divisive factions (them and us) but also to the emergence of an expansive void of uncertainty around the boundaries of vanilla and SM. For example, is restraint (by any means) the property of vanilla or SM? Tied up in such knots, it is difficult to find the answer!

Many dykes have anecdotes about being barred from events as their dress code symbolizes the SM culture or their dancing flirts with the dangerously erotic. Of course, there is more to SM than a public image, but is the dress code really that dangerous? What are we saying to each other when we disapprove of how we each get turned on? Yes, sex is political, but it seems a sad irony that in a community exiled from supposed 'normality' by acting upon our desires, we should, from the asylum of our counter-culture, merely redefine boundaries and ostracize others who transgress them. Without even a uniform to titillate, law enforcement, lesbian-style, can oppress, intimidate, re-educate and alienate. The intellectual warfare between opponents and proponents of sado-masochism becomes a battle of name calling, as labels like 'sexual radical' and 'dyke police' hinder further discussion. Most SMers live out their fantasies uninterrupted as the dyke police provide yet another scenario to be played with. However, in many countries including the UK, to engage in certain activities is to break the law. The fact that legal muscle is flexed at all in this arena has rather sinister implications.

In December 1990, following arrests under 'Operation Spanner', fifteen gay men were tried for engaging in consensual sadomasochistic sex, in the privacy of the home of one of the participants. The charges by which the eight sadists were convicted included keeping a disorderly house, drug offenses, publication of photographs and causing, aiding and abetting actual bodily harm. The sentences ranged from a year to four and a half years. Six others were either fined, given conditional discharges or suspended sentences for similar offences – one man was put on two years' probation for aiding and abetting others to hurt him. In sentencing, Judge Rant (yes, this is his real name), despite the role of consent, summed up that it was up to the courts to 'draw the line between what is acceptable in civilised society and what is not',[31] in other words, that social disapproval can be enforced by law.

Sheila Jeffreys, a radical feminist opponent of SM, informs us: 'The desire of the court to set up moral regulations may well have been hypocritical and misplaced but some limits on the indulgence of a masochism which can endanger life might be necessary.'[32] Laws are necessary to protect us from violent assault, but this is a completely different issue. When the intricacies of the legal machinery result in the unwarranted invasion of our homes, it becomes apparent that . . . 'Everywhere man or women may be born free . . . but your liberty may be at risk, if you consensually bound them in chains.' If I want to tie up my girlfriend and whip her in accordance with both our wishes and hedonistic tendencies, what gives the law the right to enter my house and stick the non-consensual boot in? It seems somewhat strange that in a country where violent offences are on the increase, the police should put so much time and energy into catching grown men (or women) in the act of hurting themselves, when they are enacting their own desires. If the participants had not consented, this would have been a totally different matter – but they had.

Those convicted appealed against the sentences in February 1992, on the grounds of consent. This was rejected on the premise that without good reason, consent was immaterial, and pursuit of sexual pleasure did not constitute a good reason. As ever, it seems like pure sexual pleasure cannot be our goal. We must seek some 'higher' aspiration, permissible for purposes of procreation and maintenance of heterosexual unions, art form, or some other philanthropic guise. With the media attention on the Spanner case, in both mainstream and the lesbian and gay press, we can be excused for thinking this was a test case setting future legal precedent. This is not the first time the law has ruled on such activities. In 1982 a sex industry worker was sentenced to six months for videoing an SM scene between herself and a non-fee-paying woman partner; her partner testified that it was consensual and that she did not want charges filed. However, the accused, Brenda Morris, was found guilty of running a disorderly house, assault, and possessing pornographic material. (I only read about this in a footnote to an article, years later.)[33] Reactive activism in the face of a constant erosion of our civil liberties produced the climate for renewed social protest in the 1990s. The march protesting against the Spanner convictions was also an outburst of accumulated anger and opposition to Section 25, Paragraph Sixteen of the Children Act, and the Embryology Bill.[34]

But it is also true that Brenda Morris lacked popular support not only because she was a woman who worked in the sex industry who enjoyed SM out of 'office' hours, but because lesbians did not have the resources available to gay men. Ironically, many in the community at this time were waging the sex wars, where SM was a burning issue.

The right-wing backlash and the government (in) action

The decade of the 1980s reads somewhat like a lesbian and gay thriller-cum-horror story: an incurable virus, hostile government forces, and the symbolic threat of right-wing activists. It is a story to cause the most horrific nightmares.

As lesbians and gays we have come a long way and our struggles, past and present, bear testimony to this. As our communities become more pro-active, visible and vocal, anti-lesbian and -gay feeling paralleled our increased presence and the British government adopted a homophobic stance. We had never been accepted and now we had pushed tolerance to the limit. While the right-wing backlash escalated, the virus too, in its early stages, seemed unstoppable. Misinformation and media sensationalism fuelled the homophobic fires and a resurgence of prejudice. The hostility, of course, had never gone away, but had become more covert. HIV and AIDS and the erroneous association with 'homosexuality' gave many people a chance to express what they had believed all along: that the gay community was deviant and sinful and had brought the wrath of god or god knows what upon themselves. This type of thinking typifies what psychologists call the just world – that people only get what they deserve.

Traditional family values and a decline in morality became the war cry of the Thatcher administration and fundamentalist religious organizations – the lesbian and gay communities and left-wing councils were their targets.

'Loony-left' councils were scapegoated at a time when the recession helped make society a fertile breeding ground for prejudice, as the government adopted the never-failing strategy of 'add sex and stir'.[35] The main target for the governmental onslaught was Haringey Council in London, as the so-called loony left were ridiculed and attacked by a government supported by an equally hostile tabloid press. Having been already denigrated by central government for its focus on racism, Haringey remained the media devil-child for several years, due to its commitment to a broad equal opportunities policy, including lesbian and gay rights. Haringey, alongside several other councils (not all in London) were acting on official Labour Party policy, adopted in 1985/6, to combat discrimination against lesbians and gay men. The 1986 local elections had returned Haringey's leadership with an increased majority. In line with its progressive electoral manifesto, Haringey planned to address discrimination via educational provision. Through its 'Positive Image' policies, it was hoped that young lesbians and gays would benefit from an increase in self-esteem, and that other students would have a better understanding of sexuality, and thus be less likely to act in a discriminatory fashion.

In the midst of a bureaucratic bungling by the council and a government enquiry into the nature of positive images, the local community responded in an atmosphere of increasing media hype and an escalating moral panic. The Parents' Rights Group, which was to become the Tories' puppet in the run-up to the general election, was formed in opposition to the council's policy, fearing that the plan was to teach children that homosexuality was a viable and acceptable alternative to heterosexuality – and that willing recruits would be given full instruction. In support of the council and its policies were the campaigning groups, Positive Images and Haringey Black Action, fighting both racism and homophobia.

The rising moral panic continued as Haringey, in its failure to articulate details of the educational policy, inadvertently allowed the opposition to convince people it was something a lot more sinister. With the media/popular focus encouraged to fall on a left-wing council, the public eye was distracted from governmental failures on a national level. Escalation of the panic was inevitable when the right seized upon a children's storybook, *Jenny Lives with Eric and Martin*,[36] to elaborate upon their own popularist fiction. Suddenly the secret was out, and in the hands of the nation's paternal tabloid press – it was official! Impressionable children were being made to read books about gay men bringing up a little girl . . . and look at the photographs, she's in their bed. The controversial text had been placed in an ILEA (Inner London Education Authority) teaching centre for teaching staff to refer to. At around the same time, the parent's rights group discovered it in Haringey's public library system and vowed to root out every copy and burn it. The book was never intended for curricular use in schools.[37] The positive image policy (which in fact was never actually implemented), was aimed at secondary education – not primary and below, as the media had people believe.

Public hostility to the policy was mobilized by a subtle form of political warfare. The implication that children were going to be encouraged to be lesbian or gay, and taught that such practice was preferable to heterosexuality, alarmed many people. Most people do not think about the nature or effects of their prejudices, and have little understanding of sexuality. In a society where this is encouraged, and heterosexuality is a given, such political manipulation was easy. By creating the illusion that the promotion of equal rights was, in effect, special rights, a clever psychological technique was employed, playing on people's existing fears and stereotypical thinking. By implying Haringey had abandoned its commitment to fighting racism and was submerging all other concerns, the Tories exploited the existence of multiple oppressions to its own advantage.

The rise of the right was evident at local level before it became the official party line – 'Back to Basics'. Prior to the 'children's story scandal', Haringey established a lesbian and gay unit in 1986 to implement anti-discriminatory policies. This action provoked a press statement from Tottenham's Conservative Party, in which it was claimed that the unit represented 'a greater threat to family life than Adolf Hitler.'[38] Soaring homophobia was being used as a warm-up exercise for Tory audiences as early as 1985, when a conference speaker declared: 'If you want a queer for a neighbour vote Labour.'[39] If only it were that easy!

In view of the rising tide of Tory homophobia, the institutionalization of it in the late 1980s was hardly surprising. The Halsbury Bill, the forerunner to what is commonly known as Section 28, was unsuccessful because its proposal fell late in Parliament's term in 1986. But it had served to whet an insatiable appetite. After her re-election, Thatcher honoured her promise (shame she never gave the electorate the same consideration) and encouraged the Bill's revival. It had been an election in which, for the first time in history, lesbian and gay issues figured prominently on electoral agendas. While Labour cautiously opposed all discrimination, on the national level 'our' vote was not courted. The Conservatives capitalized on anti-lesbian and -gay prejudice and erotophobia, using anxieties and popular misconceptions for political expediency.

Thatcher set the scene of what was to follow in her victory speech at the October conference: 'Children who need to be taught to respect traditional moral values are being taught that they have an inalienable right to be gay.'[40] Yes, this is our caring government who are attacking the overworked, underpaid and undervalued teaching profession, just in case they utter a few positive words to stop a young person who is dealing with same-sex attraction from potentially killing himself or herself. It is no coincidence that some of their homophobic election posters ridiculed a text by young lesbian and gay teenagers and that they ran full-page press ads showing how 'scared' Haringey parents were. *Capital Gay* had forewarned the lesbian and gay electorate that voting Tory was like 'a turkey voting for christmas'.[41] Thatcher was not merely expressing disapproval, she was declaring war, backed by a willing and motivated infantry.

After the election, the private member's Bill was confidently reintroduced and ultimately became incorporated into the Local Government Act of 1988 as Section 2a or 28. The opposition parties had been slow to react for fear of alienating the mainstream, and by the time they did, their objections were weak and ineffectual. The MP who introduced the bill said in an interview with the *Guardian* newspaper that his actions were motivated 'wholly by the principle of supporting normality'.[42] By whose value system are we defining 'normal'? I assume it is the white, male-dominated, middle-class, able-bodied, heterosexual system. Not all the Labour party were complacent – Bernie Grant, former leader of Haringey Council (and one of the few black MPs) made clear all the dangers: 'What else will they ban from schools? What else will the local authorities be stopped from talking about? ... If the new clause is accepted, it will be a signal to every fascist and everyone opposed to homosexuality that the government are on their side.'[43]

Section 28 stipulated that a local authority shall not 'intentionally promote homosexuality or publish material with the intention of promoting homosexuality' or 'promote the teaching in any maintained school of the acceptability of homosexuality as a pretended family relationship'.[44] Inherent in the wording of Section 28 is the assumption that sexuality is susceptible to change, that it is not instinctive but can be learned from willing teachers, eager to promote, recruit and corrupt. Thus the right had co-opted constructionist arguments to emphasize the risk to 'natural' heterosexuality, a rationale which is somewhat contradictory. By combining such arguments with ideas of the vulnerability and innocence of children, playing on hysteria generated by the moral panic, the Tories had found the recipe for success. Unlike previous legislation, Section 28 was as much against lesbians as gay men – homosexuality was an identity applicable to either gender, not just to men or male sexual acts (as it had been in the Wolfendon Report and the La Bouchère Amendment).

From the time of its introduction it met popular opposition, and not only from the lesbian and gay community. While ministers maintained it was not discriminatory, the message was clear – our lifestyle was wrong and inferior to heterosexuality. This message was carried to the people of Britain, in effect authorizing every act of discrimination and prejudice enacted on a lesbian or gay person. Prior to its incorporation into law, Margaret Thatcher, in a letter to the Organization for Lesbian and Gay action (OLGA) claimed, 'it is in no part our intention in supporting clause 28 to remove the rights of homosexuals.'[45] Taken literally, this is quite true, since 'homosexuals' or 'lesbians' have no rights to lose! As Peter Tatchell notes, 'In total, about twenty different points of law, either explicitly or by omission, discriminate against the lesbian and gay community.'[46]

The clause may have been incorporated into law, but it was met with well-orchestrated and sometimes theatrical opposition, a modern-day Stonewall, a resistance to be proud of. For many, it was a chance to get involved politically for the first time in defence of our rights; for others, feminism and gay liberation provided well-rehearsed strategies. The range of campaigning included political lobbying, demonstrations, debates and guerrilla tactics. Despite the opposition of the arts lobby, lesbians chaining themselves to BBC newscasters who were reading the six o'clock news, and abseiling in the House of Lords, the clause became law on 24 May 1988.[47]

However, we must ask ourselves how victorious the government could be in their attempt to prevent 'promotion', when the 'love that dare not speak its name' was spoken about all the time in the consistent and repetitive news coverage. Although initial confusion and uncertainty caused a wave of panic reactions as grants were pulled and performances of controversial plays abandoned, the section was more a symbolic deterrent than a law to be implemented. Legal experts emphasize the difficulty of its execution, due to its incompetent design and unintelligible syntax. Ironically, the first series of Channel 4's *Out* was commissioned within months of its passing. Television networks, publishers and individuals cannot be prosecuted – only local authorities come under the law's remit. In the 1990s, the *Out* series continued, universities offer post-graduate courses in lesbian and gay studies, and lesbian and gay publishing is flourishing. The icing for the cake, in 1994, had to be the test case in which a lesbian co-parent was awarded equal legal rights to her lover, the biological mother. The law had acknowledged a lesbian family unit, and was seemingly not pretending!

The Conservative stranglehold on British politics began with Thatcher's victory in 1979. The sluggish behaviour of successive administrations in response to the AIDS crisis nurtured a rise in social anxieties, in which racist and homophobic tendencies were apparent. Medical ignorance was used as an excuse for inactivity, as was the idea that a health education campaign could not be launched until the general public had been 'made ready' (the same excuse that had been used over the Wolfendon Report).

It was advocated by some MPs – in a fashion reminiscent of the Contagious Diseases Acts of the late 1800s – that AIDS be made a 'notifiable disease', empowering authorities to detain those deemed responsible for the 'contagion'. Prostitutes were the targets back then, now it was 'promiscuous irresponsible gay men', Although health author-ities were given 'reserve powers', AIDS was not made a notifiable disease. The fear generated around HIV and AIDS was played upon by the govern-ment to distract from other social and economic issues like unemploy-ment, and to promote its drive back to traditional family values and archaic sexual morality. In a climate where the incidence of marital and family breakdown was being brought to the public's attention, and aware-ness of child sexual abuse was increasing, the Tories rallied behind the 'sanctity' of the family. By presenting a combination of Enid Blyton-style family life with a right-wing value system, while ignoring the social realities (and inequalities of the time), the 'traditional' family was idealized. Lesbians and other sexual minorities were vilified as symbolic of the degeneration of the 'normal' family. Pretend parents and gay men with AIDS became the bogey men (and women) of the decade.

The 1980s was a decade of increasing social stress. Class divisions widened as a result of Tory fiscal policies and the attendant socio-economic repercussions; unemployment continued to rise and cost-cutting changes were implemented in key areas of the welfare state, health and education. As more and more people contracted the HIV virus, and the numbers developing AIDS increased, there were global fears of a pandemic. Sexuality became a target for many displaced anxieties. In an era when discourse on sexuality was essential, policy makers hid behind accusations of degenerating moral standards and a decline in traditional family values. It was easier to scapegoat than to address the reality that contemporary beliefs around sexual practice and identity were in urgent need of reform.

'There's nowt as queer as folk!' – from discourse to intercourse

The AIDS crisis, the resurgence of homophobia and the passing of Section 28 had generated a great deal of anger and activism which gave birth to yet another social movement within our history – queer. It is an example of what academics refer to as reverse discourse, whereby the targets of a derogatory label reclaim that label and use it themselves as a form of empowerment. We had come full circle – 'gay' was first adopted in protest to replace the derogatory 'queer'. Two decades later, when 'gay' was in popular usage, many in the community reverted to 'queer', a lot of whom belonged to a generation who had not experienced the term, first time round. Like gay liberation, queer was also a US import – in an era which was allegedly post-feminist, and post-gay-liberation, and post-political, the new movement, supposedly embracing all diversities, cast a wide net.

With the failure of the activity to stop the section, several organizations emerged in the aftermath – Stonewall, OutRage! and ACT UP (AIDS Coalition To Unleash Power). Where Stonewall (fronted by a select few with the purpose of lobbying for political change) is essentially assimilationist, trying to achieve equal rights without changing the structure of society, other organizations became the 'bad kids' in the playground with their policy of civil disobedience.

These organizations represent the new queer psyche. Queer is modern, it gets people noticed, it's not only loud and proud, it's somewhat noisy and exhibitionist, and in true 1990s marketing style – it's sexy! The epidemic has forced a re-evaluation of sex and sexuality. In the search for a new sexual ethos this movement hides nothing – it doesn't even flirt with notions of acceptance from wider society. Anything goes, under queer, with no shame – lesbian, gay, butch, femme, SM and transgender – you name it, it's queer. Although, of course, the naming is part of the problem. As a movement it emerges not only out of dissatisfaction with the identity and sexual politics of a subculture, but Cherry Smyth locates its origins in a broader socio-economic framework: 'in the wake of over a decade of the highly oppressive Thatcher regime, and in the midst of a mega recession, there was a choice to buckle under, survive the mortgage movement, or explode. Queer activism is that explosion.'[48]

In the avant-garde vernacular, queer has a new meaning:

> Each time the word queer is used it defines a strategy, an attitude, a reference to other identities and a new self understanding ... for many, the term marks a growing lack of faith in the institutions of the state, in political procedures, in the press, the education system, policing and the law.[49]

For others, it is less of a political strategy than an essential fashion accessory, a product of a consumer age, to be replaced by the inevitable next ascendant trend.

Some dykes are attracted to queer, weary of the prescriptive and desexualizing nature of lesbian feminism. In many ways, queer is the antithesis of radical feminism, adopting an anti-censorship, anti-political-correctness, and pro-objectification stance. To objectify, to see another body as an aesthetically pleasing object of desire, is criticized by radical feminism. Watney (an intellectual guru of queer) suggests that the politically correct 'way to want' infiltrated the lesbian and gay communities, and that such 'sanctimonious moralism'[50] contributed to the emergence of queer. The radical feminists have been blamed for a lot of things – now queer is partly their fault too! Political correctness has impacted on the lesbian communities, like a parent's night-time curfew, eliciting compliance from some and rebellion from others. The lesbian sex wars were as much a reaction to this as queer now claims to be.

Queer has successfully done what the GLF never even tried to do – assimilated bisexuals into our group of marginalized deviants, as well as other 'minorities within a minority'. For queer, labels are restrictive – to be queer you don't necessarily have to sleep with the same sex, you just quite simply have to be queer. By separating our desires from the constraints of gender and sexual identity, we are free to do as we please. For the new queer politics, systems of sexual classification have been identified as public enemy number one. Refusal to embrace the lesbian and gay community as a distinct minority is based on the premise that to do so would be tantamount to colluding with notions of hetero–homo polarity upon which 'the authority and legitimacy of ... state powers and governmentality depend'.[51]

This is also the basis for queer's fundamentally anti-assimilationist stance, where equality is insufficient as a political goal. To settle for equality in a structure which does not challenge the prevailing consensual reality of the sexual hierarchy, based on notions of duality, is an unacceptable compromise and a negating of all queer stands for: 'Queer culture appears as that which aims to trouble and destabilise the overall discursive legitimacy of modern sexual classifications, and the power relations they sustain and protect.'[52] In other words, while both the mainstream and counter-cultures accept the homo–hetero divide, nothing will change, as it is by subscribing to these notions of 'consensus' reality that the power base which controls us is maintained.

Queer wants the state off its back. It wants to flaunt the new politics in your face – and sit on it too! Tactics of civil disobedience embody the notion: 'We will not respect your laws because your laws don't respect us.'[53] Some dykes are suspicious of queer because it appears very white and very male, and they fear it is another movement co-opting lesbian energy while submerging our concerns. Even in view of queer's evolution in a social 'emergency', these issues need to be addressed if it is to have grass-roots success. It is all too easy to rationalize exclusions, with arguments that the necessity of immediate action hindered recruitment of the under-represented. Granted, queer may be anti-assimilationist, brave and inventive, but it is still plagued with the same problems which eroded earlier movements. Those most active are in the privileged positions to do so – privilege afforded not only by gender, race and class but in accumulated advantage related to occupation and education. Queer and the art of transgression may indeed be a new chapter in sexual politics, a 'kiss-in' does indeed make the personal political, but is that what the media and its consumers see, or do they see a load of leather-clad queers who are not so much oppressed as wearing chips on their shoulders? Likewise, under-age gay black men presenting themselves to be arrested have similar problems to those faced by black women in the 'take back the night' marches – cultural identity is as important, if not more so, than sexual identity: will the label queer protect against a racist police force?

Queer serves a similar function in lesbian and gay politics to that of radical feminism's role in the women's movement. Because it seems so 'radical' and extreme, the more moderate forces are seen as the acceptable compromise and are therefore more likely to be assimilated into society. Of course, assimilation is merely tolerance and in the grand scheme of things may change little, but many would settle for the right to love in public, leaving the revolution to others. Queer may offer that revolution, but we have heard revolutionary talk before. Queer has advantages earlier movements did not – the energy generated by the AIDS crisis and the right-wing backlash. It is also a product of a consumerist age and, like other fashions, queer adorns the political in an image that sells. Queer is a vital movement, but I wonder where it will lead us – will I cruise books in our shops in twenty years time entitled, *Look back in anger – Queer in the nineties*?

Queer is designed to overcome the limitations of identity politics by liberating sexual behaviours from the dictates of a label. In doing so, it creates a new identity politic and a different sexual standard. Smyth, writing on queer, says:

> It has been a long haul back to reclaiming the right to call my cunt, my cunt, to celebrating the pleasure in objectifying another body, to fucking women and to admitting that I also love men and need their support. That is what queer is.[54]

But surely we can do all these things while identifying as lesbian, even if we read her love of men as one of physical desire? To many lesbians, there is a legitimate divide between a lesbian identity and a bisexual identity. Queer, by transcending this, offers an inclusivity vital in a battle against sexual repression – but is the cost that we leave behind all we have fought for?

Outside the academy, arguments of sexual fluidity allow some to explore desires for both men and women; other simply do not want to and will not sleep with men or change the ways they express their desires. Is queer a throwback to psycho-essentialist notions of bisexuality or, even worse, the idea that all lesbians really want to sleep with men? I call my cunt my cunt, I fuck with women – so is this talk revolutionary or is it merely 'shock speak'? Do we embrace the long-term goals of queer and wait to see a day when heterosexual supremacy will crumble, because as a category is will be redundant? Or do we fight to maintain our separate lesbian identity in view of how much it has cost us? If we embrace queer, our communities have the opportunity to overcome gendered divisions, but is this all-inclusive utopia possible? Will queer really replace the existing structure or will the Lesbian Avengers (or their equivalent) still be confiscating papers produced by gay men on the grounds of their blatant anti-lesbian and misogynistic messages?[55]

Queer has definitely allowed many of us to discard our 'political correctness' and classificatory straightjackets with the haste with which we remove clothing in an urgent sexual liaison. It has appeared at a time when social realities necessitated change. While gay men mobilized to prevent the spread of the virus, their strategies and lessons infiltrated groups differing in sexual preference, race and ethnicity. Lesbians are visible and pro-active in this new era. With lesbian sex practices classified as low risk, when a lesbian cruising area was established, providing women with opportunities like gay men, sexual health was not the issue. Instead, the question was whether lesbians really wanted it.

Early feminism, the sex wars and queer highlight the sex as well as the politics. Queer, like radical feminism, is a dissident voice rendered audible not just because of its existence in a democratic framework, but because it shouts to be heard. However, the opposition seems intransigent, and queer is kept at bay by the constant need to respond to attacks on gay/lesbian rights. It is likely that such reactive activism will burn out this initiative in the same way as it has burnt out other movements; unable to make much progress, popular support will wane, leaving queer to become yet another subject for academic discourse.

NOTES

1. See, for example, Michael Foucault (1976), *The History of Sexuality*, Vol. 1, London; Penguin, 1990; and Jeffrey Weeks, *Coming Out: Homosexual Politics in Britain from the Nineteenth Century to the Present*, London, Quartet, 1977.
2. See Mary McIntosh, 'The homosexual role', in Kenneth Plummer (ed.), *The Making of the Modern Homosexual*, London, Hutchinson, 1981.
3. See Alfred C. Kinsey, Wardell B. Pomeroy and Clyde E Martin, *Sexual Behaviour in the Human Male*, Philadelphia, W.B. Saunders Co., 1948; and Alfred C. Kinsey, Wardell B. Pomeroy, Clyde E. Martin and Paul H. Gebhard, *Sexual Behaviour in the Human Female*, Philadelphia, W.B. Saunders Co., 1953.
4. See William Masters and Virginia Johnson, *Human Sexual Response*, Boston, Little Brown, 1966.
5. Beatrix Campbell, 'A feminist sexual politics: Now you see it, now you don't', in Feminist Review (eds.), *Sexuality: A Reader*, London, Virago, 1987.
6. Ann Koedt, 'The myth of the vaginal orgasm', in L. Tanner (ed.) *Voices from Women's Liberation*, New York, Mentor, 1970.

7. David Reuben, *Everything You Wanted To Know About Sex (But Were Afraid To Ask)*, London, W.H. Allen, 1970. His thinking had not changed much by his second book, *How to Get More Out of Sex (Than You Ever Thought You Could)*, (1976), London, A Star Book, 1986, in which he writes, 'Harrassing homosexuals in the name of morality is a tempting sport but hardly pays any longterm dividends.' p. 193.
8. Reuben, 1970, ibid., pp. 215 and 217.
9. The contemporary feminist movement is referred to as second-wave feminism as it follows an earlier movement at the turn of the century.
10. Deirdre English, Amber Hollibaugh and Gayle Rubin, 'Talking sex: A conversation in sexuality and feminism', in Feminist Review (eds.), *Sexuality: A Reader*, op. cit., p. 66.
11. See Adrienne Rich, 'Compulsory heterosexuality and lesbian existence', in Henry Abelove, Michele Aina Barale and David M. Halperin (eds.), *The Lesbian and Gay Studies Reader*, New York, Routledge, 1993, pp. 227–54.
12. Elizabeth Wilson, 'I'll climb the stairway to heaven: Lesbianism in the Seventies', in Sue Cartledge and Joanna Ryan (eds.), *Sex and Love: New Thoughts on Old Contradictions*, London, Women's Press, 1983, p. 188.
13. Linda Strega, and Bev Jo, 'Lesbian sex – is it?', in *Gossip: Journal of Lesbian Feminist Ethics*, no. 3, 1986, pp. 65–76.
14. Quoted in Katie Brown, 'Lesbian porn: Friend or foe?', *Deneuve*, vol. 4, no. 4, August 1994, p. 37.
15. Anti-pornography activity in the United States culminated in the Minneapolis Ordinance, written by Andrea Dworkin and Catherine McKinnon in 1983. Pornography was defined as a form of sex discrimination and the proposed amendment to civil law, if accepted, would have enabled women to sue the industry for damages. For a detailed overview of the anti-pornography position in general see Catherine Itzin (ed.) *Pornography: Women, Violence and Civil Liberties*, Oxford, Oxford University Press, 1992.
16. In 1986 and again in 1989 Claire Short introduced an unsuccessful private member's bill aimed at outlawing the pin-ups in the tabloid press. It was feared the legislation would be open to abuse, for example, by censoring art, and might have set a precedent for extensive censorship. Another Labour MP, Dawn Primarolo, introduced the Location Of Pornographic Material Bill, also in 1989. This measure (which also failed) was essentially a compromise allowing for the

continued production and sale of pornography but with restricted availability, by licensing vendors. For more detail see Catherine Itzin (ed.), *Pornography: Women, Violence and Civil Liberties*, Oxford University Press, 1992, p. 594.

17. See for example Catherine Itzin (ed.), ibid.
18. See, for example, Pamela Church Gibson and Roma Gibson (eds.), *Dirty Looks: Women, Pornography, Power*, London, BFI Publishing, 1993; or Lynne Segal and Mary McIntosh, *Sex Exposed: Sexuality and the Pornography Debate*, London, Virago, 1992.
19. The Sheba Collective (eds.), *Serious Pleasure: Lesbian erotic stories and poetry*, London, Sheba, 1989; and Joan Nestle, A *Restricted Country*, London, Sheba, 1988.
20. Cherry Smyth, 'The pleasure threshold: Looking at pornography on film', in *Feminist Review, Perverse Politics: Lesbian Issues*, no. 34, spring 1990, pp. 152–9.
21. GLF manifesto, quoted in Stephen Jeffrey-Poulter, *Peers, Queers & Commons: The Struggle for Gay Law Reform from 1950 to the Present*, London, Routledge, 1991.
22. Quoted in Jeffrey Weeks, *Coming Out: Homosexual Politics in Britain, from the Nineteenth Century to the Present*, London, Quartet Books, 1977, pp. 106–7.
23. David Wiltshire is the Conservative MP responsible for introducing the bill which included Clause 28.
24. Quoted in Jeffrey Weeks, op. cit., p. 107.
25. Ibid, p. 107.
26. Several lesbians abseiled down from the spectators' gallery into the House of Lords in protest against Clause 28.
27. 'Passing' is used in two ways in our community:
    i. To 'pass' as straight, to allow others to assume heterosexuality.
    ii. To 'pass' as a man; to both dress and act in sterotypical male ways so that others perceive the passing woman as a man. This phenomenon, more common at the turn of the century, is well documented by several feminist historians.
28. Quoted in Cherry Smyth, *Lesbians Talk Queer Notions*, London, Scarlet Press, 1992, p. 23.
29. Quoted by Ann Redston, 'Jennifer Saunders freed', *Lesbian London*, no. 7, July 1992, p. 1.
30. A satellite group of the direct-action politics group OutRage! Later disbanded when OutRage! dissolved the subsections.

31. Anna Marie Smith, 'Resisting the erasure of lesbian sexuality: A challenge for queer activism', in Ken Plummer (ed.), *Modern Homo-sexualities: Fragments of Lesbian and Gay Experience*, London, Routledge, 1992, p. 212.
32. Sheila Jeffreys, *The Lesbian Heresy*, London, Women's Press, 1993, p. 49.
33. Anna Marie Smith, op. cit., p. 212.
34. Section 25 was an amendment to the Criminal Justice Bill imposing limitations on gay male sexual behaviour. Paragraph 16 suggested that lesbians and gays were unfit parents, and the Embryology Bill limited lesbians' access to medically assisted artificial insemination (AI).
35. Carole Vance, 'More danger, more pleasure: A decade after the Barnard Sexuality Conference', in Carole Vance (ed.), *Pleasure and Danger: Exploring Female Sexuality*, London, Pandora, 1992, p. xxxi.
36. Susanne Bösche, *Jenny Lives with Eric and Martin*, London, GMP, 1983.
37. The text *Jenny lives with Eric and Martin* was deemed unsuitable for curricular use because the text was not written in an appropriate style – the linguistic development of the child being a priority when texts are considered for academic purposes.
38. Quoted in Davina Cooper, 'Positive Images in Haringey: A struggle for identity', in Carol Jones and Pat Mahoney (eds.), *Learning Our Lines: Sexuality and Social Control in Education*, London, Women's Press, 1989, p. 57.
39. Quoted in Stephen Jeffrey-Poulter, 1991, op. cit., p. 201.
40. Quoted in Sue Saunders and Gillian Spraggs, 'Section 28 and education', in Carl Jones and Pat Mahoney (eds.), 1989, op. cit., p. 94.
41. Quoted in Stephen Jeffrey-Poulter, 1991, op. cit., p. 199.
42. Cherry Smyth, 1992, op. cit., p. 15.
43. Quoted in Sarah Roelofs, 'Labour and the natural order: Intentionally promoting heterosexuality' in Tara Kaufman and Paul Lincoln (eds.), *High Risk Lives: Lesbian and Gay Politics after the Clause*, Bridport, Prism Press, 1991, pp. 179–96.
44. See Madeleine Colvin and Jane Hawksley, *Section 28: A practical guide to the law and its implications*, London, National Council for Civil Liberties, 1989, p. 1. A subsection of the clause stipulates that nothing in the above shall prohibit activities designed for the 'purpose of treating or preventing the spread of disease', which is not only ironically timid phraseology, but insidious in its equation of gay sexual practice and HIV infection,

45. Quoted in Kath Pringle, Tara Kaufman and Paul Lincoln, 'Clause 28 in practice', in Tara Kaufman and Paul Lincoln (eds.), 1991, op. cit., pp. 4–12.

46. Peter Tatchell, 'Equal Rights For All: Strategies for lesbian and gay equality in Britain', in Ken Plummer (ed.), 1992, op. cit., p. 237.

47. It should be noted that, because of the outcry the section provoked, several other insidious little clauses passed unnoticed which, without this distraction, would probably have been opposed. Section 28 is a civil law, not a criminal law, and can only be invoked against a local authority, not an individual or organization. However, despite the technicalities and limitations of application, the psychological impact of fear, confusion and lack of precise definitions did produce the very reluctance to act that its authors obviously intended.

48. Cherry Smyth, 1992, op. cit., p. 16.

49. Ibid., p. 20.

50. Simon Watney, 'Queer epistemology: activism, "outing", and the politics of sexual identities', in *Critical Quarterly*, vol. 36, no. 1, spring 1994, p. 18.

51. Ibid., p. 25.

52. Ibid., p. 23.

53. Peter Tatchell quoted in Cherry Smyth, 1992, op. cit., p. 59.

54. Cherry Smyth, ibid., p. 27.

55. In response to the misogynistic overtones of an article entitled, 'Dicks and dykes divided?', in MX *Magazine*, 9 September 1994, the Lesbian Avengers took action by removing the magazines from lesbian/gay venues and disposing of them in a recycling bin.

2

representation: prime-time fictions and real-life stories

If you don't know that there's a group of people who engage in a particular sexual behaviour, it makes it much more difficult to imagine yourself ever being able to do it.
Pat Califia[1]

The problem, for lesbians, is that the images produced are in the context of oppression, and it can feel as though the cost of media representations of lesbian sex hugely outweighs the benefits. Perhaps our best bet is to settle for positive portrayals of female friendships and to forget about graphic depictions of lesbian sex?
Jenny Kitzinger and Celia Kitzinger[2]

Oppressed people resist by identifying themselves as subjects, by defining their reality, shaping their new identity, naming their history, telling their story.
bell hooks[3]

'Does it matter if they did it?', a radical feminist demands in her impassioned rhetoric.[4] The thrust of her scholarly enquiry is an attempt to move debate beyond whether or not the women we claim as part of our history experienced 'genital initiation' (read, sex) and to elevate discursive practice onto a higher plain[5] (read, the oppressions of heteropatriarchy). Sex, she argues, should neither be the focus of our consciousness nor central to our identity. However, it is precisely in such an 'emotional universe' of lesbianism that sex gets lost in an expansive cosmos, eclipsed by struggles of gender inequality (to which it is intimately related). To equate any prioritizing of sex with patriarchal prescription is as misleading as the belief that such a priority will, by its revolutionary nature, end oppression and liberate the libido.

Sex has surfaced but briefly in social movements. Its appearance on the agenda of second-wave feminism was brief, buried under the more pressing concerns at the time. Lesbians in the movement were silent on this issue, not only to avoid offending or threatening, but because they bore the burden of a 'woman's true essence', and to discuss anything which tarnished the icon would not have fallen far short of heresy. Lesbian and gay liberation, too, became entwined in more immediate issues. And so, in the 1970s and 1980s, the 'sex' fell from sexual politics, as questions of identity, social location, and related dimensions of oppression became of prime importance. There was a lot of talk, but little was said about sex. Even the much-acclaimed lesbian sex wars were as much forums for the necessarily wider issues of censorship and prohibition, as for debating the actualities of practice and the perplexing nature of lesbian desire. If the sex fell from the politics in previous decades, it can now equally be contended that from the late 1980s into the 1990s, the politics fell from the sex.

In a changing society, sex is increasingly looked to for the meeting of needs which other ideologies and institutions (like religion and the family) become less likely to fulfil. Sex, more than ever before, is a dominant theme in western capitalist cultures. It is the common denominator which never fails to captivate public interest. And while the harness binding it to ideas of love and romance has been loosened, the connections remain, collectively creating a fixed lens through which the world is viewed. It is a prism through which many wants and experiences relating to material wealth and personal happiness are projected. On an almost daily basis we are confronted by both overt and covert messages, constantly reminding us to think about, if not perform, an activity which is supposedly so natural and intrinsically reinforcing, it needs no prompt or promotion.

When, as is so frequently the case, the message reads 'heterosexual', we can ignore this point, or more likely, translate it. This cultural obsession with sex crosses the ever-permeable boundaries of sexual identity. With the growth of the counter-culture, its industries and modes of production, the preoccupation with sex has become just as ubiquitous (within the confines of the censorious structures imposed by a heterosexist parent culture). Sex sells, constructed and commodified – the lesbian and gay culture too subscribes to this manufactured naked need.

As long as sex and sexuality remain so heavily regulated, lesbian sex has the potential to be a site of resistance. It is vital, however, to realize that the relative freedoms won by civil rights struggles, feminism, and lesbian and gay liberation do not constitute freedom itself. In understanding that the individual and private world of sex cannot be divorced from power relations and material structures, it is essential that practices of sex and love are not dismissed. The pleasures and the pains of lesbian sex, love, and relationships, form one of the day-to-day levels on which many of us operate.

Despite a reclamation and redefinition of the label lesbian, we have been less confident in owning the sexual component. And although this may be central to a mainstream stereotype, it is also pivotal to many lesbians who not only 'surpass the love of men', but submerge themselves in the love of women, be it emotional, spiritual or explicitly sexual. It does matter if they did it, do it, talk about it, don't talk about it, film it, photograph it, write about it or assertively advertise it. Lesbian sex, like sex generally, is trapped by the taboo which keeps it in the public (or in the counter-cultural confines) arena while holding it simultaneously just beyond our reach.

This book is being written in a cultural moment when few literary endeavours ensure such popular (or specialist academic) interest as those which in some shape or form lead back to sex. The field is kept fertile through different narrative styles and theoretical positions, as publications proliferate. This textual practice is a primary method of counter-cultural reproduction, a mechanism through which we pass on history, and cultural traditions, a contemporary commentary through which we can reproduce ourselves. We found ourselves in books, long before we were skirting across television screens and large-scale filmic productions, in fictions which were built upon romantic convention and sexual allusion. These novels, in more recent times, are dismissed as 'pulp', diminished by the anti-romance stance of lesbian feminists.[6] As the fictional genres diversify, lesbian relationships and sexual intimations are still popular themes. Allusion, however, has become increasingly less closeted and metaphors progressively more graphic, as the salacious becomes less suggested and more stated. The imagination of the reader has to initiate less and less. In a cultural metamorphosis, sexual meanings multiply as the erotic evolves, allowing explicit sex to surface.

Barbara Wilson, author of the novel *Cows and Horses*,[7] employed the portrayal of sex to convey its intimate connection to loss – a technique which she now retrospectively sees as conventional erotica.[8] This was a shift from earlier genres where it was commonly deployed as the quintessential coming out event or as a means to assert lesbianism in a concrete way. While mainstream reviewers issued predictable censure, it was well received by lesbian audiences: 'for every reader who said to me "that was a wonderful description of the grieving process", there were three who said "great sex scenes".'[9]

It was this increasingly visible and vocal market force which had come of an age to be receptive to the more explicit – some would say pornographic – literature, for example Sheba's *Serious Pleasure*.[10] In the introduction the editors pre-empted many likely condemnations, in a fashion less apologist and more reminiscent of a feminist agenda that had long lain dormant: 'We decided to publish a book of lesbian erotica because quite simply, we wanted to read it and we knew that we were not the only ones, a huge number of lesbians "out there" would want to read it too.'[11] And they were not wrong. The book dedicated to 'doing it' was followed by others of a similar ilk, to an extent that some would argue that if nothing else, the market got saturated.[12]

In real terms, the number of books dedicated to explicit erotica, as compared to the fictional/autobiographical narrative generally, is not that great. The choice, however, saves an intrigued reader from scrutinizing entire publications to glean the odd sexual sentence, and guarantees she will come across sex in a matter of pages, if not before. The imagery is not only graphic, it is probably more inspiring and instructive than the few lesbian sex manuals available. We are now told what happens when, either by night or day, they are not divided:

> When Annie felt the movement she pressed downward against Louise. The hot lips of Annie's cunt burned against the mound of Louise's arse. Louise pushed upward to meet Annie's clit and Annie quickened her movement. It happened so fast Louise wasn't certain Annie had come . . .
>
> Jewelle Gomez[13]

> Again she teased with erect nipples, feeling her clitoris tingle as Celeste moved with her this time, silently. Celeste arched her hips. Jenny grasped at the top of her hip bones, pulling her up to her knees she slid one hand between her legs and into the wetness of Celeste's vagina, fingers moving round and deep . . .
>
> Jo Whitehorse Cochran[14]

The sex scenes in more general fiction may touch on similar explicitness, the difference being that it is diluted throughout the story. It was the adaptation of a lesbian novel into a televised serial drama that marked the beginning of what is proving to be popular culture's short-lived romance with lesbianism. The text translated well onto television, and *Oranges Are Not the Only Fruit*[15] got, in general, favourable reviews. The inclusion of sex scenes, while making the relationship 'real' for the straight audiences, added to the ambience already created by the subtle cues, more readily picked up by lesbian viewers. It also reinforced the sexual reality for many lesbians. The producer commented in an interview with the *Daily Mirror*: 'We decided to make it obvious the girls were having a sexual relationship . . . not a wishy washy thing . . . we wanted to face the question everyone asks . . . what do lesbians do?'[16] But any comprehensive attempt to address such a query would have most likely ended up on the cutting room floor.

With the floodgates open, there followed a steady trickle of occasional serial dramas, incidental and ongoing storylines. Cult followings generated by the reading of lesbian subtext in programmes like *Cagney and Lacy* were overshadowed by 'real' lesbians in both British and American soap operas and serials. The ratings in many a lesbian house soared, as did the phone bills, as the excitable rushed to the phones with 'Quick, turn on the TV, there's a couple of dykes in . . . *Brookside, EastEnders, Emmerdale Farm, Between the Lines, Casualty,* L.A. *Law, Roseanne* . . . . For the briefest moment we were not only 'Out on Tuesday' but on most other weeknights as well.

Much has been written about these representations, especially in sensationalist press commentary, as the stories unfolded. And while the portrayals were not beyond criticism for many reasons, sexual innuendo and overtone were not as absent as many predicted. Complaints were made by those offended and outraged by the pre-nine-o'clock-watershed screening of lesbian kisses – no doubt most of them would have sat up half the night to observe the same offence and dutifully complain. As for more explicit sexually suggestive scenes, there was little to object to, apart from their relative non-existence. Whatever status lesbian sex may have as being innocuous, in the eyes of the censors, script writers and production companies, it remains a highly risqué practice.

For lesbian audiences disappointed with the diluted TV imagery, the Lesbian and Gay Film Festival provides a more concentrated sequence of lesbian stories, with an inevitable generous helping of sex. Yet even here, some are dissatisfied with cutting-edge material, as the approximations fall short of expectations. Over two consecutive years, the festival has opened with the lesbian films *Go Fish*[17] in 1994 and *Bar Girls*[18] in 1995. As potential barometers of changes in the subculture, familiar reliance on romantic conventions was accompanied by the depiction of different relationship styles and sexual appetites. Storylines not long out of the closet (where mainstream movie-making is concerned), dragged sex out from behind closed doors.

Go Fish is the subject of analysis later in the book, and while it too included sex scenes, the most elaborate episode of Bar Girls is of more interest at this point. What is striking is not so much the performance *per se* as the motives behind it. The two women involved are not tucked up in a warm and loving relationship but driven by mutual dislike, mistrust and sexual rivalry (sex has always been prematurely postmodern, it its potential for multiple meanings). However, after teasing with sex on the sinister side, the story returns to the softer sensibility as fractured formula romance is restored, with the film concluding with the ultimate in affair repair. Any fears of intimacy or betrayal are forgotten in the desire for a second chance, which of course leaves the way open for the sequels, in true Hollywood style: *Drunk on Desire, Fizz Goes Flat with Fusion* and *Dyke Divorce!*

The variations on sexual themes depicted in text, television and on film reflect the sexological scripts, moralistic fashions and elaborate psychological theorizing tailored into the fabric of everyday life. They mirror how it seems to be, or more importantly how we think it should be. Everything seems so 'natural' in a world where, undisputedly, significant others are so necessary. Where we do need to love and be loved, to touch and be touched. To be part of an idealized couple, to have that special someone with whom we can recount the trials and tribulations of the day and transcend them at night, seduced in her arms. Yet in such fictional representations we are given less insight into the inevitable conflict where our fantasies clash with reality.

Commercial fictions constitute only some of the narrative frameworks through which we come to understand sex, and identify with the experiences. We each have our own unique sexual stories to tell, but many of the themes are shared, recurring in the stories of others. The different narratives are not only permitted but encouraged by particular audiences. In the remainder of the chapter I will be looking at some of the sexual stories commonly told in the lesbian community. The coming out story is one such narrative, of which we all have a personal version. The changes brought about by HIV/AIDS have created frameworks through which we can discuss sex and sexuality. With the increasing exposure in our communities to alcohol use, its role as a social lubricant is brought into focus via the functions of intimate disclosure and sexual exploration. The chapter ends with a discussion of sexual abuse, stories which while increasingly told, are still those less likely to be heard.

Broken Silences

Coming out, the realization of same-sex attractions and emotional affinities, is a reconstruction of self in relation to society, a rite of passage, with every lesbian having her own unique version. Such confessions can bring about transformation both personal and political, being part of the cohesion that binds the counter-culture together. As well as being stories through which we assert our presence and difference, a challenge to the socio-sexual order, they are also accounts of desire and an accepted way through which to talk about sex. For many, the experience of sex with another woman is synonymous with coming out. As an identity which is in part defined by sexual difference, we will often look towards this act for proof of who and what we are. Recollections of coming out (no matter how recent) often take on an almost essential quality of predestiny as the past is retrospectively interpreted through lesbian eyes. And thus licensed to tell, we recite the frustrations, passionate yearnings, wants and almost desperate needs.

Once afforded great significance, coming out is routinely expected, a necessary developmental stage, a lesbian adolescence. Yet while people are coming out at younger ages[19] and the experience is necessarily different as the lesbian and gay culture is now so much more visible and collectively confident, we are far from the day when such an act would be 'easy'. As the counter-culture has changed, so too has the function of the story. And while there are continuities in theme and content, the narrative seems to have undergone a shift in significance. While still undeniably a political act, it is no longer the only medium through which to discuss our desires, sexual preferences and practices. Although still not able to utilize all the avenues available to those in possession of full sexual citizenship, we now have other frameworks through which to view and talk about sexual attraction and experience. The continual change in the community reflects the psychological approach to the individual journey of coming out – we, like our community, progress through stages, and one will at all times inform the other. There is now less talk of how we came to feel this way and more of what we do with it. For those currently coming out onto inner-city scenes, lifestyle seems more important on the surface than political consciousness. And the sex in many respects has returned to the centre stage of the definition, if it every really left at all.

Lesbian communities seem less political and more preoccupied with lifestyle and sex as old-style consciousness-raising has been replaced with consumerism. The transition and its tensions have replaced the traditional coming-out themes in films and textual practice. The *Go Fish* girls are battling not with a stigmatized identity, but how to make 'a catch'. The transformation of Ely in that film (discussed in greater detail later) can be read as a symbolic reconstruction of the community. Stereotypically 'Seventies', she is quite literally recreated, and the stories are not about coming out but going out . . . with other women.

Debate and discursive practice

When Cindy Crawford said publically that lesbianism was a safe way to be sexual in the age of AIDS,[20] shocking as this may have been coming from a seemingly heterosexual sex symbol, her comment was merely reflecting what appeared to be common knowledge about lesbian 'immunity'. The public image of lesbianism contradicted health promotion messages which asserted necessary separation between action and identity. This contradiction lay in the assumption that lesbian sex equalled safer sex, thus confounding ideas of low risk groups with low risk practices (an association health educators sought desperately to shatter). From the beginning of the epidemic, lesbians had been defined either in relation to gay men, or as symptomatic of the neglect of lesbian health generally – marginalized and ignored. While initially lesbians and gay men were erroneously equated with the HIV virus in an era of resurging homo-phobia, the image of lesbians at least (gay men still face such ignorant bigotry), changed from that of high risk group to practically the safest 'group'. And with such a translation, the stereotype of lesbian sex being less than real sex because of the absence of penetration with a penis, met a contemporary interpretation that real sex equals high risk practice. This reflects a tenacious belief that the HIV/AIDS educators were up against the idea that intercourse was sex and everything else foreplay. Lesbians have long been aware of this particular fallacy.

This supposed low-risk group with low-risk practice was also low in priority in terms of research and accurate information provision. The medical establishment was not overly concerned with lesbians; compla-cent, yet strangely confident considering the lack of empirical data. In addition, if such expert assumptions were in some way informed by a common understanding of the parameter of lesbian sexual repertoires (and other risk behaviours), then medicine was remarkably way ahead of most lesbians who shared no such clear consensus. It was in this context that lesbians (and a few community organizations), prompted debates and dialogues within the community. If we had been waiting for some 'higher purpose' to discuss sex, then the moment had arrived. On the ground, response was mixed, ranging from disinterest and dismissal to an enthusiastic proliferation of opportunities to discuss lesbian (safer) sex.

HIV and AIDS provided a language and a licence to talk about sex. In the debris of shattered silences, sex with men and intravenous drug use were forced onto the agenda. In the absence of any prior lesbian sex education, we fumbled in unfamiliar territory, in all-embracing debates of practices and politics. And here, in many ways, was yet another avenue to circumvent discussing sex purely as a pleasure principle. While working to elaborate on what lesbian sex was and how it felt, the wider meanings were often hurried over as practices were written up in charts of low, medium and high risk. The pros and cons of the dental dam[21] were privileged over any other aspect of cunnilingus, as lesbian sex became theorized through layers of latex. The safer-sex materials, which were creatively appropriated in a stroke of genius, were not initially designed for lesbian sexual practice. And what had fast become folklore of lesbian low risk, was institutionally endorsed by the lack of specifically designed protective barriers. While several attempts were made to redesign and improve the dental dam for lesbian purposes, mass production did not take off, reflecting the fact they were rarely, if ever, used.

Awareness on the ground led to serious safer sex for some and a mounting resistance from others. In an age when lesbians wanted to reap the freedoms won by feminism, gay liberation and the expansion of lesbian sexual representation, it appeared as if sex was undergoing an unnecessary sanitization. Workshops and other localized initiatives complemented attempts at more national outreach, such as the printing of advisory leaflets by the Terrence Higgins Trust and Lesbian and Gay Switchboard. However, many were to remain oblivious to the whole debate, existing beyond the domains through which such messages were carried. Many were living outside cities and the thriving scenes, or disinterested in the new erotic genre in publishing, or largely unaware, in a parent culture where lesbians and HIV were simply not an issue. Even for those in the cut and thrust of city life, with access to a community, health education was relatively sparse.

The Terrence Higgins Trust (THT) targeted lesbians as part of its health promotion initiatives. The first of two posters (part of national campaigns), showed an image of two naked dykes with the explicitness contained by their physical positioning. It was accompanied by the advice, 'Wet Your Appetite for Safer Sex.' The Trust, at this stage, was endorsing the uncertainty and the need to play safe. The poster made its debut on the front page of London's *Evening Standard*, which was covering the launch of a national campaign to raise awareness, on Valentine's Day 1991. The accompanying text did include a passing reference to lesbians, with the style of this new educational imagery in general being described as 'controversial'.

Whether lesbians needed targeting at all was a contentious issue, although any controversy, from a lesbian standpoint, was perhaps more applicable to the second poster in the lesbian series. In an image where clothes had been put on, safer sex on the larger scale had been taken off. It seems we had got wet for nothing, as the update mirrored a more confident belief that lesbian practices were predominantly lower risk. Under the question, 'Lesbians and HIV: What are the risks?' is the answer, 'Very low risk in oral sex . . . so ditch those dental dams, don't bother with gloves unless it turns you on, if you share toys, use condoms', and underneath in smaller print is the vital but all too easily forgotten caution, 'However lesbians have been infected with HIV through sharing "works", sex with men and donor insemination.'

What had been the general consensus among many lesbians anyway, had gained the official backing of one of the best-known organizations in the country. It was inevitable that such a pronouncement would be emotive in a climate of sexual uncertainties. Here was yet another bone of contention to add to the debate in which accusations of 'virus envy' became a derogatory means of silencing those articulating anxiety. With the emphasis on whether the THT should have taken such as assertive, almost authoritatively paternal stance, the reference to latex fetishes went largely unnoticed. And yet protective barriers are not only fetishised but are used to signal sex and sexual intent, since this is actually one of the most familiar languages of latex love.

More comprehensive provision came in the form of A *Lesbian Guide to Sexual Health: Well Sexy Women*, a London-made video.[22] Funded by the THT, redemption was available, if sought. It combined a frank round-table discussion by a panel of lesbians, interspersed with explicitly choreographed safer-sex scenes. The discussion brought down many myths by presenting the facts (as we currently know them to be) and following through with all-girl action shots. This was not just a film about sexual health, it was about sex, and more precisely safer sex. In the absence of an emphasis on romantic or relationship themes, the safer-sex message was the overall narrative thread, setting the sex in context. This thread was successful, and the film continues to score highly over a more recent production on lesbian sex, *The Lesbian Kama Sutra*[23] (or 'How to caress a lesbian while allowing sex with men to enter the conversation at every available opportunity'). Capitalizing on the currency of lesbian sex, the film-makers promised everything and delivered very little – leaving *Well Sexy Women* safe from competition and definitely well sexier.

As is a common criticism made of much available sexual representation, *Well Sexy Women*, (in many ways) did not go far enough. It did not show all there was to see, and I'm not talking about technique or position. Although anchored in the reality that sex is frequently spontaneous, negotiated physically rather than verbally, the separation of talk from action is in part problematic. A similar split is found in erotic texts like *Serious Pleasure*, where the 'facts' of safer sex are segregated (for the most part) from the fictional pleasures and flights of fancy. Literature as art, of course, does not have to be a vehicle for education. The video, however, effective in its depictions of how safer sex can be assimilated, did not demonstrate how to get to this point. The film bypasses the unsexy and definitely unromantic connotations STDs have in wider society. Encouraging as it was to see precautions seductively portrayed in sexual episodes, the fact that no one batted an eyelid in surprise, giggled, balked or objected, set the film apart from many lesbians' experiences. In the sex scenes, the universal language of sex needed no translation, every sexy signal was readily understood. Frankly, if a partner was to don costume dress and a dildo adorned with a condom, I'd like to talk about it first – especially the costume dress! Watching the scenes, we could convince ourselves that discussion and negotiation had occurred previously, that these women were now 'old hands' at safer sex, because they had been doing it so long. (The filming of which would be the script of an ongoing lesbian serial drama, as opposed to a fifty-five minute take.)

Alternatively, we can allow for a different reading of the film. Primarily about sex, its 'safer' element was seen as little more than erotic licence. Questions about what was missing from the film were not asked in the public forum, because they were not an issue. In one sense this was less about avoiding transmission (of anything) and more about representations of sex.

As well as being protective barriers, condoms and latex serve another function. Like toys, they are tangible symbols of sexual practice, proof that we are actually doing 'something'. Safer sex materials are not only signs of bad girls behaving good, or good girls behaving badly but safely, but are a currency for sex – for innuendo and invitation. From this position, we can see that the language of latex has more than one meaning, as communicated through the lesbian mother tongue.

Social lubrication

With the proliferation of text, theory and a media articulacy around sex, it is another matter as to whether this public discussion is replicated in the personal and private dialogues we have with sexual partners. Open communication is no longer the prerogative of the sexually adventurous, but a necessity for all who are sexually active. Encouragement comes from the enticing idea that such conversations will make the experience not only safer but also better. But to converse we need a suitable vocabulary and the confidence to use it. The role of language, a recurrent theme throughout this book, is the focus of the next chapter. Of interest here are not the words or lack of them, but how we find the voice.

In the early stages of a relationship or liaison, straight talk about pleasures, preferences and prohibitions may not come easy. Intimate disclosures usually take time as trust and emotional investment grow. Initially, much of the excitement resides in that which is not spoken, as she gradually reveals who she really is, and we compare this to the all-encompassing fantasy of who we think she is. During such a process, it is often easier to expose our physical selves than any psychic foundations. We are reticent to broach the subject of safer sex, for fear of introducing another kind of barrier. The more we invest in a sexual encounter in a particular person, the more loaded the dice in a dating game that we are forever reminded we must play to win.

While lesbian politics may challenge such metaphors, they are pervasive in everyday understanding of sexual relationships. In our communities, as well as the pressure to be coupled, there is pressure to be sexual. And while there have been shifts to separate the two, the latter is still largely seen as a quest for the former. But meeting other women is not always easy when, in everyday interactions, lesbianism often remains illicit and disguised. Groups for discussion and/or political activism are one source of contacts, and will be among the motives of a number of women joining organizations like the Lesbian Avengers, for example. Indeed, this very temptation was stated quite clearly (in a recent television interview) by Sarah Schulman,[24] founder of the original Avengers in New York. We also meet in the bars and clubs of the scene, where social lubrication is sought in the form of alcohol.

This is not restricted to the subculture. Alcohol is renowned for this very function, in a society where its use is sanctioned and encouraged by an advertising industry that intertwines drink with the wider peddling of seduction, sex and romance. Unlike some other drugs, alcohol is not taken to enhance the physical sensations of sex, but is part of the wider routine. While it is, in fact, a depressant drug (as opposed to a stimulant), the commonly experienced effects of increased confidence, relaxation and disinhibition are as much to do with a cultural expectation as with the complex psycho-pharmacological properties acting on the brain.

Provisional research[25] reflects what is in many ways taken for granted – that a number of lesbians drink alcohol when initiating a sexual encounter (36 per cent 'sometimes', 23 per cent 'usually/always'). It is also interesting to note that in questions relating to drinking motives of the lesbian community at large, the enhancement of sexual intimacy was commonly cited by respondents. This is not to say high levels are being consumed by everyone, nor that lesbians can only connect when drinking. However, evidence suggests that lesbians are three times as likely as other women to develop problems of alcohol misuse and dependence. Any multi-faceted explanatory model for such findings should examine the social and sexual dynamics of interaction. Reluctance to do so will stem in part from an awareness that sexual practices were central to earlier patho-logical theories, and from the fact that discussion of sex and of alcohol misuse have both been silenced – the latter still is. The role alcohol plays in sexual behaviour has become a priority in research projects investigat-ing its compromising effects on an individual's ability to negotiate and implement safer sex. There is, however, another side to this enquiry – that moderate amounts of alcohol may actually enhance the likelihood that such frank and exploratory discussions are undertaken.

Talking the taboo

It has been easier to raise awareness around issues that do not seem too close to home. Hence HIV and AIDS has a higher profile than issues like breast cancer or sexual abuse. While the former is discussed later in the text, elaboration of the latter is essential to any overview of lesbian sex. Brought into the public domain by feminist activism, incest, rape, and sexual abuse are no longer the familial and private secrets they once were. The women's movement has created safe enough environments for some of these stories to be shared, both in consciousness-raising (CR) and support groups, and in print. Such speaking out is particularly encouraged in some lesbian communities in North America, where ideas of therapy and recovery are a facet of the culture.

The concept of safer sex as disease prevention, while vital, is too narrow. For many women, the impact of emotional, physical and sexual abuse means that sex does not always feel 'safe' emotionally. This fact is rarely mentioned in books which discuss sex, other than those focusing on abuse. This serves to perpetuate the taboo, to keep it 'out there', as does the failure of videos, leaflets and posters to mention the subject.

With the demise of CR-style groups which created shared realities, it becomes a knee-jerk reflex to seek qualified help, a further profession-alization of our private lives. Partners often feel ill-prepared to offer support as there seems little on-the-ground discussion or representation. Histories of abuse can and do interfere with our sex lives (though this is neither inevitable nor permanent). If we are to continue to unravel lesbian sexuality and desire, while also acknowledging the need for safety, then this issue needs to be returned to the arena with the energy, care and commitment shown by the feminists who put it there in the first place.

There is more to making a woman feel safe than clingfilm and latex. There are more ways to open old wounds than neglecting to manicure your nails. There is potentially more to a sexual history than a list of consensual acts: with whom, when and where. The available self-help literature is useful, and the better approaches build on those conveyed in *Strong at the Broken Places*,[27] where one is not forever controlled by earlier hurts. The word 'survivor' was carefully chosen to replace 'victim' for a reason. Many women feel their experiences of abuse have little more impact on their sexual and emotional lives than any other life event, while others may feel the effects erratically or for protracted periods of time. And yet, to look at our available sexual representation and where it places the emphasis would appear not to be an issue.

Sexual abuse in particular, and 'the dysfunctional family' dynamic, have a higher profile in the therapy industry of the USA, but so too does so-called 'false memory syndrome'. 'Discovered' only after the high preva-lence of sexual abuse was exposed, this is where accounts of abuse are the result, not of actual experience, but of suggestions by therapists or cues from books. (The much-acclaimed *The Courage to Heal*[28] is a text which figures frequently in disputes in the United States.) Evidence frequently used to support the notion of false memories is the sudden recollection of events from the past: proponents of false memory syndrome choose to ignore the mechanisms of repression and remembering. Some of the explanations on both sides of the debate are credibly based on current psychological theories of how our memories work. However, the scientific community is reluctant to acknowledge the wider implications of prevalence estimates – i.e. the dangers inherent in some social and family systems – and consequently produces the larger fictions. Arguments over false memories or 'false syndrome' become yet another distraction from the painful realities of sexual abuse and the necessary political analysis of gender inequality.

In lesbian theory, associations have been made between sexual abuse and the lesbian sexual styles of the 'stone butch' and sado-masochistic practices (returned to in Chapters 3 and 5). This analysis is vital to a greater understanding of lesbian sexuality and desire, but can be as oppressive and disempowering as it is insightful and liberating. Some survivors practise SM. A number of these women make conscious associations between early experiences and their current sexual practice, seeking empowerment, control and a right to sexual pleasure through the cathartic experience. But others make no such link, and those who insist that they should – in the absence of invitation or consent from these women – need to look a little closer at the pervasiveness of abusive practice.

It is inevitable that we seek explanations for behaviour. Establishing motives for ourselves and others allows us to feel in control of our social worlds. Who we are and what we do at any one moment is not just contingent upon the situation we are in at that time, but is powerfully shaped by life experience, especially that of our early years. Infancy and childhood are formative parts of our lives – it is during these years that we learn the basic rules of love, trust, autonomy and attachment. Yet the process is not always as flawless as the image of the perfect family suggests. While we need to appreciate this fact, we could become in danger of attributing every act to events of the past. It is problematic to describe every practice which deviates from the norm in the language of 'coping strategies', or the 'acting out' of distress or earlier hurts. These descriptions are accurate in some instances, but individual women may or may not want to engage with them. And while involving a necessarily complex analysis of conscious and unconscious motives, such language can also operate as an over-simplification – as, for example, when all actions of survivors are attributed to their abuse.

Consensual acts involving the manipulation of power are not sexual abuse. Much lesbian feminist theory offers a somewhat contradictory analysis here. For in the same breath as talking of empowerment and support such theory robs women of the right to act under their own sexual agency, and claims that they are driven instead by distress. Politicized, this becomes 'false consciousness'; psychologized, it becomes symptomatic of 'dysfunction' and 'denial'.

The fact that many lesbians recount experiences of abuse does not mean more lesbians have been abused than have straight women, but that the counter-culture is more accommodating to disclosure (in some respects). Our friends and lovers can be very supportive. Statistics drawn from the Pride Survey, a lesbian sex study (see Chapter 4) showed that 43 per cent of the respondents (who numbered 278), reported being sexually abused by a man. No information is available on whether these events occurred in childhood, adulthood or both. The majority of women who specify rape are also represented in the general 'sexual abuse' category; but, again, further detail is lacking, and one cannot tell whether the responses refer to the same or separate events. However, based on earlier findings from Diana Russell,[29] Judith Lewis Herman[30] and JoAnn Loulan,[31] it is likely that, in a large number of cases, these women are reporting *both* childhood sexual abuse (which may or may not be defined as rape) and later adult assaults (which may or may not be defined as rape). In an age where so much weight is placed on 'statistical truths', the Pride Survey shows that practically half the respondents report the experience of sexual abuse, and a quarter report rape.

The potential horror escalates when other women are identified as the perpetrators. From the same study, 8 per cent of the sample report being abused by another woman (with a further 4 per cent uncertain, which compares to 8 per cent uncertain in relation to male perpetration). And while comfort may be taken from the vast difference between the numbers of female and male perpetrators, over-emphasis of this point prevents the necessary support structures from being put in place for those who have been abused by women. Again, the survey's limited design allows for little detail, thus the range of experiences may include childhood abuse by mothers or strangers, and assaults in adulthood. In a number of cases the respondents will be describing abuse from women who were/are their lovers/partners.

The exact prevalence of same-sex assault in our communities is difficult to ascertain, and it is an estimate which many of us are reluctant to make. Place the figure too low, and we invalidate painful realities; too high, and we distract from issues of male violence, and blur the differences between male and female power and behaviour. One study into sexual coercion[32] in gay and lesbian relationships found that from a sample of thirty-six lesbians, 31 per cent reported being subject to forced sex by their current or most recent partners. Of the total sample, 8 per cent were pro-active in coercive practice. Violence was less likely to be used in sexual coercion by the lesbians than by the gay men in the study. Without challenging the reality, the problems of research using small numbers of student populations must be borne in mind, as must the limitations of this particular method of research – these issues are dealt with more fully later in the text.

The groundbreaking book on violence and abuse in lesbian relationships *Naming the Violence*[33] has been followed by *Lesbians Talk Violent Relationships*.[34] While awareness of such abusive power dynamics is slowly being raised, the authors of the latter text note that, when it came to discussing sexual abuse, 'the women who told us their stories found it hardest to speak of.'[35] The hidden terror of rape, assault or abuse within our communities is still largely taboo. And as the unspeakable becomes spoken, the community must respond on a collective level.

NOTES

1. Pat Califia, *Macho Sluts*, Boston, Alyson, 1989, p. 22.
2. Jenny Kitzinger and Celia Kitzinger, ' "Doing it": Representations of lesbian sex', in Gabriele Griffin (ed.), *Outwrite: Lesbianism and Popular Culture*, London, Pluto Press, 1993, p. 19.
3. bell hooks quoted in Ken Plummer, *Telling Sexual Stories: Power, Change and Social Worlds*, London, Routledge, 1995, p. 30.
4. Sheila Jeffreys, 'Does it matter if they did it?', in Lesbian History Group (eds.), *Not A Passing Phase: Reclaiming Lesbians in History 1840–1985*, London, Women's Press, 1993, p. 19.
5. In the article, Jeffreys discusses the debates surrounding Lillian Faderman's book, *Surpassing The Love of Men*, which is seen by many writers as desexualizing lesbianism. See, for example, Sonja Ruehl, 'Sexual theory and practice: Another double standard', in Sue Cartledge and Joanna Ryan (eds.), *Sex and Love: New Thoughts on Old Contradictions*, London, Women's Press, 1983.
6. See, for example, Carol Ann Uszkurat, 'Mid twentieth century lesbian romance: reception and redress', in Gabriele Griffin (ed.), op. cit.
7. Barbara Wilson, *Cows and Horses*, London, Virago, 1989.
8. Barbara Wilson, 'The erotic life of fictional characters', in Judith Barrington (ed.), *An Intimate Wilderness: Lesbian Writers on Sexuality*, Portland, Eighth Mountain Press, 1991, p. 203.

9. Ibid., p. 204.
10. Sheba Collective (eds.), *Serious Pleasure: Lesbian Erotic Stories and Poetry*, London, Sheba, 1989.
11. Ibid., p. 8.
12. The fact that Sheba went out of business raises the question of the strength of the lavender pound (as opposed to the combined lesbian and gay pink one) in the publishing market place. The publishing of titles by excellent writers like Audre Lorde and Joan Nestle was insufficient to fight off the recession.
13. Jewelle Gomez, 'White Flowers', in Sheba Collective (eds.), op. cit., p. 58.
14. Jo Whitehorse Cochran, 'Guaranteed a Story', in Tee Corinne (ed.), *Intricate Passions: A Collection of Erotic Short Fiction*, Texas, Banned Books, 1989, p. 95.
15. Jeanette Winterson, *Oranges Are Not the Only Fruit*, London, Pandora, 1985. Winterson adapted the script for a televised serial drama, first screened in January 1990 on BBC 2.
16. Quoted in Hilary Hinds, 'Oranges Are Not the Only Fruit: Reaching audiences other lesbian texts cannot reach', in Sally Munt (ed.), *New Lesbian Criticism: Literary and Cultural Readings*, New York, Harvester/ Wheatsheaf, 1992, p. 165.
17. *Go Fish*, Rose Troche, 1994.
18. *Bar Girls*, Marita Giovanni, 1994.
19. See, for example, Ken Plummer, op. cit.
20. Quoted in Annamarie Jagose, *Lesbian Utopics*, London, Routledge, 1994, p. 159.
21. A dental dam is a square sheet of latex rubber used by dentists to isolate teeth for dental procedures. It has been adopted by the lesbian community as a protective barrier through which to have safer oral sex.
22. *A Lesbian Guide to Sexual Health: Well Sexy Women*, a Pride Video production made in association with the Terrence Higgins Trust and the Unconscious Collective.
23. *The Lesbian Kama Sutra*, Triangle Productions, 1995.
24. Sarah Schulman in *We Recruit*, Optomen Television, screened on Channel 4, 9 September 1995.
25. Elaine Creith, Ph.D in progress, Middlesex University, London.
26. See, for example, Deborah L. Diamond and Sharon C. Wilsnack, 'Alcohol Abuse Among Lesbians: A Descriptive Study', *Journal of Homosexuality*, vol. 4, no. 2, 1978, pp. 123–142; Lillene H. Fifield, J. David

Latham and Christopher Phillips, *Alcoholism in the Gay Community: The Price of Alienation, Isolation and Oppression*, a project of the Gay Community Services Centre, Los Angeles, 1977.

27. Linda T. Sanford, *Strong at the Broken Places: Overcoming the Trauma of Childhood Abuse*, London, Virago, 1991.

28. Ellen Bass and Laura Davis, *The Courage to Heal: A Guide for Women Survivors of Child Sexual Abuse*, London, Cedar, 1990.

29. Diana Russell, *The Secret Trauma*, New York, Basic Books, 1986.

30. Judith Lewis Herman, *Trauma and Recovery*, London, Pandora, 1992.

31. JoAnn Loulan, *Lesbian Passion: Loving Ourselves and Each Other*, San Francisco, Spinsters/aunt lute, 1987.

32. Caroline K. Waterman, Lori J. Davison, and Michael J. Bologna, 'Sexual Coercion in Gay Male and Lesbian Relationships: Predictors and Implications for Support Services', *The Journal of Sex Research*, vol. 26, no. 1, 1989, pp. 118–124.

33. Kerry Lobel (ed.), *Naming the Violence: Speaking Out About Lesbian Battering*, Seattle, Seal Press, 1986.

34. Joelle Taylor and Tracey Chandler, *Lesbians Talk Violent Relationships*, London, Scarlet Press, 1995.

35 Ibid., p. 18.

3 language: louder than words

In the transformation of silence into language and action it is vitally necessary for each of us to establish or examine her function in that transformation, and to recognize her role as vital within that transformation. For those of us who write, it is necessary to scrutinize not only the truth of what we speak but the truth of that language by which we speak it.

Audre Lorde[1]

Discourse, then, is entirely within, yet not necessarily in the service of, mechanisms of power. Consequently, the most efficacious task for lesbian theorists is not to secure a body or sexuality beyond networks of power but to understand that body, that sexuality, as incoherently constituted through discourse.

Annamarie Jagose[2]

Writing is a resource, to be played with, chewed over, debated, and above all used; but never trusted . . . writing is less a gift of the few than a craft that can be deployed by and for the many.

Jeffrey Weeks[3]

The devotion of a chapter to language, in a book dedicated to sex, may seem like yet another technique for talking about sex without actually saying very much. However, language cannot be divorced from sex, for without it there would be no 'sex' of which to speak. As the primary mode through which we communicate, language does not just allow for the sharing of ideas and experiences, it structures and shapes them. It is a resource and, like other resources, is not subject to equal distribution. Looking at this from a socio-political perspective[4] allows for the examination of the ideologies embedded in language, how speech is determined by context, and how its use empowers some groups over others.

I will begin this chapter by looking at the changes which social movements – specifically, feminism and lesbian and gay liberation – have made to linguistic order. The overview will include several terms and labels coming under close scrutiny. This will be followed by a focus on sex-speak: the conditions in which we do or don't talk, the functions and consequences of both silence and revelation, and how we discuss and define lesbian sex with a limited vocabulary.

Not a passing phrase

Language has been a weapon of oppression throughout history, and remains so even when the more obvious structural inequalities in law and civil rights have been successfully removed. But black activism, feminism and lesbian and gay liberation movements have all demonstrated how language is a site of resistance, a tool for change. The struggle does not stop with the demand for freedom of speech, but confronts the very words we have available. A language which reproduces phallocentric (male centred), sexist, racist, able-bodied and heterosexist assumptions and ideologies, however subtle, ensures the survival of these mechanisms at both psychological and societal levels. When vocabularies reflect nothing but the dominant order, others are invisibilized, cultural difference is denied, and non-conformity is contained. Through the strategies of reclamation, redefinition and innovation, disenfranchised groups have translated and transformed contemporary speech as a means of empowerment.

It is upon such strategies that the lesbian and gay communities are built. Naming ourselves is not only a defiant act of resistance but asserts our presence; we become and remain visible despite efforts at erasure. Self-definition, and ownership of the terms, both speak and spell out a powerful message. While, in isolation, naming does not result in total change, the postmodern anxieties around the constraints of labels should not detract from its impact. Our labels and vernacular are mechanisms through which we reproduce ourselves and recreate our culture. Countercultural codes are passed down through the generations; we inherit a history, a sense of the present, and a way to express our shared realities and meanings. These codes and colloquial conventions are among the customs through which we have come to recognize ourselves as a subculture and community.

A vocabulary which had already been expanded, with the words lesbian and gay to replace the generic homosexual, has been widened more recently to include not only queer and dyke but, significantly, the terms zami and khush – which carry wider cultural messages of race and ethnicity than those terms which define sexuality alone. As with other changes to language, adoption and assimilation is far from universal. Engaging critically with the words we speak is not something we are taught to do. Those who do not experience racism, sexism or heterosexism may never even think about language in this way. And some who do think about it will continue to resist translations, to protect the dominant structure of which they are part. Thus initiatives are dismissed as fads of the loony left (as was typical of the media distortions around Haringey Council's anti-racist policy), feminism gone too far, or exhibitionist queers.

This is not to say that changes to language have not have been effective, because many have. More general changes of sexist and racist language are now reflected at institutional levels. Lesbian and gay are terms which are widely used in the parent culture and subculture, although they are also used as insults by those patrolling the gender divide. But radical feminist respelling of the words herstory and wimmin (to eliminate the male 'essence' of history and women), while widely adopted in some (mainly radical) feminist circles – particularly parts of the lesbian community – remains largely absent in the mainstream.

The words with which we speak are not only indicative of our backgrounds (and all that entails in terms of education and class) but affiliations to philosophies and ideologies within the counter-culture. In particular, the splits in our community over the role of sexuality have resulted in certain words being imbued with negative meanings when deployed in specific contexts. Thus, lesbians resisting the anti-porn movement became identified as 'sex radicals' or 'libertarians', and those preoccupied with anything other than lesbian politics became 'lifestyle' or 'lipstick' lesbians. Radical feminists are similarly branded with labels like 'repressive', 'puritanical' and 'politically correct'. This last term has also been adopted, in the mainstream, to denigrate affirmative action policies – which aim to implement social change and eliminate inequality.

An example of how words can shape our thoughts is found in the term 'homophobia'. This expression came into circulation around the same time that the American Psychiatric Association removed homosexuality from its official list of mental disorders[6] (an event seen as a turning point). Its literal meaning is 'fear of sameness' but it is used to mean 'the irrational fear of homosexuals'. And while many of us use the term to describe the prejudice we encounter, it is argued we should identify it more accurately as prejudice, discrimination and lesbian hatred. Homophobia is problematic because of its psychological connotations. An irrational fear, a phobia, is the property of an individual. It is his or her particular response to a trigger – in this case, homosexuals. And as such, society is not to blame for homophobia. Ironically, we cease to be sick when those who are prejudiced against us become pathologized. This distracts from the fact that anti-lesbian and -gay prejudice is endemic in the parent culture. Individuals do not become fearful; they are socialized into believing there is something wrong with those who make lesbian and gay choices. This prejudice (like many) is a social norm, operating at all levels.

Celia Kitzinger,[7] in her radical analysis, cleverly subverts the meaning of homophobia and the equivalent, lesbophobia. With reference to the radical feminist goal of bringing down heteropatriarchy, the fear, she argues, is far from irrational: if revolutionary intent poses a threat, it will be feared. In addition to the term homophobia, many of us use the phrase 'internalized homophobia' to refer broadly to the negative images of lesbians and gays we have absorbed, which may in part affect our self-esteem, feelings of shame, and ability to disclose. And while this term is similarly limited, any fear we have is far from irrational. Coming out or being identified by others can have many negative consequences, which is why many lesbians describe a sixth sense when deciding whether or not it is safe to state their preference or orientation.

Having established a language of identity and articulated the discrimination we face, we still have a spartan vocabulary in many respects. When it comes to describing those who occupy important places in our lives, we can still find ourselves stumbling at this public and private hurdle. What do we call the women in our hearts, heads and, most probably, our beds? 'Lover' is a common choice and, while conveying the sexual component, the emphasis might make us feel a little uncomfortable. As an expression, it is very 'forward'; and it may not be sufficient to convey the other feelings and connections we have with these women. 'Significant other', meanwhile, may be considered too intense – and it is a bit of a mouthful. Closeted references to flatmates and friends leave us completely invisible. If heterosexism were not so pervasive, validating our partners and our own choices would be so much easier.

'Girlfriend' has a far wider circulation and currency. And while it can be confused with a reference to a straight woman's friend or with camp

(North American) colloquialisms, the context usually clears up any confusion. The word does have something of a youthful quality (which is no bad thing) as, in the mainstream, it signifies a developmental stage prior to fiancée, wife and, possibly, widow. Another widely adopted term is 'partner'. While this term can be dismissed as symbolic of male possession, an alternative interpretation is that it denotes a relationship status, even after death – thus the role of the other is witnessed. It is increasingly adopted in the parent culture by those unhappy with the oppressive overtones of 'husband' and 'wife', the growing numbers of unmarried couples, and those sensitive to dyadic (couple) diversity. The difference is that, when it comes to the paperwork, she is often not counted as our partner, even when it is scrawled all over the page, as well as in the box provided! Likewise, we cannot marry (even if we would want to) and we are denied any official avenues through which to publicly assert any commitments and statements we might want to make. This lack of partnership recognition and public status is paralleled by the relative scarcity of appropriate terminology. And while not endorsing institutions like traditional marriage, which function to keep women oppressed, I do believe our lack of language and of ceremonial opportunity impacts upon our lifestyles and relationships. This, along with other major inequalities faced by lesbians and gay men, has been identified for legislative change by the lobbying organization Stonewall, in its proposed 'Homosexual Equality Bill'. If successful, such legislation could eventually be assimilated into changes in language, labels and how people think – although a great deal more would have to happen for such a radical reformation of society and its sexual hierarchy.[8]

Names and identities have a function not only in the public domain but in intimate and exclusive contexts. One way of enhancing such exclusivity is the use of pet names and characterizations unknown to anyone else. This type of romantic role-play has been largely analysed in relation to heterosexual couples,[9] where the adoption of 'cute' animal-like personas allows for the communication of needs which would otherwise be prohibited. Whether similar numbers of lesbian couples enter such worlds is unknown. There is potentially less need, as communication may be easier without gendered barriers and the emotional illiteracy traditionally associated with masculinity. In addition, such characterizations may be consciously resisted, as a different style of relating is favoured to that dictated by commercialized and sextyped conventions of romance. Alternatively, their use may be exaggerated, to assert the intimacy which straight society so frequently ignores. There is also the possibility that such personas function less as a vehicle for intimacy and more as a currency for sex.

While the role of romance is looked at more closely in relation to butch/femme dynamics, of interest here is the more general vocabulary for the language of love. And on closer scrutiny it becomes apparent how pervasive some ideas are. We 'fall in love', we cannot help ourselves – whether it is her magnetism or our attraction, it seems to be a force we cannot resist. This image fits snugly into wider notions of the compelling nature of sexual attraction, inevitable and seemingly unstoppable. We are driven by insatiable urges for love and sex. A more accurate description might be that we are less likely to fall than to jump in with two feet, albeit often without looking. Or we are pushed by cultural pressure. As long as we continue to speak of love and sex in this framework, it is but a small step to the powerlessness of addiction.

But what can we put in place of banished images of romantic love? Lesbians often rewrite romance, but a framework survives through which we understand our experiences. And while romance is no longer a necessary licence for sex, the two are still closely related in many women's minds, even in situations where the sex is felt first. Romance and love provide narratives in our lives, guiding expectation and creating meaning. There is a lot of love in our communities – falling in and falling out. In another departure from the model of the parent culture, many ex-lovers stay friends, becoming part of an intimate friendship network (which may make for an easier life in small communities). When the definition changes from ex-lover to friend is the subject of another book.[10]

For the *hopeless* romantic frustrated by the shortage of superlatives through which to convey thought and feeling, the search for sexual articulacy is even more daunting. A much cited example of linguistic wealth is that Eskimo culture/s have over 100 words for snow. That's probably more words than we have to describe our entire sexual repertoire. And although much of this text is concerned with the emergence of a new sexual dialect,[11] the adoption of this visibility and vernacular has its limits. The translation of public profiles, dialogues and discourse into the private arena is far from inevitable.

Talking about sex

Being a sex radical means being defiant as well as deviant. It means being aware that there is something unsatisfactory and dishonest about the way sex is talked about (or hidden) in daily life.

Pat Califia[12]

Our failure to find simple comfortable ways of talking about sex perpetuates lopsided attitudes with adverse effects upon personal and natural health and happiness . . . finding a common language with which everyone can talk comfortably about sex is a persistent problem.

Antony Grey[13]

Sexuality is as much about language as it is about the sexual organs.

Jeffrey Weeks[14]

'Sex-speak' can take many forms. Ranging from the debates and conversations we have in public, to the intimacies of talk with a sexual partner prior to, during or after the acts we define as sex. Despite the prevailing myth that sex needs no discussion or negotiation, the therapy industry has effectively convinced us, for several decades now, that sex talk is good for our sex lives. An added incentive in contemporary times is that such discussion will also make it safer. Yet when it comes to sex, we also communicate in non-verbal ways. We can have entire 'conversations' where no one has to say a word. When vocalizations do punctuate the practice, they become part of it: signals of pleasure, directives, questions, elaborate running commentaries of fantasy, and the passionate exclamations and declarations, which might otherwise be known as pillow talk.

Unsurprisingly, these articulations of the sexual meta-language have been little investigated. The counting of isolated acts is seen as intrusive enough, but to ask people what they say to each other or think about while performing these acts goes beyond the imagination of sexologists – although not beyond the curious minds of some feminists. Yet even amongst feminists, intimate revelations and comparisons of experience have been largely absent, as energy has been directed to 'more important issues'. Feminist lesbians have found themselves doubly silenced, burdened by naive notions that women loving women have perfect egalitarian sex and that to break this myth would be little short of heresy.

Despite these social silences we are supposed to maximize our pleasure by turning our bodies and our minds into sexual information superhighways. We can read, watch videos and look at pornography to develop our erotic infrastructures. But when it comes to talk, what do we say and how do we say it? Words are scarce, much of what is available being medical, heterosexualized, pejorative or 'obscene'. We become shy, embarrassed, labouring under a lifetime's socialization and sex-role stereotyping. And while breaking the taboo on talk is an act of resistance, which is exciting, there is the underlying anxiety that if we take the mystery out of sex, there is nothing left. If the erotic charge of the illicit is diffused and desire is domesticated, sexual fluency will have lost its purpose.

It is unlikely that, in western, over-sexualized, capitalist economies, we would ever reach (en masse) such a place. And while we are powerfully reclaiming a number of words in identity politics, and expanding our own sexual economy through the medium of popular culture, sex – like our salaries (if we have them) – remains largely undiscussed.

Take the situation where a friend asks about your new girlfriend – the woman who preoccupied your fantasy life for six months before she asked you out. In response to the question 'what does she do?' (asked in some misguided notion that, if she invites you to talk about this woman, you just might exhaust yourself and manage to change the subject before the end of the evening), what do you say? A conventional answer would be to state her interests and activities. An alternative might be: 'Well, we've slept together twice (Friday through to Sunday, and Wednesday night), and she seems particularly adept at finding the right place with her thigh, she is figuring out just how much penetration I usually like (although she's not quite there yet), and I think she's placed a homing device on my G-spot. She hasn't found out yet that my ears are sex organs, and I'm trying to figure out how to tell her – I mean it's not the thing you talk about, is it?' The listener, meanwhile, hurriedly retrieves her chin from the floor.

An alternative scenario is that your friend's question was, in fact, asking for just such a disclosure, in which case you may have been left shifting uncomfortably in your seat, wondering about her potential motives and voyeuristic tendencies. Because, after all, the privacy protecting what remains unknown to others helps to keep sex 'special'.

Even in those rare forums designed for sexual discussion, the level at which we talk varies. We fear judgment, censorship, being laughed at. What if we've been doing it wrong all these years, or if we don't do it at all or never have? And besides, the lights are still on! It is by looking at the lists we compile in lesbian sex workshops, of the breadth of our sexuality, that we appreciate that the actualities of action are but one part. But they are a part that a number of women want to talk about. And silences are shattered, bonds forged and secrets shared. It was after facilitating one such workshop that I was approached to write this book. When I was advised of the publishers' cautionary concern[15] – 'We don't quite know how you're going to do it, we only know it has to be done right' – I was left thinking that they were far from alone in their expectations of another's performance of lesbian sex. As with the nature of sex itself, the book is far more complex than I initially imagined – falling just short of the fantasies I had been entertaining.

Lurid lexicons and sexual semantics

In a book seductively entitled *Undressing Lesbian Sex*, well might you ask, what exactly am I undressing? So far I have spent more time stripping the layers off the culture than disrobing the performers and their practices. So what is this amorphous 'it' that so many of us do and fantasize about? The 'it' that some even talk and write about? Forever avoiding a concise definition, it may be that sex is too fluid to be pinned down to a succinct synopsis. But defining what constitutes lesbian sex is vital to our debates. Imagine being confronted by a Martian who wanted to know what lesbian sex was (stay with it – consider this an exercise in creative fantasy enhancement which is bound to improve your sex life!). Resorting to a text-book definition may render the task less arduous: 'any sex that happens between two women';[16] but this leaves the alien visitor little the wiser. And besides, she has read the entire contents of the local women's bookshop in a nano-second, so she probably knows this much already. No, she's on a mission and she's determined to be successful. She has five arms totalling twenty fingers, the softest skin and a handy little detachable joy-stick from the space-ship ... someone should tell her!

The definition of sex must ultimately reside in context and intention. We don't have to be in a relationship, in love or even in bed. But when does lesbian sex officially 'begin' and 'end'? How can we be sure we've had 'it'? We could map out the episode according to Master and Johnson's 'Human Sexual Response Cycle',[17] a model largely seen as definitive of the sexual experience. Thus 'sexual stimulation' triggers 'excitement' (as indicated by physiological change) after which we progress through the stages of 'plateau', 'orgasm' and 'resolution'. However, despite its scientific credibility, this model is not universal. Not only does it neglect an entire psychology, but their research was conducted after the theory was in place – only those whose responses came close to the model were selected for research.[18] So although the eighty-two lesbians selected got turned on Masters-and-Johnson-style, many more were turned away. A problem with relying on such a model is the emphasis placed on orgasm, a goal-oriented approach which many women have condemned.

An alternative model which allows for the psychological perspective is JoAnn Loulan's adaptation.[19] This model begins with willingness, progressing to desire, excitement (emotional), engorgement (physical), orgasm, and pleasure (an experience which accompanies all other stages). These are, however, maps of response and feeling, defining a potential destination as opposed to a route. And while they may contain parts of what we would define as sex, the description remains incomplete. To define, we need to know explicitly what we do and what we don't do. A question on the Pride Survey asked women to describe what, for them, constituted sex. This particular question followed others including: number of sexual partners, age of first sexual experience, frequency of sex, and changes in practice made as a conscious choice of safer sex. Thus one thing is clear: in the absence of a definition, up to this point, each woman had her own ideas of what sex was. These answers yielded some of the most informative and interesting findings from the survey. What follows is a selection of the answers, some in full, others in part.

Lesbians were asked, 'What would have to happen between you and another woman for you to call it sex?'
And they answered . . .

'Well it starts when she looks at me and goes on from there.'

'Don't know.'

'Mutual masturbation.'

'Mutual fucking.'

'Finger penetration or penetration with a vibrator or dildo.'

'Ooh, difficult question! All sorts of things . . . A lot of mutual pleasure . . . Enjoyment of each other and experiencing each other's reactions to pleasure . . . Kissing and sucking and licking and stroking and feeling her in me and me in her.'

'Kissing, caressing, touching breasts, touching genitals, but not necessarily penetration.'

'Touching, caressing, licking, stimulating each other's clitoris.'

'Intimacy – both or one of us having an orgasm.'

'Penetration by some means and oral sex.'

'Some form of genital contact.'

'This is not something I have ever thought about before. I think for me it would have to involve the genitals, with or without penetration, but to include touching, stroking, etc. I would not consider kissing or fondling breasts, cuddling, etc., to be sex.'

'I suppose it would have to culminate in orgasm either by finger stimulation, oral stimulation or any other kind of stimulation. Kissing wouldn't constitute sex.'

'If I go to bed with a woman and oral sex does not play a part in what we do, I do not really consider it to be full sex, even though we may have stimulated each other digitally and come as a result of rubbing, deep kissing, massaged each other, etc. . . . Also includes an amount of role-playing such as being tied up and feeling relaxed and trusting each other so that you can explore other reactions over and above 'vanilla' sex.'

'A very good question! I've thought about this before. I suppose as soon as non-clothed genital contact happens, this is where I feel sex begins.'

'Genital contact – kissing and breast contact would not make it! Having a grind standing up wouldn't be, but lying down, I'd probably call it sex. Having a sexual conversation might come pretty close.'

'With my girlfriend I am constantly making love to her . . . When it comes to straighforward sex I think there are several stages which go together to define sex: 1) Kissing/light stroking/seduction. 2) Arousal/ stroking/talking (usually naked). 3) stimulation/oral sex/fingering etc. 4) Climax.'

'Good question! Extensive touching, both intimate, i.e. of clitoris, labia etc., and more general. (orgasm and/or penetration are not essential).'

'Very interesting question – something I think about regularly, talk with friends and my lover a lot. It's definitely not got to involve orgasm, but however much I try not to focus on genitals, I find it hard to think of sex not including some touching of genitals. I'm not happy about this – in my head I know sex should be defined in a much broader way, but defining e.g. a good snogging session is hard work.'

'To call it sex between me and another woman, we would both have to orgasm.'

'For us both to agree that what we had was sex.'

'I would call anything that aims at achieving orgasm sex, even if orgasm does not actually occur.'

'Going past heavy petting, naked . . . '

'Varies according to the partner.'

'Depends what I was doing and who with! Kissing, for example, with my partner could be sex, but with someone else . . . '

'Consenting physical contact with the mutual intention of arousal and orgasm.'

'Anything that made me feel vulnerable!'

'To touch, kiss, etc. her (consensually) and be touched in return, including the vulva – it's really difficult to write – terms either seem clinical or have been used as terms of abuse.'

'Anything that got me wet!'

'Anything involving cunts.'

'Sex: any of the following – stimulating the genitals, oral sex, humping, tribadism. Making love: caressing, massaging, deep kissing and any of the above with someone you love.'

'Oral stimulation downstairs.'

'To kiss properly on the mouth; to both get genital arousal from one another's actions, to probably be undressed.'

'Direct clitoral stimulation, possibly with vaginal penetration – with lots of kissing and nipple sucking thrown in for good measure.'

'One or more (usually more than one) of the following: either active or passive or both! Stimulation of the clitoris, breasts, penetration of the vagina, tribadism (each of above) with hands/mouth/tongue/sex toy.'

'Penetration of vagina (by anything) of either partner by either partner i.e. I do not include naked fondling etc. unless at least one partner orgasms.'

'Impossible to answer – too many possibilities! (But you'd know at the time that was what you were doing).'

'There must be an attempt to arouse sexual desire or express it. Must involve sensual touching and would be unusual if done in public.'

'Touching each other, intimately.'

'I would class snogging, touching, etc. as sex.'

'Both of us would have to be turned on, i.e. become wet down below! It's the working toward the wetness that is a big part of sex – and the sexiest bit – next to coming.'

'An intimate one-to-one experience where one or both partners specifically intends to arouse the other. This does not necessarily have to lead to orgasm (but if I'm honest, if it does it helps).'

'It would vary greatly depending on if I was in a relationship with the woman or had just met. I suppose anything done with passion.'

'Sexually stimulated to at least plateau phase by physical (tactile) contact from another woman.'

'What we label as "sex", as individuals, will be different at different times with different people.'

'I think there's a difference between "sex" and something "sexual". For it to be sex I think it has to involve the genitals (either mine or hers or both).'

'To both enjoy bringing each other to the point of climax point of no return – and to both be very dirty in talk or behaviour.'

' . . . would definitely involve the touching of erogenous zones to the point where it's impossible to keep control . . . I think the morning after is when you really know whether you've had sex or not.'

'The more intense the desire, the less has to happen for me to feel I am "having sex".'

'Any expression of desire – passionately or exquisitely gently. There isn't, for me, one act which means it's "sex" we're having.'

'Penetration by both partners.'

'Intimate, erotic interaction, e.g. phone sex to SM play.'

'Deep kissing and almost any physical contact that is consciously and deliberately done between women who have discussed being sexually attracted to each other.'

'Any physical or eye contact that wouldn't take place with my platonic friends.'

'Passion with tenderness: physical and spiritual communication with our bodies leading to sexual arousal and stimulation.'

'You're with another woman in a relatively private place and you're throbbing as a result of the interaction between the two of you. If this goes on for more than ten minutes, you're having sex! For those more bold – the place doesn't have to be private and you could be with more than one woman.'

'I don't believe that sex necessarily has to be genital, hence caressing and stroking of the whole body would be considered sex to me. Similarly a massage could be very sexual. I think it's very personal what is considered sex, |it| really is more a feeling that what has happened is sexual.'

'Would have to be genital contact – all other contact which is sexual, such as some massage, caresses, etc., I would think of as sensual contact rather than sex. However, I would class SM as sex, regardless of whether there was contact or not, as when I do SM, the main aim for me is to intensify sexual pleasure and tension, whereas the aim of caressing, massage, etc., is simply to gain pleasure from those acts themselves, rather than necessarily lead to sex.'

'It's a state of mind and something shared rather than a physiological action/reaction. Is that nebulous and pretentious enough?!'

'The determining factors would be feelings of attraction and desire . . . but mainly it would involve moving into physical and emotional territory which is generally out of bounds to other women . . . '

'An activity in which one or both women try to bring the other to the point of orgasm. Not necessarily physical – mind sex – verbal sex.'

'When calculating the answer to Q7 I included people where orgasms and/or penetration was involved.' |Question 7 asked about the number of sexual partners.|

'I have a broad definition of sex, from talking about it, i.e. fantasies, to actually doing it.'

'One or both partners masturbating the other/each other. Anything involving touching genitals with any part of the body by one or both partners. However I think this question is somewhat irrelevant – was it Sheila Jeffreys who wrote "Does it matter if they did it?" '

Even within the constraints of language, selection of answers demonstrates the varied configurations through which lesbian sex can be described. The words employed cover the whole range of clinical to colloquial sex-speak. While themes recur, many of the answers are very different, reflecting the diverse priorities and meanings we assign to sex. There is no one term, either describing a particular part of the anatomy or a specific practice, that is mentioned uniformly across all 278 answers.

Although orgasm is commonly referred to, its inclusion is used by some women to stress that it is not necessary. A range of practices are referred to in the same vein. Of particular interest is the role of kissing. A number of respondents were keen to say what would not constitute sex, as well as what would. Kissing was most commonly cited in this respect. And although kissing was included by the others as part of what would 'have to happen', 'deep kissing' was the preferred term here. In a climate where there is a pressure to assert 'real sexuality', many women may contend that 'kissing is not sex', to defy the popular image that kissing is all lesbians ever do. There is also the fact that kissing is not genital sex and may be considered foreplay. However, having said this, research suggests that lesbians kiss during sex more than other couples (see Chapter 4), so it is obviously vital to many of our repertoires, and this is reflected across a range of the 278 responses. It may be that, in the absence of freedom of affectionate/intimate expression in public, kissing remains more erotically charged, as we are less able to take it for granted. Then, of course, there is the fact that, for many women, sex involves a lot of activities as well as genital sex.

Many of the answers refer to the genitals, or specifically genitally related practice, either directly or with metaphors. General touching and caressing are also frequently cited through a range of words. Language is both graphic and explicit, as would be expected from the nature of the question. For many of these women, quite a lot 'has to happen' for them to call it sex: from kissing to penetration, from 'mutual intention' to engaging in 'physical or eye contact' that wouldn't take place with friends. These descriptions are of course relative – a fact which was highlighted by a number of respondents. While some clearly prioritize physical practices and pleasures over other aspects of intimacy, others struggle with the belief that they shouldn't, even though they do. A number of women in the survey defined sex in a wider context of intimacy. However, interpretation of the answers is necessarily limited. For what we do not know are the wider meanings of what these sexual episodes represent to these women. Vital as it is to see what women actually consider sex to be and the words they use to describe it, we need more information to gain insight into the nature of lesbian desires and the functions of sex. Some answers do point to this expansive area, like the brave and telling reply, 'anything that made me feel vulnerable.'

Considering the high profile of the SM versus vanilla debates, the range of answers demonstrates that such a framework is not the only one through which to talk about lesbian sex. (Vanilla, in this context, is a general term to describe sex practices classed as not SM – as opposed to a term used by some black women to describe white sexual partners.) The range of practices detailed (throughout the questionnaire) also shows the problems of establishing the parameters. Fisting, for example, is the insertion of the whole hand or fist into the vagina (or rectum), which affords sensations of deep and full penetration. Yet more women enjoy the practice than are happy to label it with a word which has such aggressive connotations and has the image of being the property of SM. The term handballing is even less popular, seen primarily as a gay men's practice. Restraint and bondage, also commonly reported, have SM associations. In the Pride Survey, there is a notable disparity between the numbers who practise it and those who identify with the SM roles of either top or bottom.[20] Isolated acts, however, do not constitute SM sex, in the absence of the wider dynamics. It is not just about what you do, it is about how you do it – consciously manipulating positions of power, with mutual consent, in the quest for sexual pleasure.

The suggestion that many lesbians are abandoning vanilla practices in favour of serious SM scenes is exaggerated. Many lesbians are practitioners of SM, but others enjoy the appeal of a surface style and one or two behaviours which play on power or involve props and toys, as opposed to adoption of a complete new sexual persona. Either way, this sexual 'otherness' is the subject of much debate, defence and damnation across lesbian communities.

The term sado-masochism is derived from the writings and practices of two men, the marquis de Sade and Leopold von Sacher-Masoch, familiarized in the works of psychiatrists Krafft-Ebing and Freud in the late nineteenth and earlier twentieth centuries. Recent proponents of SM are careful to point out how neither de Sade nor Sacher-Masoch fits perfectly into the modern-day definition, which relies on reciprocity, concern and respect.[21] In a world with so much unwanted pain, suffering and oppression, the very notion of SM may appear irreconcilable with ideas of sexual pleasure. The important difference is that the orchestrated scenes of SM are based on consent, not coercion. A counter-argument here is that the very notion of consent amongst oppressed peoples is almost illusory, as it is less a choice than a symptom of false consciousness. But, while I agree that consent is an issue for ethical appraisal, writing off sexual desire as oppressive practice is premature foreclosure.

SM – which may also be described in terms of dominance/submission (D/S or S/D, sub-dom), bondage and discipline (B/D), or more idiosyncratically by individuals using terms like power and trust[22] – appeals to lesbians for a number of reasons. It is rich in language, labels, rituals and visual codes. Terms like top/bottom, dominant/submissive, mistress/slave and sadist/masochist allow for the articulation of a particular sexual preference. Although these terms can be interchangeable, this is not always the case, as, for example, when a bottom likes to 'serve' and be dominated, but does not get off on physical pain. In addition, there is an available vocabulary to name sexual practices, as evidenced by the glossary at the back of Pat Califia's book, *Sensuous Magic*.[23]

Talk is also vital in SM, not only to allow for the setting of the scene and the simmering of sexual tension, but to ensure physical and emotional safety. Creative strategies included in *The Lesbian SM Safety Manual*[24] show how such discussions can playfully be incorporated in to the assuming of unequal roles. The notion of safety in SM practices is far from a contradiction in terms – for experienced practitioners it is an essential requirement. 'Safe words' are agreed as a signal to lessen the intensity or terminate the scene altogether. Words like no, stop, and mercy tend not to be used as exit clauses, as such protestations are often deployed in the scene itself as part of the psychodrama. Honest discussions about sex are a ritual requirement for SMers, unlike many other sexually active individuals who do not talk and plan in the same fashion.

Stylistically, SM fashions make sex visible through the recognized paraphernalia of leather, body harnesses, piercing and hankies worn to the right (passive/receptive) and left (active), which communicate particular practices depending on the colour. This outlaw look has appeal for many lesbians, not all of whom follow through with pre-scripted elaborate manipulations of unequal power relations.

Amongst the explanations for the enjoyment of physical pain is the high caused by the surge of the body's naturally produced opiate-like pain-killers, the endorphins. This 'high', together with the psychodrama, enhances the complete sexual episode. This rationale is also readily adopted by addictionologists eager to prove the compulsive or addictive element underlying SM sex. The experience of pain under invited conditions is not the same as non-consensual violence. When physical sensations are incorporated into an erotic scene, any 'discomfort' element is perceived differently, as moving pain thresholds allow for pleasure to take hold.

But pain is not the central reason why SM meets with so much resistance from lesbians. The objection is to behaviour which is considered to re-enact oppressions. And while practitioners argue that the power dynamics do not overspill into everyday life, when Pat Califia[25] boasts that the nature of her non-monogamous relationship makes her partner 'think twice' before using her safe word, this may be seized upon as evidence to the contrary. Sites of particular controversy are the symbolic themes of child sex abuse, Nazism and slavery. The roles of adult/infant recreated in sex scenes is considered offensive and disrespectful to those who have experienced such assault. However, there are some survivors of sexual abuse who see such role-play as cathartic (this is explored elsewhere in the text).

Although many of the props for scenes are kept in the 'dungeon' (a place designed and kitted out for SM scenes), styles are symbolically incorporated into the dress code. Texture and clothes fetishes are communicated by leather and uniforms, chains being a sign of captivity, ownership, and dominance/submission. The adoption of the Nazi uniform prompts, quite justifiably, great condemnation. The swastika, originally a Buddhist symbol, was reversed to become the international mark of the Nazis. It still carries the same meaning today, whether in East London, South Africa or anywhere else. And to many, including myself, the eroticization of an emblem with such a violent history is beyond comprehension. However, this emotive aspect of the SM scene must be kept in perspective. While seized upon by opponents, to encourage the complete rejection of SM sex, the appropriation of the swastika is actually condemned by most SMers. Sophie Moorcock[26] (of *Quim* fame), has written a powerful and compelling criticism of such practices, while identifying as an SM dyke.

That chains and manacles are less broadly condemned reflects not only the fact that they are general symbols of captivity, but also the nature of British imperialism. While the horrors of the war and the Nazi regime are kept in circulation, the history of slavery is less publicized, as is Britain's involvement in the slave trade. Some of the most articulate critiques of the adoption of chains, roles of dominance and submission and the ownership language of slavery, are written by black women, who encounter a racist society built on the economies of the slave trade and imperialist exploitation and the ideologies of racial and ethnic inferiority.

The experiences of racism and heterosexism (if separate) have similarities and differences. White lesbians cannot challenge a system for ignoring sexual politics, if we are then going to quietly collude with failure to respect difference along other dimensions. In our struggles, we would do well to remember that oppressions exist beyond those of sexuality and gender, and that wider experiences – of racism and anti-semitism, for example – must be equally prioritized if we are to make any further progress with the complexity of sexual politics.

Although SM is portrayed as the daring, exciting, sexual other, 'vanilla' sex is hardly dull, impoverished or boring. And in a patriarchal heterosexist society, it is hardly the acceptable face of sex, either. I would argue (as would many others) that it lacks nothing in comparison to its big bad little sister. But this returns us to the question of what is 'vanilla' sex, because many of us will do a range of things, including using sex toys, without identifying as SMers – although the more fundamentalist may brand us so. The vernacular we have to describe stereotypical vanilla practices is not only limited but vague, masking differences which, while subtle, could function as distinctions if we wanted to get more specific both behaviourally and verbally. Tribadism, that all-embracing term for 'she who rubs' (from tribade, another word for lesbian!) is used interchangeably with frottage or humping to describe all acts of body rubbing. That is if these acts are actually named at all. These terms ignore all variations in positioning and the accompanying genital geography. Even in the 'missionary position' (one lying on top of the other, facing each other) genital-to-genital contact is not inevitable, as one partner may get more direct sensation from the more general pubic region or the upper thigh. Then there is lying on top. both facing downwards, rubbing against her arse – potentially also stimulating her clitoris while she's underneath. Is one act higher up the lesbian sexual hierarchy than another? Other positions include kneeling, standing and straddling chairs, in a most admirable display of polymorphous perversity, and yet it all gets submerged under one name.

In terms of amorphous catch-alls, 'mutual masturbation' is one of the most difficult to tie down. My objection to this expression is that it is vague. Masturbation, which was the sin of sins before the moralists, puritans and medical profession discovered homosexuality, is self-stimulation. Deemed responsible for a range of social ills over the years, attempts at prohibition have even taken the form of dietary deterrents – I guess eating Kellogg's cornflakes is one way of ensuring your hands are kept above the table. Masturbation: sex with 'five finger mary' (Loulan), someone you love, or the ideal date – you don't have to dress for the occasion and you don't have to be a mind-reader to know what she wants. Feminists and sex therapists alike recognized its potential for self-appreciation, pleasure and a way to learn about our bodies so we could please ourselves and instruct others on how to do the same. The Victorian myths have finally lost their grip – no more short-sightedness or hairy palms – people masturbate and they enjoy it.

Solitary and partnered sex are different. And while valued, masturbation still carries connotations of something less than real sex. Recognizing that this needs further challenge, until there is more of a change in attitude, the term will continue to cause me some problem when it is applied to dyke sex. It not only subtly reinforces notions that lesbian sex is not the real thing, but invalidates our partners – as if we would feel just the same without her, taking ourselves in hand. And when we mutually masturbate what are we actually doing? Do we take turns to get ourselves off in front of our partners? Or does she touch her vulva as she touches ours? Is the touch of self and/or other done serially or in tandem? Is it mutual if only one partner is genitally stimulated? Are we talking clitoral stimulation, or penetration or both? How about the role of toys, talk, pornography or guided fantasy? All of the above have meaning and words as acts of lesbian sex, and masturbation is something different. This diversity also has very real implications for the marketing of mutual masturbation as a safer sex technique. Wendy Castor in *The Lesbian Sex Book* bravely pins it down, describing mutual masturbation as 'simultaneously touching each others clitorises, often to the point of orgasm.'[27] So if this is mutual masturbation, does this mean other acts are merely a variation on a theme? Is tribadism masturbation without any hands? According to a leading authority on lesbian sex, this would seem to be the case. In the results of her first sex survey, JoAnn Loulan[28] lists it under 'methods of masturbation'. It seems we are in a no-win situation here – we're either ripping off heterosexual sex or we're masturbating.

Sexual language is indeed a complex matter. Throughout the course of writing about lesbian sex, I have been faced with yet another dilemma – how to describe who does what to whom. This is commonly communicated in the terminology active/passive, inserter/insertee, or fucker/fuckee.

This language of 'doing' and 'having done to' has oppressive subject/object connotations. We are both giving *and* receiving in the exchange. The 'passive' or 'recipient' partner may have initiated the sex, she may be far more physically active than her partner. The other phrases cited are more readily associated with gay male sex, and although they can be used for lesbian penetrative sex, active/passive is more generally adopted. The words we have are at times too vague and, at others, too specific. The use of butch/femme is looked at in more detail later in the text. It is clear that if we want to talk more about lesbian sex and the subtleties of it, we need a broader language which we will feel comfortable using.

If, as Marilyn Frye argues in her formative essay,[29] sex is an inappropriate term for what lesbians do, then what do we call it? While the actualities of what we do may evade succinct description, replacing the familiar shorthand will not automatically produce a much-sought-after clarity. Sarah Lucia Hoagland offers a similar analysis to Frye's: 'I want to try and leave behind the word sex and focus on desire ... we need a new language and meaning to develop our desire.'[30] I could not agree more with her latter premise. Elucidation of desire would offer some much-needed insight into the complexity of sex and sexuality, providing the momentum to look at sex in new ways. By [re]defining our desire/s, we take charge of an area through which we are controlled, as desire is mainly defined by the dominant order. In such a redefinition, caution is necessary to avoid setting narrow, prescriptive parameters. There is also a risk that, in taking Hoagland's advice, we do not break the circle, but merely shift our focus to another. Lesbians do have sex. They also have desire. We need to be able to articulate the personal meaning before we can succeed in a counter-cultural transformation and translation. And, although expanding the vocabulary and securing new meanings is not easy when so much is invested in maintaining contemporary interpretations, post-modernity potentially renders this more possible.

NOTES

1. Audre Lorde, 'The transformation of silence into language and action', in *Sister Outsider: Essays and Speeches by Audre Lorde*, Freedom, CA, Crossing Press Feminist Series, 1984, p. 43.
2. Annamarie Jagose, *Lesbian Utopics*, London, Routledge, 1994, pp. 4–5.
3. Jeffrey Weeks, *Against Nature: Essays on History, Sexuality and Identity*, London, Rivers Oram Press, 1991, p. 8.

4. This approach to language study is broadly known as Discourse Analysis. See, for example, Erica Burman and Ian Parker (eds.), *Discourse Analytic Research: Repertoires and Readings of Texts in Action*, London, Routledge, 1993.

5. The name zami has Caribbean origins, khush is an Urdu word originally from Indian culture. See, for example: Audre Lorde, *Zami: A New Spelling of My Name*, London, Sheba, 1982; Valerie Mason-John and Ann Khambatta (eds.), *Lesbians Talk Making Black Waves*, London, Scarlet Press, 1993; Helen (charles), '(Not) compromising: inter skin colour relations', in Lynne Pearce and Jackie Stacey (eds.), *Romance Revisited*, London, Lawrence and Wishart, 1995, pp. 197–209.

6. Homosexuality was taken off the American Psychiatric Association's Diagnostic and Statistical Manual III in 1973. The term 'homophobia' was coined by George Weinberg in 1972.

7. Celia Kitzinger, *The Social Construction of Lesbianism*, London, Sage, 1987.

8. For discussion of the Bill and its implications for equality and citizenship, see either: Peter Tatchell, 'Equal rights for all: Strategies for lesbian and gay equality in Britain', in Ken Plummer (ed.), *Modern Homosexualities: Fragments of Lesbian and Gay Experience*, London, Routledge, 1992, pp. 237–54, or Simon Watney, 'Practices of freedom: "Citizenship" and the politics of identity in the age of AIDS', in Simon Watney, *Practices of Freedom: Selected Writings on HIV/AIDS*, London, Rivers Oram Press, 1994, pp. 156–68.

9. See Wendy Langford, 'Snuglet Puglet loves to snuggle with Snuglet Piglet': alter personalities in heterosexual love relationships', in Lynne Pearce and Jackie Stacey, op. cit., pp. 251–64.

10. The experience of relationship break-up and the transitions into friendship are charted by Carol S. Becker in *Unbroken Ties: Lesbian Ex-Lovers*, Boston, Alyson, 1988.

11. A phrase coined by Arlene Stein in 'The year of the lustful lesbian', in Arlene Stein (ed.), *Sisters, Sexperts, Queers: Beyond the Lesbian Nation*, New York, Plume (Penguin Group), 1993, pp. 13–34.

12. Pat Califia, *Public Sex: The Culture of Radical Sex*, San Francisco, Cleis Press, 1994, p. 11.

13. Antony Grey, *Speaking of Sex: The Limits of Language*, London, Cassell, 1993, pp. 9 and 12.

14. Jeffrey Weeks, op. cit., p. 3.

15. In conversation with Christina Ruse.

16. Wendy Castor, *The Lesbian Sex Book*, 1993, Boston, Alyson, p. 7.

17. William H. Masters, Virginia E. Johnson and Robert C. Kolodny, *Masters and Johnson on Sex and Human Loving*, Macmillan, London, 1986.
18. For further discussion see, for example, Leonore Tiefer, *Sex is Not a Natural Act and Other Essays*, Boulder, Westview Press, 1995; or Janice Irvine, *Disorders of Desire: Sex and Gender in Modern American Sexology*, Philadelphia, Temple University Press, 1990.
19. JoAnn Loulan, *Lesbian Sex*, San Francisco, Spinsters/aunt lute, 1984.
20. Out of those reporting sex with a regular partner (231) 13 per cent (thirty women) practised SM. Of these, eighteen have switched between roles, reporting both top and bottom, six report being a top only, and six report being a bottom only. Of the seven women reporting SM practices with casual partners, one has experienced both top and bottom; five, top only; one, bottom only. A more detailed description of other practices with regular and casual partners is discussed in Chapter 4.
21. See Ted Polhemus and Housk Randall, *Rituals of Love: Sexual Experiments and Erotic Possibilities*, London, Picador, 1994.
22. See Juicy Lucy, 'If I ask you to tie me up, will you still want to love me?' in SAMOIS (eds.), *Coming To Power: Writings and Graphics on Lesbian S/M*, Boston, Alyson, 1987, pp. 29–40.
23. Pat Califia, *Sensuous Magic*, New York, Richard Kasak, 1994.
24. Pat Califia (ed.), *The Lesbian S/M Safety Manual*, Boston, Lace (imprint of Alyson), 1988.
25. Pat Califia, 1994, op. cit. note 12, p. 228.
26. Sophie Moorcock, 'Context counts', in *Capital Gay*, issue 660, 2 September 1994.
27. Wendy Castor, op. cit., p. 115.
28. JoAnn Loulan, op. cit., p. 197.
29. Marilyn Frye, 'Lesbian "sex" ', in Jeffner Allen (ed.), *Lesbian Philosophies and Cultures*, State University of New York Press, pp. 305–315.
30. Sarah Lucia Hoagland, *Lesbian Ethics: Toward New Value*, California, Institute of Lesbian Studies, 1988, pp. 167–8.

4 *a l*esbian's *v*ital *s*tatistics

The institute for sex research was commissioned by the National Institute of Mental Health to conduct the most ambitious study of homosexuality anywhere in the world ... Never before had so many people from every walk of life been so extensively interviewed. Never before have the sexual circumstances, the social lives and the psychological adjustment of homosexual men and women been so thoroughly explored ... This comprehensive study examines in depth the dimensions of sexual experience, including sexual partnerships, sexual techniques and sexual problems.

Alan Bell and Martin Weinberg[1]

The amount of speculation and discussion of sexual behaviour stands in stark contrast to the lack of reliable empirical evidence.

Kaye Wellings et al.[2]

We hope to persuade the reader, not that we know all the answers or that we have all the facts right, but that the facts can be obtained through scientific enquiry and that they should be pursued and encouraged, then debated, clarified and interpreted.

Edward Laumann et al.[3]

The social and behavioural sciences have an important role to play in increasing society's knowledge and understandings about lesbians, gay men and bisexual people.

Gregory M. Herek et al.[4]

Of all the influences that shape our thoughts, feelings and actions around sex, science plays a formidable role. With the position it occupies in westernized belief systems, science both has and is the power to define reality. Operating within the positivist paradigm (that is, the philosophies and methods of the natural sciences) it is widely believed that only through rigorous research can the objective truths of sexual behaviour be accessed. In this chapter I will be dealing with the results of a particular type of rigorous research, the sex survey.

Sexual surveillance in this form has become increasingly common. The methods of questionnaires and interviews remain the favoured scientific approaches to penetrate ever deeper into the private world of sex, to produce raw data and hard facts. This approach is far from problem-free and, arguably, can never be completely objective. Science formulates its own questions and answers. Every generation seeks faith in beliefs, and builds upon its own theories of human behaviour, including those explaining the nature of sex. But sex statistics are not free-floating facts awaiting discovery in a cultural vacuum. They are products of a particular type of search, which take on meaning in a specific cultural context, relative to the scientific fashions and social mores of the day.

The cultural practice of storytelling has a history as long as sex itself. The sexual story thrives in the contemporary climate, from media reports to the most personal and private revelations. Sexual scientists contribute numerical narratives in the form of commentary and documentary, which create the impression of fact, not fiction. Meanwhile, the popular media capitalize on the respectability of numbers with their own surveys, reported in the same statistical language.

It is upon such findings from both scientific surveys and popularized adaptations that this chapter is largely based, nestling in a bed of fertile lesbian theory. The story is one of passion, love, intrigue and infidelity, with detail of the most intimate of sexual practices. Salacious yet scientific. But do the data match the reality of lesbian 'sex lives'? By undressing lesbian sex, I aim to leave science exposed. Many studies and surveys will be cited throughout this chapter, from both scientific texts and popular journalism, with further details referenced in the notes. The presentation is thus not that required by scientific pro forma, but a more accessible approach.

There are, however, several key studies which I will introduce at this point, because recurrent reference is made to them: The National Survey of Sexual Attitudes and Lifestyles in Britain[5] (1994), hereafter referred to as the National Survey, or by its collective authorship, detailed in the scientific style, Wellings et al. A National Survey of Sexual Practices in the United States[6] (1995) will be cited throughout as the US Survey/Study, or under the authors, Laumann et al. A Study of (North) American Couples[7] (1983) is hereafter called the Couples Survey or Study, or referenced by authors Blumstein and Schwartz. The most frequently cited study is one which, up until now, has gone unpublished (this is the intrigue I mentioned!). A questionnaire entitled 'Lesbian Sex Survey'[8] was available at the Pride festival in London, 1992, and the resulting data, based on responses from 278 women, will hereafter be referred to as the Pride Survey/Study.[9]

We will begin with a familiar line of enquiry: the issue of prevalence – how many women in the population are lesbian? A common fanatical focus, it distracts from many other questions surrounding sexuality, not least those of sexual practice. As a point of entry it allows for elaboration of the politics and problems of scientific methods which seek to quantify sexual behaviour.

The prevalence of perversity: Seen one, act one . . . is she one?

The question of exact figures is one raised for both humane and hostile purposes. Despite our often antagonistic relationship with the scientific establishment, we too take recourse to its findings for reasons both personal and political. The much quoted 10 per cent or 'one in ten people is lesbian or gay', is not, as commonly believed, a Kinsey finding.[10] Amongst his dry academic tables and text – in which we can read of the variety of female animals known to have 'sex' together, including the propensity of cows to mount cows – we find that 2–3 per cent of his female respondents reported being exclusively homosexual for at least three years of their lives. The cumulative figures show that by age forty-five, 28 per cent of his female sample reported homosexual experience, 13 per cent to the point of orgasm.[11] Included in the many methodological problems of this research is that the sample (those women surveyed) was not representative of the wider population. His all-white sample did not reflect the diversity of variables like class, race, ethnicity and socio-economic status found in the wider society. Accessing a sample that is representative is one of the most difficult tasks facing social scientists, inadequate approximations being one of science's (much-defended) weak spots. Yet, like a mutating gene, science has ensured a mechanism for its own survival. Study after study critiques what has gone before, claiming to have done better. Methodologies are improved, never abandoned. Successors to Kinsey pay polite homage to his legacy, forever trying to avoid the mistakes which are, by now, well-documented.[12] Other studies which also use non-probability methods of accessing samples, are limited in application in similar ways to Kinsey's. Studies like those published in *Psychology Today*[13] and *Playboy*,[14] and those from Shere Hite,[15] although having high numbers of lesbians in the sample, tell us more about the particular respondents than about the population generally. This limitation affects many of the studies reviewed in this chapter.

Even with the most advanced techniques of quantitative research, prevalence estimates are little more than cultural artifacts. The meaning of the measurement changes. The scaling down of sexuality to numerical values creates the impression that the score reflects some fixed and underlying trait, but this is more illusory than real. Whatever is being measured is not a permanent position determined by nature, but a fluid and dynamic characteristic, contingent upon social context. There are several ways we can assign someone a label of sexual identity: how they define themselves, what they think of doing, and what they actually do. While there may be continuity across these three dimensions, this is not always the case, as will be seen throughout the following discussion. Two of the most recent estimates of the prevalence of homosexuality have been produced by national investigations into the sexual behaviour of randomly selected members of the population. These two unrelated surveys were conducted across Britain[16] and North America.[17]

After a period of governmental complacency about the spread of the HIV virus on both sides of the Atlantic, it began to look as if centralized funding would be made available to finance extensive investigation into people's sexual behaviour on an unprecedented scale. However, this was not to be the case, as amidst administrative pontifications, New Right agendas prevailed, unchallenged. In North America, the introduction of a bill by the well-rehearsed arch-homophobe Jesse Helms[18] prevented any application for funding ever being made. In Britain, the government's untimely withdrawal from research occurred well into the actual negotiations, initiated by several senior ministers including the then Prime Minister, Margaret Thatcher. The imposed veto was defended on several grounds: that there were already similar studies underway and that any replication would be an inappropriate use of public funds; that such an enquiry constituted an invasion of privacy; and that the validity of the results would be held in question (when had this ever bothered them before?). In addition to this list, which was never officially communicated to the researchers but reported by the press,[19] a more insidious agenda existed. The conflict, uncertainty and general moral panic generated by widespread anxiety distracted from governmental failures in social welfare. The resistance to investing in health education directed at so-called minority groups, combined with the fear that, if the resulting prevalence estimates were high, the struggle for lesbian and gay rights would be strengthened, further deterred government involvement. Both projects were salvaged in the fashion of economic liberalism characteristic of the Thatcher reign, by the intervention of the private sector. Between 1990 and 1991, nearly 19,000 members of the general public in Britain underwent an intimate probe into their sex lives.[20] In 1992, 3432 men and women in North America agreed to a similarly styled interrogation.[21]

Just as with the publication of the Kinsey data in North America decades before, when the National Survey in Britain went into print, few findings gained as much publicity as those pertaining to homosexuality. This time, the outcry of shock and disbelief hailed from within lesbian and gay communities, as opposed to a horrified general public. The low figures authoritatively laid Kinsey's inflated estimates to rest. When the survey was reported in the broadsheet press, to safeguard public sensibilities readers were not exposed to the same details of frequency and practice that they had the option of reading in relation to heterosexuality. Rather, the thrust of the article in the *Independent* entitled 'The facts of homosexual life'[22] was whether or not 'we' constituted a fact at all. The prudence advised by the researchers themselves in relation to the figures was markedly absent from a front-page article in the same paper, which relied purely on deference to expert knowledge for impact: '*Academics* who carried out Britain's *biggest survey* into sexual behaviour . . . rejected charges they had grossly underestimated the number of lesbians and gays'[23] (emphasis added). These estimates were produced by analysis of both the responses given in the face-to-face interview and those written on the self-complete questionnaire. Unremarkably, there was a large difference between the numbers reporting such practice or preference in the interview and those detailing them on the questionnaire. During the interview, less than 0.25 per cent described their sexual experiences as exclusively or mostly with other women. On the questionnaire, 3. 4 per cent reported any homo-sexual contact, 1.7 per cent detailing genital contact. Only 0.6 per cent reported having a female partner within the two years prior to the survey.[24] Such time frames are often employed in sex research to maximize the accuracy by reporting the most recent and current behaviours. A result of this is that many of the transient same-sex explorations in childhood/ adolescence are discarded as isolated episodes in sexual development, as they are often not repeated in adulthood.

While this trend is common in research into sexual behaviour, it was not the case in the US Study. In this survey, the pattern proved stronger for men than women: those women who reported sexual experiences with another female between puberty and eighteen years, also reported experiences after the teenage watershed and into adulthood.[25] Not only did many of the findings differ between the two surveys, but the criteria of measurement of homosexuality also differed. Wellings et al. focused primarily on reported behaviours. The fact that 2.6 per cent of their female sample reported same-sex attraction but no experience was used to support the contention that the majority of women do not harbour unrealized fantasies. While Laumann et al. also had a behavioural emphasis, homosexuality was assessed along two other dimensions: self-labelling, and desire, which was ascertained by reports of same-sex attraction and/or the appeal of sex with another woman. While only 1.4 per cent of women in the sample identified as lesbian or bisexual[27] (an equitable finding to Wellings et al. by scientific standards), a combination of all three categories produces a maximum figure of 8.6 per cent.[28] However, by far the largest group were women who reported same-sex attraction and/or the appeal of same-gender sex, in the absence of any concomitant identity or practice. As well as offering an interesting angle on the 'American (wet) dream', the authors use this to demonstrate the wider parameters of a homosexual scale, while showing that lesbians are not the only women to experience same-sex attraction or to find the idea of sex with another woman appealing. Working within the time scales provided, in the two years preceding the National study, 0.6 per cent of women participating in the survey had a female partner. In the year prior to the US survey, 1.3 per cent of women surveyed had a female partner. This is not a whole lot of lesbian sex!

Low prevalence estimates such as these can be explained when we look at gendered patterns of sexual socialization, societal oppression and the scientific methods employed. It is well documented that women are less likely to register subjective experiences as potentially erotic or sexual.[31] The chances of recognizing such sensations are further reduced when the inevitable stigma is added. Then there are the very serious risks involved in disclosing lesbian identity, practice or desire, in addition to the stresses of any psychic sex-shame we may have internalized. Rejection, loss of employment or custodial rights of children are just some of the penalties paid by women asserting such desires. Wellings et al. found that 65 per cent of men and 59 per cent of women surveyed considered that sex between two women was always or mostly wrong,[32] a finding which held across all age groups, thus challenging the ageist myth that such hostile views are the sole property of 'older' generations. These statistics reflected trends which had already been identified in a range of surveys since the mid 1980s, including the British Social Attitudes Survey, in which the growth of hostility to lesbian and gay relationships was considerable between 1983 and 1987.[33] If women were sexualized with the same sense of sexual entitlement and autonomy as men, and society were not structured around inequalities and prejudices, the prevalence estimates would inevitably be higher. But then again, if our culture were to undergo such a radical transformation, the quest for such estimates would be redundant.

One of the greatest methodological strengths of 'Britain's Biggest Ever Survey' is also its academic Achilles' heel. The sampling frame, widely accepted as one of the most reliable techniques for accessing probability samples,[34] does not accommodate the particular demographics of a mobile sexual subculture. The rationale behind this method of accessing a representative sample is that population characteristics are randomly distributed. Thus, the number of lesbians in the sample will be proportionate to the numbers in the general population. This, however, cannot be the case when the pattern of migration of lesbians and gays to the larger cities – and, increasingly, to gay ghettos within these conurbations – is taken into account. In both the US Study and the National Survey, this social drift is found to be stronger for men, which may be related not only to a range of socio-economic variables but to gendered differences in sexual style. The cities afford not only greater anonymity, but the services of the scene, and a larger field of 'sexual availables'. Many contemporary lesbians and gays may move less in search of self-discovery and more on the hunt for the sexual 'other'. The Pride survey reflects this city bias, although the heavy London weighting is partly a result of the location of the study. It may also be a result of the younger generation of more confident lesbian women, bound less by traditional and familial gender roles.

Wellings *et al.* themselves conclude that 'there is a large difference ... between different regions of Britain in terms of prevalence of homosexual orientation ... men and women who report having a homosexual partner are far more likely to report having moved to London than those who did not.'[35] So it would seem the unusually mindful politicians had a point: the data was not beyond question. The authors themselves acknowledge that, 'we have not yet moved into a culture that tolerates sexual variety',[36] and I would suggest that, until we do, the canons of scientific enquiry will continue to replicate false or questionable estimates.

Number crunching and pelvic grinding

Gay and lesbian sex plays by many of the same rules as heterosexual sex.

Robert T. Michael et al.[37]

We have learned, among other things, that the values and experiences of homosexual couples are similar to those of heterosexuals in many ways. Whatever their sexual preferences, most people strongly desire a close and loving relationship with one special person.

Letitia Anne Peplau[38]

Findings that lesbians are more orgasmic in their relationships than heterosexual women confirm the idea that lesbian sex tends to be very satisfying.

Suzanna Rose[39]

There are several recurring and often contradictory stereotypes surrounding lesbian sex: that it is always satisfying and orgasmic, that it occurs either constantly or infrequently, that it involves lots of tender caressing, that lesbians instinctively know how to please each other, that sex equals love and we don't sleep around. To trace the origin of such ideas would lead us to many sources, sexual science being one of the most formative. Although contemporary research reflects the theoretical shift from lesbianism as a pathology (sickness model) to the current vogue of 'alternative lifestyle' (liberal humanism), it is apparent that lesbian communities are viewed somewhat as a natural laboratory, exemplars of essential femaleness devoid of male influence. When any differences are identified between lesbians and straight women, they are often used to subtly disenfranchise lesbian sexuality, while also diminishing women's sexuality more generally. And differences will be found between lesbians and heterosexuals, just as they will be found within groups of lesbians and groups of heterosexuals. It is now generally agreed by social scientists, however, that lesbians are more similar to 'other women' than to their gay male counterparts, especially when it comes to sexual and emotional behaviours. Reassurance of gendered norms should not distract from the limitations of the behaviourist approach in the analysis of sexual repertoires, where the numerical values assigned to every physical act are privileged over the wider meanings of sexual scripts. All action is usually read according to one perspective, that of hegemonic heterosexuality.

Sexual behaviour is shaped and profoundly influenced by a multitude of social, economic, political and cultural factors. Age, gender, class, place of residence, religious affiliations, race, ethnicity, health status and self-esteem are just a few of the variables researchers have examined in relation to sexual practice. Wellings *et al.*[40] identified particular patterns of action in relation to such trends. While the data on lesbians are sparse, anyone drafting a lonely hearts advert might find some of the specifications useful for recruitment purposes. Of the women sexually active with other women, the most active age band is twenty-four to thirty-four years; 'younger' women report more oral sex; 'older' women, more non-penetrative sex. The fact that the levels of activity 'peak' almost a generation later than that reported for heterosexual activity is consistent with patterns of a later onset of lesbian career: that women become involved with other women usually after an established history with men. This is further borne out in the Pride Survey, where the average age of first sexual experience with a male partner was fourteen, compared to nineteen with another woman.

The fact that age-related trends in sexual practice were identified by Wellings et al. is not a lesbian phenomenon but the result of the cohort effect (that respondents were born in different generations and will thus inevitably have different experiences), and of social transitions in sexual fashion. Oral sex, for example, has become increasingly acceptable and popular since the 1950s, and as it is further normalized the generational differences will probably become less marked. New patterns will emerge, however, as sexual activities diversify even further.

The ambitious scriptwriter of the lonely hearts ad may become a little down-hearted when she realizes that everything these amorous women are doing can be contained in the categories 'active or passive oral sex' or 'non-penetrative sex' – an amorphous catch-all which is used interchangeably by Wellings *et al.* with the even vaguer 'mutual masturbation'.[41] This privileging of oral sex reflects the popular conception of oral sex being to lesbians what intercourse is to heterosexuals – the definitive sex act. The Pride data shows that approximately 90 per cent (in the year prior to the survey) of the sample practised both active and passive oral sex, and while this statistic relates to incidence (whether it occurred at all) as opposed to frequency (how often) it does suggest more lesbians do it or try it than were picked up by trends in earlier studies.[42] It is also over double the incidence reported in the National Survey,[43] a fact which may be linked to how the reporting women identify. It would seem that self-identified lesbians are more likely to engage in oral sex,[44] partly because of sub-cultural sexual expectations, confidence, experience, and regularity and familiarity of partners.

If oral sex constitutes some sort of definitive sexual ritual, then it should occur during most episodes defined as 'sex'. From the (North) American Couples Survey we can see that only 12 per cent of the lesbian couples participating in the study engaged in oral sex during every episode, 27 per cent usually, 38 per cent sometimes, 19 per cent rarely, 4 per cent never.[45] While to some it may be as pleasing as it is popular, it is not to eveyone's taste. Even in the face of evidence that it is a favourite technique of many[46] this does not equate with elevating its status to that of the definitive act of lesbian sexual practice. Having correlated the statistics on oral sex with other findings, Blumstein and Schwartz conclude, 'the more oral sex lesbian couples perform and receive, the happier they are and the less they fight about sex'[47] – hardly surprising if we're being sold the idea that we can't beat the taste of the real thing. Such a deduction not only neglects the limitations of correlationary statistics but is deeply embedded in the modernist mentality that sex is vital to health and well-being. It is possible that Blumstein and Schwartz have overlooked other variables, and even that they have reversed cause and effect. Lower incidence of sexual antagonism may result in more oral sex, the frequency of which may be determined by broader measures of happiness. Oral sex may be a barometer for numerous other factors like trust, feelings of entitlement, confident sexual agency and desire. Sweeping scientific assertions like that above are less the answer to all our problems and more potentially the cause of a few new ones.

Returning to the narrow categories of the National Study,[48] they not only exclude the more specific details of genital and body contact and the use of sex toys, but ignore entire practices like anal sex, which is only considered if a male partner is involved. Wellings et al. are not the first to omit anal eroticism from a lesbian sex inventory. As one of the last taboos in the current sexual climate, unless its inclusion is vital – as it is with the monitoring of gay male practice – it is simply ignored. This necessarily limits the realization of one of the study's objectives, which was concerned with lifestyle factors not only in relation to HIV, but to other STDs as well. By omitting anal sex completely from the female-to-female repertoire, the risk of infections like hepatitis from oral–anal contact (rimming) is simply not considered.

While the Pride Survey is not without its own omissions, one of its strengths is the explicit database it produced on the actualities of sexual practice. Not constrained by an epidemiological emphasis, the questionnaire covered areas beyond a high-risk-related inventory. Based on practices spanning the twelve-month period prior to the survey, over 96 per cent reported clitoral stimulation (both active and passive), oral–breast contact (sucking and licking – both active and passive), penetration of the vagina with the fingers, general body caressing and deep kissing. The latter has been commented on elsewhere, as it seems lesbians kiss more than any other couples during sex.[49] Approximately 90 per cent of the Pride respondents reported tribadism, the incidence of which seems higher than in other studies,[50] which challenges any notions of its being an ageing practice sliding lower down the hierarchy. Just over three quarters document talking explicitly about sex during the episode, just under three quarters having reported fantasizing at some stage during the sexual encounter. Less than a third discuss their fantasies in a sexual context, under half the sample acting them out (40 per cent). Under a quarter of the sample reported any of the following: dressing up, corporal punishment, or specific SM role-play.[51] Accounts of anal eroticism varied, 44 per cent detailing active digital penetration, 42 per cent receptive, 13 per cent had experienced rimming, and 2 per cent penetration with toys.

Given the publicity and coverage bestowed upon the sex toy industry and the interest toys seem to generate, the implication is that they are an essential accessory of the 1990s. However, the available statistics suggest that the high profile is disproportionate to patterns of actual usage. A third of lesbians replying to a survey in the now defunct London listings magazine *City Limits* reported toy use.[52] Of those replying to a survey in a lesbian magazine (also no longer in existence, *Lesbian London*), 20 per cent 'admitted' to ownership, with a smaller (but unspecified) percentage reporting that they were used.[53] Thus in no recent study can I find the almost universal application of inanimate objects as described by Saghir and Robins in 1973[54] (phrased in a style reminiscent of Havelock Ellis and his phallic phantasy). Nor could other researchers working around the same time. Barbara Ponse, in her study into lesbian identities, found that only a few women reported toy use, a finding supported by an earlier study which she cites.[55] Even amongst the 'younger urban' respondents of the Pride survey, toy use is reported by less than a third. Vibrators were the most popular (23 per cent), followed by the dildo (15 per cent) and to a lesser degree the 'strap-on' (13 per cent) (all of which were predominantly detailed in relation to vaginal penetration), with butt plugs being used by fewer women (2 per cent). This pattern may change with the rapid expansion of commercial outlets including mail order companies, although availability is only one of many considerations including cost and the possible wider meanings of sex toy use. Held manually, these objects often take on a different meaning from in a harness, and as long as toy use is bound in such debates, it is unlikely we will see universal assimilation into ideas of what constitutes the lesbian sexual repertoire. In the popularized version of the US Survey,[56] while sex toy use is included in the remit of lesbian sexual practices in a fashion undocumented in the more academic companionate reader,[57] no further commentary or statistics are provided. The number of women using toys is low, which probably meant the number of lesbians in this category was too small to analyse. Yet toys continue to maintain a high profile in the popular imagination of what lesbian sex involves.

Toys, like other material objects, mythical fantasy or the most carefully scripted psychodrama, add other dimensions to the sexual experience. Absence of any of the above does not constitute an impairment, no matter what badgirl bravado may imply. But a less-recognized point is that they can be useful in situations where energy levels are low, physical sensation or mobility limited or where movement-related pain is a constant. Allowing activity or passivity, they can provide another route to pleasure. But for those of us living with disabilities, either visible or invisible, these toys remain a facet of preference, not compensation. The available lesbian sex texts are amongst the few manuals of this genre that engage with the issues of disability and long-term illness, which are as absent from research as from other forms of popular representation. Many of us take health and physicality for granted.

Sex toys are politically volatile but no one should be marginalized from the debate, which is frequently inaccessible due to the lack of recognition and visibility of physical difference. 'How often', and 'who with' are but two of the taboos that need breaking down around sex. As sexual politics has so sharply demonstrated, where there exists a majority there will always be a minority – and gender and sexual orientation are only two of the avenues in which women's lives are marginalized, oppressed and ignored.

Until this point in the text, all findings drawn from the Pride database have referred to activitites practised with partners who were described as regular. An innovative aspect of the survey was that many of the same questions were asked in relation to casual partners. This was hardly revolutionary from the epidemiological perspective, but a clear recasting of the public image of lesbian sexuality. The reputation of casual sex is as confused and contradictory as the wider world of sex. Interwoven with prescriptions of morality, monogamy, and the pressure of almost compulsory coupling, the casual liaison basks in the mystery and excitement of the unfamiliar other, and is often endowed with more than a hint of the conquest mentality. This in turn co-exists in a climate of punitive politi-cized aspersions of aping male prowess – and psychological justifications, as stories unfold of personal failure and inadequacy in the urgent and unsuccessful quest for Ms Right. Entire performances are pathologized and reframed as fears of intimacy, sex addiction or the manifestation of the clamorous need left by unfulfilled childhood bonds. The unwritten lesbian lores are conflicting and, in the confusion, it seems quite difficult to go out and have sex just for the sake of it.

The term 'casual partner' was not defined on the Pride Survey, inviting reports of any experience with partners judged by the respondent to be 'non regular'. There was not the space to compile a complex relationship demography and to draw on its wider meanings. Thus the range of these encounters will probably have included, for example: one-night stands, ongoing affairs, sex in club toilets and sleeping with a former lover. Approximately three quarters of the sample report *ever* having had a casual partner, 29 per cent of whom report interludes in the year prior to the survey – half of whom detail more than one partner in this category. Looking at the averages, for those who have had casual partners, they average more casual than regular partners.[58] The trends identified in the Pride Survey did not replicate those of other researchers,[59] who had found that the incidence of unconventional sex acts was higher with partners deemed transient or more exciting – characteristics which could be assumed to be part of a casual dynamic. If (drawing on current knowledge) we consider manual genital stimulation, oral sex and tribadism to be conventional, then, according to those studies, we would expect to see a higher incidence of other, more unconventional acts in casual sex. While clitoral stimulation, vaginal penetration and body caressing were reported in a large percentage of encounters (80 per cent) there was markedly less oral sex (50 per cent) and low prevalence of anal sex, SM practice and toy use. If the episode is spontaneous, then the lack of props is hardly surprising – unless this is the real reason some lesbians carry handbags! One finding that does stand out is the greater percentage of women who discuss their fantasies with casual partners, relative to the same practice with regulars (79 per cent versus 29 per cent). This disparity is reversed when it comes to the *enactment* of such flights of fancy, with nearly four times as many reporting this activity with regulars than with casuals (42 per cent versus 11 per cent).

It may be that the appeal of casual sex lies in the detail of the sexual scenario, and more in the unconventionality and thrill of the unfamiliar encounter. If the duration is short, then inhibitions are as likely to stay intact as to be thrown off in a wild display of abandon. Especially when our communities, at times, seem so small, we are less able to ignore what she will think of us the morning after. The disparity between scripts with casuals and regulars fits with commonly reported attitudes that sex is 'better' with a familiar and regular partner, with whom increasing intimacy creates a climate for diversifying practice. However, some lesbians do have the 'trick mentality' more readily associated with gay men where 'once is recreation, twice is courtship'.[60] The murmurings of desire for this sexual style are becoming increasingly audible in some sections of the community. But they are not new. As early as 1975, writer Rita Mae Brown bemoaned the lack of sexual choices for lesbians. Having infiltrated a gay male bath-house by dressing as a man, she wrote of the experience:

> I want the option of random sex with no emotional commitment when I need sheer physical relief ... it is in our interest to build places where we have relief, refuge and release ... it is the desire of a woman to have options. Like men we should have choices.[61]

Brown can boast to being a forerunner of many lesbian desires: casual sex, drag, Martina ... which, ironically, look more at home in the 1990s than they did in the 1970s. Is this 'evolutionary' trend moving us ever closer to the position which sex therapist Margaret Nichols claims is best suited to us, the 'most advanced state of sexuality within pair bonding known to human kind'[62] combining 'gay men's sexiness and lesbians' connectedness'.[63] There is definitely an undercurrent of what might seem like 'deviant desire' to some. An example of this sexual market-force was the attempt to set up a lesbian cruising zone on a London heathland, which already functioned as a notorious pick-up point of gay men. While its failure can be attributed to a lack of patrons, it was also relatively inaccessible, given little publicity, and realistically overshadowed by the attendant dangers accompanying such public sex. Lesbian communities have also yet to acclimatize to the idea of casual sex and 'tricking'. There has been no dramatic counter-cultural shift to normalize it as an expectation and attempts to force this meet with great resistance. Our venues (some more than others) function as much as a 'market-place' for contacts, both socially and sexually, as do straight or gay establishments – the difference being that, in contrast to the latter, the agenda is less overt, the expectation less ritualized. Stereotypically, if a dyke meets someone at a club, consummation may be followed by their withdrawal from the scene together, or their attendance as an 'item', as opposed to a knowing nod the following week as the hunt begins all over again.

Moving from casual sex to non-monogamy and acts of infidelity, I can make little comment from the Pride Survey as this area constitutes one of its glaring omissions. While instances of 'casual sex' may have involved one or both of the above, commentary would be little more than speculation. Looking to other studies, a recurring theme is that, unsurprisingly, more lesbians subscribe to monogamy in theory than in practice.[64] Non-monogamy may partly be attractive as an act of resistance to patriarchal models of relationship, but equally, monogamy appeals because of all the accompanying benefits of socio-emotional security. While serial monogamy may be a norm, non-monogamy is not uncommon. Importantly, its meaning has largely shifted from that of an act of resistance to the patriarchal institution of marriage, to a rebellion against those who scripted the original battle plan, the radical feminists. The politics of coupling also has much personal resonance, impacting on our everyday lives and styles of relating. Psychologizing has largely replaced politicizing. The focus has moved from strategies of defiance, to the functions which different styles of relating serve for the dyad (couple) and the individuals involved. Thus, one such model[65] is stable and couple-oriented types of non-monogamy are negotiated, resulting in clearly defined boundaries between primary partners and those of secondary status. This strategy has currency to counteract the effects of merging – where the couple get so close that any awareness of being separate disappears – and also to prevent sexual boredom (for further discussion see Chapter 5). Symbolic non-monogamy is the open relationship, where the couple remain behaviourally monogamous. Self-oriented non-monogamy has primarily individual benefits of self-discovery and growth. Another form with which many of us may be more familiar is what is diplomatically called 'transitional non-monogamy', a period of overlap between old and new relationships. This chaotic unnegotiated adventure is a common strategy in a culture where every constructed insecurity, need and desire is tweaked on a regular basis, as we are forever reminded that we can improve not only upon ourselves but, in the fashion of consumerist coupling, upon our partners as well.

Blumstein and Schwartz offer some interesting if predictable findings in this area. According to their survey, lesbians more often than not have enduring affairs, as opposed to isolated encounters, with secondary relationships being the most common form of non-monogamy. In situations where the non-monogamy has not been previously negotiated, disclosure or discovery leads down one of two well-worn routes: termination of the secondary liaison, with a re-invigorated primary relationship, in which further infidelity is unlikely; or (alternatively) the end of the original primary relationship, with the secondary partner elevated to primary status. Is this beginning to sound a little like *Dallas*? What about the scenario where it all goes hideously wrong and everyone ends up single, angry or in therapy, or a combination of the three? Or when the 'betrayed' and the 'affair' elope after a whirlwind romance, which began while the former object of their mutual desire was moving house . . .

Returning to the Couples Survey,[66] the findings are explained away with the theory that lesbians, labouring under the affliction befalling the female gender generally, cannot separate sex from love. The related findings, that in relationships of ten years or more, lesbians are second only to gay men in acts of infidelity, elicit little comment.

Relationship status is a prime factor influencing an individual's sexual behaviour. When it comes to research on lesbian relationships, we see that, although lesbians are the most couple-oriented of all possible gendered combinations,[67] successful in both seeking and maintenance, there is also a high incidence of relationship breakdown.[68] While lack of institutional endorsements like marriage may make leaving easier, it may also render us more vulnerable, because of a lack of public 'witnessing'. Another contributory factor could be that lesbians, contrary to popular belief, want continuity in both sexual as well as intimate exchange, and thus they leave the relationship when the balance shifts. Such an interpretation comes from established psychological theory, where analysis of relationships is communicated through economic metaphors. Social and sexual reciprocity take on meaning through the terminology of investment, profit, loss and return. So pervasive is this framework that it affects many populist perceptions of sexual and romantic interactions, having resonance in the individualizing therapeutic approaches, discussed later in the chapter. Whatever the outcome of lesbian liaisons, it is a fact that we were forerunners in establishing alternative and enduring styles of commitment, prior to the contemporary move towards the dismissal of marriage as an antiquated relic of Victorian morality.

Whatever functions relationships serve – tactile needs, esteem, affiliation, a framework to render one's lesbian identity intelligible to others, or a romantic licence for sex – at any one moment, a number of us are single. Despite partnership pressures in the subculture, some are single through choice; others, obviously not. For those seeking a significant other or even casual sex, the lonely hearts columns can provide a rich hunting ground.

Even these varied compositions do not escape the scientist's roving eye (or that's the story they tell us when caught reading the *Pink* personal columns while surreptitiously sliding a letter beginning 'Dear Horny from Hounslow' out of sight.) While 1990s lesbians may be out and proud, advertising or replying to personal ads is still a closeted practice for many, tapping into ill-founded notions that it constitutes a last resort, the destiny of the desperate. In fact it can be a useful strategy. As a method of consumer courting or scheduled sex, it allows for clearly articulated specifications, which – while not guaranteeing success – may give us the edge over those match-making exercises employed by over-zealous friends.

Analysis of the 'personals' tells us a little about the person and their sexual styles, but more about the culture in which they are written. Yet interpretation usually takes the form of the psychology involved, rather than any dissection of the wider cultural context. One such study[70] shows how, when it comes to self-promotion and recruitment, lesbians place less emphasis on physical characteristics. Personality traits figure more, as do references to 'long-term' potential. Lesbians are less likely than either straight women or gay men to ask for a photograph. Conducted in the 1980s, the study reflects common ideologies of the time – that lesbians were less concerned with cultural definitions of beauty or with 'sexy appearances'.[71] While, arguably, this remains a tenacious organizing principle for desire, there have been shifts in this dictate, which I deal with elsewhere in the text. (I must confess to finding the requests for photographs a little off-putting. I have a recurrent nightmare that, if I was to comply I would later walk into one of the trendy bars of London – where the clientele look like a combination cast of the *Clothes Show* and *Baywatch* – only to be confronted with a life-size enlargement of myself surrounded by flashing neon words like 'single', 'desperate' and (perish the thought) 'unresolved separation anxiety'!) But for now let us return to where, inevitably, many of these correspondences will lead – to sex.

Sex statistics only become meaningful because they are relational. They are a way of comparing our 'performance' to other dykes and other couples. Lesbian, gay, straight, or bisexual 'scores' of sexual frequency, orgasm and satisfaction create a mentality of sex as a sporting event. It is one of the few physical events involving undignified positions that people are not only encouraged to talk about outside the medical arena, but are actually supposed to boast about. Hence the humour: 'What do you call four hours of lesbian sex'? . . . 'A quickie.' A survey in which heterosexual men, women, gay men, lesbians, and bisexual men and women were compared on a range of variables found that, on average, lesbians took longer to have sex with regular partner/s than did any other group.[72] So it would seem that in terms of sexual stamina we win hands down. Why? Are we using cues other than penetration and orgasm to signal the beginning and end of sex? Do women take longer to come? Or is it that we wait to call it quits until after the sixth orgasm? From the same study, we see that the trend is reversed with casual partners, as we complete sex in less time than all the other groups. Again we wonder how this trend can be explained. It may be that casual partners, acting in a more orgasm-centred way, take less time to reach this goal. Alternatively, coming may be *less* important in these encounters, and so not even 'worked towards'. It could be that a narrower repertoire is practised, due to potential unfamiliarity with each other, or that more time is spent on the build-up as opposed to the 'act itself'. (It could be, of course, that lesbians engaged in casual sex save the disparate ten minutes by not having to declare eternal love, plan a moving-in date or negotiate custodial rights for the cat!)

If lesbians take so long to have sex, is this why we seem to have it less often? Until recently, existing data suggested that lesbians had sex less than any other couples. From the outset, according to the [North] American Couples Survey,[73] lesbians had sex less than married heterosexuals. In couples who had been together ten years or more, only 1 per cent of lesbian couples reported sex as frequently as two to three times a week, compared to 15 per cent of married couples. The contrast becomes increasingly stark when looking at the category for sex once a month or less. Here we find 47 per cent of the lesbian couples compared to 15 per cent of the heterosexuals.[74] Findings such as these are commonly echoed by lesbian therapists, who articulate discontent on behalf of their clients. While the aforementioned study has found its way into many a lesbian text, more recent evidence contradicts it. The authors of the US study not only find no difference between the sexual frequencies reported by lesbian and heterosexual women, but stress that the population generally is having less sex than commonly imagined.

Comparisons between studies conducted in Britain further suggest that there is little difference between the sexual frequencies reported by a lesbian and bisexual sample – the Pride respondents – and those detailed by a predominantly heterosexual population, responding to a survey in *Elle* magazine[75] (hereafter cited as the *Elle* Survey). 51 per cent of the *Elle* sample report sexual frequencies ranging from two or three times a week to daily,[76] compared to 50 per cent of the Pride respondents. What also emerges from both surveys is a general desire for more sex. Is this yet another responder bias motivating women to answer? It is already documented that those who answer sex surveys are often more experienced[77] (there is an entire psychology as to why people volunteer for research in the first place). Perhaps the women in these surveys waited eagerly for the publication of the results after which they left the report open on the relevant page, on their partner's favourite chair night after night!

Following an extensive review of sexual practice, it was inevitable that I would reach orgasm sooner or later. And here we stumble across some of the most colourful lesbian folklore. Following the rather naive boast in *The Joy of Lesbian Sex* that 'lesbians always reach orgasm in their lovemaking',[78] JoAnn Loulan, in the more recent *Lesbian Sex*,[79] warns against colluding with the tyranny of orgasm, because of the unnecessary pressure placed on sexual performance as a result. Knowledge that not all women orgasm all the time, some never, is now well established, disseminated by the likes of Kinsey, Masters and Johnson and Shere Hite. And it is their legacies that make up many beliefs reflected by lesbians. Kinsey, upon finding a high prevalence of orgasm amongst women engaging in homosexual practice, concluded:

> it is generally not understood either by males or females who have not had homosexual experience, that the techniques of sexual relations between two females may be as effective or even more effective than the petting or coital techniques ordinarily utilised in heterosexual contacts ... it is of course quite possible for males to learn ... heterosexual relationships could however become more satisfactory if they more often utilised the sort of knowledge which most homosexual females have of female anatomy and female psychology.[80]

Origin of inevitable orgasm myth number one. Masters and Johnson continued in a similar vein, once they had proved that lesbian and heterosexual women had the same physiological orgasmic response. (They had to watch numerous straight and dyke couples having sex to figure this out.) As the scientific establishment insists that heterosexual intercourse remain the definitive yardstick against which all other acts must be compared, reports of high incidence of orgasm during lesbian sex[81] contrast with reports that 70 per cent of heterosexual women do not orgasm by intercourse alone.[82]

The inclusion of orgasm on the Pride enquiry took the form not of incidence but of the importance placed on it, in relation to the self and to partner/s. Amidst rhetoric that women were not orgasmcentric, this claim was put to the test. The data show that the greater the importance placed by a respondent on orgasm generally, the more generally this was applied to both self and others. Though, in line with earlier research, greater emphasis continues to be placed on the partner's orgasm. It is hard to let go of the idea of a definitive marker of sexual pleasure, and, even if we can relinquish such a goal ourselves, there is much invested in a partner's signal of satisfaction.

The results of the Pride Survey show no correlation between reports of orgasm and those of satisfaction, but the latter did appear to be related to frequency of sex with regular partners. But measurement of sexual satisfaction is a difficult task. Any judgment will be influenced by perceptions of general life satisfaction and happiness. One of the most recurrent themes from existing research is the high level of reported relationship satisfaction and sexual satisfaction amongst lesbian samples. The Pride profile did not differ greatly from the *Elle* statistics. Just over three quarters (77 per cent) of the Pride sample rated satisfaction of their sex lives from 'quite to very'; and just under three quarters of the *Elle* respondents (74 per cent).[83] We did not replicate the findings of another study where there was a significant difference in satisfaction ratings between straight and lesbian women, where dykes came out on top.[84] Considering that much of the debate around lesbian sex rests (ironically) on whether or not we should be seeking debate and representation, statistics from the Pride Survey overwhelmingly show that, for these lesbians at least, sex is a priority in their lives. Close to 90 per cent (86 per cent) described sex as 'important' or 'very important'. While not necessarily translating into a hunger for non-monogamy or erotic representation, sex is important. In some cases it is not only sex with women which is prioritized.

A large proportion of women who currently identify as lesbian have had sex with men in the past. It is usual for between 75–95 per cent of any lesbian sample surveyed to report heterosexual histories. Studies involving self-identified lesbians (as opposed to random populations representing the diversity of sexual identity), may skew toward the lower parameter, as there will be an over-representation of women who have never been sexual with men. Hence, in the National Survey, 95 per cent of the women sexual with other women had heterosexual histories,[85] compared with 87 per cent of the Pride respondents. In this subgroup of the Pride respondents, the average total of male partners is ten which compares with an average total of eight female partners, across the entire response set. A number of women who identify as lesbian have sex with men in the present. The relationship between sexual practice and self-labelling is variable, and while necessary and functional, sexual identity is at all times provisional.[87] The National Survey found that 45 per cent of all women who had been sexual with other women in the two years prior to the survey, had also been sexual with men during the same time-frame.[88] Interpretation is limited, as no information as to how these women identified is available. It was also found that 39 per cent of women who had been sexual with other women also reported having had over ten male partners.[89] While the authors tentatively suggest diversity is sought in gender as well as numbers, I prefer the idea that their sexual explorations signal a search for quality as well as quantity!

The percentage of Pride respondents who had been sexual with men in the year before the survey was predictably lower, falling at less than 10 per cent (8.6 per cent). In actual terms, twenty-eight women of the 278 who responded reported sex with men in the time-frame specified. Of these twenty-eight, 10 per cent of cases involved sex industry work. In addition, a third of this sample was acting in accordance with their chosen identity – identifying as bisexual. Exactly half the bisexual women in the study reported being sexual with men up to twelve months prior to the investigation. But although recourse to categories renders this finding intelligible, the limitations of such associations are apparent when we consider that the remainder of those who were sexual with men identify as lesbian and do not report sex industry work. This figure is potentially lower than the true figure, because of under-reporting. Dykes who sleep with men still meet with a hostile response in some sections of the community. Often self-doubt arises from the discrepancy between self-identity and sexual prescription. However, such behaviour is now being touted, ironically, by proponents of the queer and sexual postmodern philosophies, as a daring act of outlawry. A number of lesbians have and will continue to have sex with men. For some, this is out of necessity or coercion, for others, desire. While not subscribing completely to the new queer politic, loosening the harness that binds identity to practice allows for exploring wider possibilities, without being forced to relinquish lesbian credentials. Because, of course, there is more to being a lesbian than what we do in bed!

When it comes to safer sex she really doesn 't give a dam

Where are the statistics? How can it be real for me when there is no proof?
                                                      Patricia Stevens[90]

I want to hear some numbers about lesbians and there are none. Until then, nobody is going to tell me I can't have sex the way I always have.
                                                      Patricia Stevens[91]

The story of the HIV epidemic is told and recreated through many different histories: medical documentary of the virus and the battle to find a cure; political discourses of the racism, sexism and homophobia present in theory and pervasive in practice, personal testimonies and commentaries on anger, activism and loss. While lesbians are by no means absent from the above, we also share a history, one which is constantly evolving as the facts emerge from the fictions. So, as lesbians, what is our story? It is a fact that a number of women across the globe, living with HIV and AIDS, identify as lesbian and/or have sex with other women. Exactly how many is impossible to ascertain, as lesbian sexual practice is not classified as an exposure category. Neither the organization responsible for monitoring national epidemiologies in Britain (Communicable Disease Surveillance Centre, CDSC) nor that in North America (Centers For Disease Control, CDC) identifies lesbian sexual practices as a separate exposure category.

That lesbians live with and have died from AIDS is not questioned. What is contested is the route of transmission – how these women were exposed to the virus. The existing evidence[92] points overwhelmingly to high-risk behaviours like sharing works (needles and syringes) for injecting drugs, and unprotected sex with men, there being little 'proof' to date to implicate sex with other women. There are, however, several cases documented in the medical journals which do suggest lesbian sexual practices were the most likely routes of viral transmission. In one report,[93] one of two lesbians seen had a history of injecting drug use, which was identified as the mode of transmission. Her partner, however, reported no such history, and in the absence of other risk practices, lesbian sex was considered the most likely explanation. The practices detailed include cunnilingus and analingus during menstruation, as well as activities which 'traumatized' the mucous membranes of the vagina, thus increasing the risk of transmission. A second documented case[94] also concludes that lesbian sex was the most likely route of transmission. The only practice specified is oral sex, the position of which in the hierarchy of risk practices is extremely controversial. Saliva carries an extremely low density of HIV and, in addition, seems to have an inhibitory action on the virus. The same, however, cannot be said about vaginal/cervical secretions in which HIV is present in infectious quantities, the levels of which increase during menstruation and in the presence of certain std's. However in conjunction with the scarcity of medical documentation vis-à-vis lesbians, there are a number of cases in which lesbians themselves are uncertain as to how they contracted the virus – accounts which must caution against premature conclusions.

So where does this leave us? It is now generally agreed that, as a route of transmission, lesbian sex is 'inefficient' and unlikely. But this must be qualified by the actualities of practice. Acts involving fluid exchange and exposed vulnerable tissue pose a greater risk: 'Although female to female transmission is apparently rare, female sexual contact should be considered a possible means of HIV transmission among women who have sex with women.'[95] Of the existing studies looking at lesbians, the data are a sober reminder that it is meaningless to talk of 'high' and 'low' risk groups (in which lesbians are dismissed as the latter) and that it is not who we say we are, but *what we do* that can expose us to the virus. Statistics drawn from research conducted in San Francisco show that 1.2 per cent[96] of the sample of lesbians and bisexual women had tested positive for the virus, and that this was three times higher than the prevalence rate amongst women generally in this area. However, from both this and a second study,[97] injecting practices and unsafe sex with men were identified as the risk behaviours. These lesbians are not taking precautions in these two known risk areas. Acting on an illusion of identity-determined immunity, lesbians are in effect enacting high-risk behaviours. Thus there is a need for effective health promotion, specifically aimed at lesbians, which takes such psychological barriers into account.

The above studies have been publicised throughout the lesbian and gay press, to inform, to educate, and to encourage behavioural change where necessary. An article in San Francisco's *On Our Backs*[98] magazine carries a particularly sinister warning, equating the prevalence pattern found in the lesbian studies with that identified in the early stages of the epidemic in the gay community. This is compounded by the wider history of the epidemic, where neglect to target certain groups with health education has resulted in a rapid rise of transmission. But it is unlikely that HIV and AIDS will ever savage our communities with the ferocity experienced by gay men and by heterosexual populations in developing countries. More recent data further suggest the inefficiency of lesbian sexual practice as a route of transmission.

This study,[99] reported throughout the lesbian/gay press,[100] found no evidence of the virus being passed from partners of positive status to those testing negative. In no case was safer sex adopted through either the use of barrier methods or act avoidance. The range of acts reported include oral sex, 'mutual masturbation', sharing sex toys and rimming. However, this study only spanned three months and dealt with a small sample. While significant, it can by no means be considered the final word.

The problem in letting this cultural construction[101] of immunity prevail unchallenged is that notions of low risk translate into no risk, which is quite simply not the case. Health promotion aimed at lesbians is often erratic and localized, and while pro-sex magazines like London's *Quim* (now defunct) and texts of erotica carry information, not all lesbians read them. Out in the community there are (broadly) two competing trends: the first and more widespread is behavioural complacency and resistance to change; the second is the attitude and action of the uncertain, rigorously advocating the adoption of safer sex. And it is here that we need balance in the form of reliable, accessible, well-disseminated information, to allow us to make our own informed choices. Knowledge is essential and vigilance is vital. As long as healthcare provision remains characterized by inequalities in service delivery – reflecting a deeply embedded institutionalized racism, sexism, homophobia and heterosexism – as communities we need to take responsibility for ourselves. Healthcare providers often make assumptions as to the nature of our sexual activities or the lack of them, based on stereotypes activated when confronted by difference. If information is not forthcoming, we have to ask for it. Proaction is not always easy. But as the British healthcare system becomes more overtly driven by market forces, we can capitalize on the change to raise the profile of lesbian health issues. The viability of specific services is evidenced by the success of the lesbian sexual health clinics in London. If service delivery is poor, we need to familiarize ourselves with our rights of redress, such as complaining to local Community Health Councils.[102] Negative reactions from healthcare providers are all too frequent, and deter us from entering the system – an effect which may be detrimental to our health. One strategy for getting round this is to take a friend or partner with you, which provides you with support, a reality check, and a collective front of resistance.

When the lesbians completing the Pride Survey were asked 'Has the risk of HIV/AIDS changed your behaviour in anyway at all?', two thirds said yes (66 per cent). This compares with 14 per cent of the women in the National Survey,[103] who said yes to a similar question. This is a dramatic finding considering the apparent indifference of many lesbians. That such a large percentage of women should change their behaviour in the absence of continued and orchestrated health promotion – which might not itself have guaranteed such high figures – is interesting. But 'perception of risk' and cognitive interventions like health education messages are only two factors infuencing our health beliefs and actions. The search is ongoing to elucidate the complexities shaping how we act in relation to our health. Psychologists have long been aware that the attitudes held by a person are complex and often contradictory and that the relationship between them and behaviour is far from straightforward. We often act in contrary ways to our attitudes. When it comes to safer sex there is more going on than a 'clinical' risk assessment. We may never make such an assessment, or after due thought may proceed unprotected anyway – in situations of both high and low risk. But, from the Pride Survey, it appears that lesbians were changing their behaviour and were not acting on assumptions that 'HIV would never happen to them'.

Although possibly explicable as an index of previously unrecorded levels of anxiety, there is a more probable explanation for changing behaviour: our proximity to the gay community. Bound together in sexual exile, we were close enough to feel the powerful aftershocks stemming from gay epicentres. Even for those not personally affected through social or occupational networks, it was difficult to avoid the upsurge of anti-gay and -lesbian hostility. And in such a situation it was almost as if we inherited the expectations of safer sex, for reasons including the communication of empathy and a sense of community.

When these women reported behavioural change, what exactly were they doing? Over half of this subgroup asked their partners about their sexual histories (58 per cent); over a third avoided certain acts (38 per cent, with a further 2 per cent specifying abstinence from oral sex during menstruation); just under a third cited washing hands and toys (19 per cent) as a precaution, 17 per cent reported using latex gloves/cots, with only 15 per cent using the dental dam. Smaller numbers reported reduction in male or female partners (14 per cent reported male reduction, 11 per cent female). These findings are similar to the limited analysis of the National Survey where, in accordance with prevailing trends, differences in safer sex practice were attributed more to gender difference than socio-sexual choices and identities: 'the preventive strategies of women reporting a homosexual partner and women with more than one heterosexual partner are very similar, with emphasis on sticking to one partner, using a condom and knowing your partner before having sex.'[104] However, to qualify, while history-taking and partner reduction may be behavioural change, this is not, in isolation, 'safer sex practice' *per se*.

Available evidence suggests lesbians, like other sexually active people, prefer risk reduction strategies to abstinence. However, these usually lean more on exclusivity and communication than latex -- reflecting not just a women's gendered tendency toward verbal negotiation, but an appropriate approach to the realities of risk assessment, and the lack of a serious widespread endorsement and adoption of the dental dam as a viable strategy. Theoretically at least, the adoption of barriers protect not only from HIV, but a number of other infections. And although the prevalence of such infections is generally considered lower amongst lesbians (or those whose *behaviour* is lesbian), we can and do pass infections from one woman to another. Statistics from the audits of London's lesbian clinics[105] reinforce some of the few findings already documented. It is generally accepted that gonorrhoea, syphilis (rare in Britain at this point in time) and chlamydia are unlikely to be passed on via lesbian sexual practice. However, there is always the proviso of theoretical risk. If, for example, two women were to swiftly exchange the dildo without washing it, penetrating quickly and deeply, then, what are, in effect, fragile organisms, might just survive.

Although the risks of transmitting/contracting these infections seem negligible, the same cannot be said for bacterial vaginosis, the herpes simplex virus, candida (thrush), crabs and human papilloma virus (HPV), commonly known as 'wart virus'. Many of the practices we readily recognize as sex, such as rubbing/tribadism, manual–vulva contact and cunnilingus, can result in the transfer of such infections. Women who are immuno-compromised – through HIV, auto-immune diseases, the effects of long-term alcohol dependency, or diabetes – may find the duration of such infections prolonged and the possibility of re-infection more likely. In addition to the message of self-protection and individual responsibility, the low profile of HIV and AIDS in our communities masks another communicable reality – you may be far more 'dangerous' to her health than she is to yours (or vice versa). This is common knowledge on the gay scene, where continued latex love may protect from another strain of HIV.[106]

Vaginal infections are commonly clinically identified through examination and the results of swabs taken from the vaginal walls or cervix. This brings us to yet another contentious issue in the communitities: the need for cervical screening or the 'smear test' or 'pap test'. While statistically there seems to be a lower prevalence of cervical cancer amongst lesbian women, lesbians do get cervical cancer. Although what little is known of its aetiology does implicate penetrative sex with men, there are other risk factors like smoking, drinking, environmental toxins and – a theory gaining increasing medical support – that HPV may cause changes in the cells of the cervix. Having wart virus does not make such changes inevitable but may increase the risk, and this is yet another reason why lesbians should seek regular screening. We often fail to get such care because very many of us do not approach the medical establishment in need of its contraceptive or reproductive technologies. This often means we neglect to get breast screening, which is particularly significant in the light of evidence that suggests the prevalence of breast cancer amongst lesbians is up to three times higher than in women generally. Breast cancer is more common in women over fifty who have never had children. There is potentially something about the hormone changes during pregnancy and lactation that may decrease the likelihood of developing this type of cancer. This is but one identified trend and many younger women, including those who are biological mothers, develop breast cancer. Much remains unknown and we have yet to find a cure.

A result of the impact made by the HIV and AIDS epidemic in western countries is that medical attitudes to sexual diversity have finally been put on the agenda. Another consequence has been the heightened profile of breast cancer, forced into the arena by lesbians angry at the disparate resources available to the lesbian and gay communities for research and care into HIV and AIDS compared to breast cancer. The continued neglect of women's health issues in relation to men's needs takes on a re-invigorated politic of gender inequality, as breast cancer is seen as the invisible epidemic overshadowed by gay men's concerns. The debate simmers, intermittently voiced in the lesbian and gay press, as lesbians point to the amount of lesbian energy which has gone into work around the epidemic, while gay men continue to ignore our issues. It is argued and widely believed that if the situation were reversed, men would not mobilize in our defence. Behind the front of collective action around the epidemic lurked the strains of gendered disharmony, which obscured underlying tensions related to race and ethnicity, another less publicized vector in the political economy of health.

This information on health is a vital component of sex education in a broader context. Desires are shaped by many forces and subjective experiences of illness, health and disability, like the wider politics surrounding them, are all too frequently ignored. To exclude such issues would result not in the undressing of lesbian sex but dressing it in society's fashionable wardrobe. Now that the cultural production line of sexual representation is a continuous flow, a wider range of experiences need to be included. The impact of disease or disability on our mental and physical lives could be discussed effectively through our popular culture. Until we see greater awareness at a community level of the effects of drug treatments and invasive surgeries like mastectomy as a treatment for breast cancer, we can hardly blame gay men for our own apathy, ignorance and denial.

Sexual practice and therapeutic perfection

The results of this survey of 1566 lesbians can be used by all those working with lesbian women ... One must glean the specific sexual activities of clients and, with this knowledge, establish goals for the therapeutic process.

JoAnn Loulan[107]

Inhibited sexual desire is the most common clinical problem of lesbians presenting for sex therapy.

Margaret Nichols[108]

The sexual diffculty that the homosexual women were most likely ever to have had was feeling that sexual contact was too infrequent. In terms of whether their sex difficulties constituted problems for them, the few lesbians who did have such problems most often cited trouble finding a suitable partner.

Alan P. Bell and Martin S. Weinberg[109]

There's nothing like a bunch of sex statistics to make you feel like you've got a problem.

Cathy Winks and Anne Semans[110]

A net result of the widespread acceptance of sex as a quantifiable behaviour has been the continued and growing professionalization of sex in the public domain, as evidenced by the expanding list of disorders and dysfunctions from which we can now suffer. The range of experiences to come under the expert gaze goes far beyond the traditional problems of mechanical difficulties of intercourse. This proliferation of sexual patholo-gies is symptomatic of more than the ascendancy of medicine as an arbiter of social order and moral values – it points to the evolution of particular individual and social needs. Some of these contemporary complaints are not the property of the medical establishment *per se* and not included in the clinical guidelines. Sex addiction and codependency, for example, are largely defined and treated by the self-help industry and recovery movement, of which 'twelve step' programmes, modelled on Alcoholics Anonymous, are common. By contrast, Inhibited Sexual Desire (ISD), recently relabelled Hypoactive Sexual Desire Disorder (HSD),[111] does have 'clinical' endorsement and is treated by those working under the auspices of the medical/scientific establishment. The above 'conditions', if unrecognizable by their names, consist of broad symptomologies which might be more familiar. The therapeutic ethos and jargon is growing steadily in Britain, though not on the magnitude found in the home of popular psychology, North America. The growth of such individualizing microcultures can be found in the lesbian communities where 'psychobabble' and 'psychology speak' increasingly occur in everyday language.

From the lesbian standpoint, this new breed of sexual problems is particularly interesting. Scripted as they are in relation to social codes and expectations, these sexual problems are about as (un)natural as sex itself. Both are cultural contingents – cut out of social fabric and tailored to the fashion of the time. Sex addiction and inhibited sexual desire (ISD)/ hypoactive sexual desire disorder (HSD) fall at opposite ends of the same continuum – either we crave, want or have sex too much, or not enough or not at all. Unsurprisingly, women tend be over-represented in the latter, men the former, reflecting the prescriptions of sex-role socialization. In earlier decades of the twentieth century, no one suffered from ISD/HSD. This is not to say society functioned free from sexual anxieties, but that experiences were interpreted with reference to the dominant theories of the time. As sex became more significant in an increasingly individualizing society, cracks began to appear in the social structure. The evolution of ISD (as it was then) marked the shift in the way sex was understood. This all-embracing category was as applicable to lesbians as straight women, returning lesbians to the arms of experts, despite having only recently broken free of their clutches. Based on heterosexualized and [medically] male ideas of frequency and normality, an early diagnostic criterion of ISD, 'chronic failure to initiate',[112] if applied, would have pathologized an entire generation of femme lesbians,[113] who were operating under different sexual codes from those found in the parent culture. While, at this stage, lesbian inclusion in sexological practice was marginal, this has changed with the development of our own therapeutic industries. Since the 1980s, this low or absent desire seems to be the most documented aspect of lesbian sexuality, to the extent that any commentary ignoring what is colloquially known as 'bed death', would appear woefully inadequate.

Indicative of the wider mysteries of sexual desire, there are numerous competing and complementary explanations of the origins of the condition: 'Organic causes, stress, sexual identity conflict, performance anxiety, drug and alcohol abuse, childhood trauma, basic sexual guilt, fear of intimacy, disappointment with sexual repertoire and anger.'[114] The list, while making no pretence to be exhaustive, is missing a further motive – especially notable since the source is a gay and lesbian self-help guide for 'building relationships that last', and this is one of the most frequently cited lesbian phenomena ever 'discovered'. Merging, or the blurring of individual boundaries, is the loss of a sense of self as separate from the significant other (discussed in more detail later in the text). Passionate declarations like 'I don't know where you end and I begin', once intended as the ultimate in soul swapping, passion and the abyss of exclusive intimacy, are now more likely to be interpreted as a warning signal of boundary breakdown and imminent 'bed death'.

Conciliatory words of wisdom reassure us that we are not alone in the languishing libido; 'discrepancy in sexual desire between partners, or the absence in both partners of erotic feelings are the problems reported most frequently by lesbian couples.'[115] But the demise of desire, for whatever reason, is not just a lesbian issue. The American Psychological Association estimates that 20 per cent of the population experience symptoms of absent or low desire.[116] Statistics from the US Survey show that a third of the female sample lost interest in sex for a period of several months or more (they also found 'problems' like inability to orgasm, not enjoying sex and performance anxiety, reported by one in ten women).[117] We could add to their liberal reassurance that 'gay and lesbian sex plays by many of the same rules as heterosexual sex',[118] that lesbians are not the only members of the team to pull out of the game. The fact that a disproportionate amount of our interest seems focused on this could be responsible for a subcultural, self-fulfilling prophecy. It also highlights the need to balance the role of individual and couple psychology with an analysis of the wider cultural forces that shape our sexual psyches, not least those that erect goals for sexual frequency.

The longer the relationship, the more inevitable the fluctuations in sexual frequency. The difference today is that what was once taken for granted is now taken to heart and to the expert. But it is an unrealistic expectation – and probably a physical impossibility – to prioritize sex above all other aspects of daily life on a permanent basis. There are times when sex does occupy a large part of our lives: usually at relationship onset, the honeymoon phase (what psychologists call limerance), the beginnings of a cycle. It is usually from the position of retrospective yearning that we exaggerate the importance, meanings and possible values of sex. When the flames of passion subside into a warming glow (if they are not extinguished altogether), adjustment is not always easy as we are constantly reminded of the sexual high and bombarded with suggestions of rejuvenation. Experts map out sexual and relationship patterns in stages to reassure us that changes are inevitable, while at the same time recommending styles of resistance to these changes, which can very easily slide into discontent. 'Hot monogamy'[119] (keeping the interest in one partner) is encouraged to fan the flames of passion, to prevent one getting one's fingers burnt elsewhere – as, of course, folklore answers to sexual boredom are often sought on the couch of another. Hot monogamy is not only potentially 'safer sex' but is a restraining hand on what is seen as a progressively permissive society. Interestingly, the number of partners is policed more than the practices themselves, and – as will be seen later in the book – strategies to rekindle the sexual appetite need only meet one criterion for the sexologists and their clientele: that they work.

Such an approach is almost the antithesis of the therapeutic philosophies underlying the treatment of sex addiction. While proponents of the recovery movement advocate the inclusion of sex addiction in the nomenclature under the label 'hyperactive sexual desire disorder',[120] the motive is one of medical recognition and endorsement as opposed to the adoption of medicines and treatment regimes. And although such clinical reification is resisted by sexologists who insist that sex addiction is 'a media term that doesn't have any scientific validity or meaning',[121] the establishment may shift in the future as the widespread success of the recovery movement threatens its dominant position. JoAnn Loulan, who straddles the schools of sexology and recovery in her West Coast style, includes sex addiction in her commentaries of lesbian sexuality.[122] Central to the concept of what are broadly called the 'process addictions'[123] (sex, romance, shopping, gambling and watching soap operas) is the notion of loss of control. In line with the traditional model of the formative twelve step programme of Alcoholics Anonymous (AA), collective support aims to enhance individual responsibility – it is we who have lost control and it is only ourselves who can keep us in 'sobriety', that is, clean of the toxin which we crave, be it alcohol, shopping or sex. Because of the power of the appetite, the treatment imperatives are abstinence and restraint – reminiscent of the temperance and social purity movements of bygone eras, when uncontrolled sex or alcohol consumption were signs of depravity, a threat to both the soul and social order.

While existing theories of the origins of sex addiction are as diverse as those of alcohol dependency, most locate the problem within the individual, and are uncritical of a sex-obsessed culture. 'Diagnosis' of such an addiction, however, leans towards the problematic when it becomes clear that it is so clearly related to established norms and social mores. How much is too much is, on the one hand, the decision of the individual, but on the other, it is a value judgement of society. A product of the same industry and of the AA model of addiction is 'codependency' – a term which is gaining currency in lesbian communities. Originally conceived as the co-addict or 'enabler' – the one who cleaned up and covered up for the alcoholic – she unconsciously perpetuated the addiction, and was herself considered to be addicted to a need to be needed.[124] Sexual co-dependency is now an addiction in its own right. With an insecure sense of self, the codependent allows others around her to define who she is. Her craving is not for sex, but for the security a relationship can provide – the symptomology is one which, potentially, even more lesbians would recognize than the numbers identifying with ISD/HSD.

'Diagnosis' or recognition of these problems, initially at least, is made by the self or a significant other. Whether in response to inventories in self-help guides, disgruntled partners or a growing awareness that the experience does not match up with what we've been led to expect, the labels are one way to confront any accompanying feelings of inadequacy, loss of control, desperation or unhappiness. There is an abundance of literature, and in the large-scale recourse to bibliotherapy, answers are sought within the pages to problems between the sheets. This is indicative not only of consumer demand, but of the fact that in the aftermath of shifts in morality, cultural values and expectations surrounding sex and relationships, something is amiss. As we increasingly turn to specific individuals to fulfil a variety of needs the wider community cannot meet, it becomes apparent that these exclusive worlds are not quite what we anticipated. It is in such a fertile climate that self-help psychology guides begin to read like symptom-bound horoscopes. The pain described is almost palpable. They provide a diet similar to that of daytime chat shows like *Oprah* and *Vanessa*, as people make the most intimate of testimonials which, once publicly witnessed, are then subject to expert commentary. We are moved, we are angered, we identify and we learn.

In *Women, Sex and Addiction: A Search for Love and Power*,[125] with the tantilizing footer, 'The book that tells you how to break out of destructive relationships', it is hard to resist taking the ideas on board, especially as lesbians are included in the text. I defy most of the women I know to read this book and not see aspects of themselves reflected. Here we are not only offered the light at the end of the tunnel but, for those lost in the search, Kasl cuts through the psychic undergrowth to show where the tunnel begins. The net cast for our symptoms is far-reaching. Familiar events, experiences and heartaches suddenly become illuminated in neon. Some of the questions to ascertain addiction include: 'Do you have a pattern of unsuccessful love relationships in spite of longing for a permanent relationship?', 'Have you engaged in sadomasochistic (S&M) relationships?' and 'Do your sexual fantasies or obsessions about roman- tic involvements interfere with your concentration or abilities?'[126] . . . now where was I? Codependency – which, the astute Kasl herself notes, is little more than the exaggerated norms prescribed as a women's role – is revealed by such questions as: 'Do you focus more attention on your partner's sexual wants than your own?', 'When someone is sexually attracted to you, does your self esteem go up?', 'Are you embarrassed to speak of your sexual behaviour with another person or a professional counsellor? (The answers refer to pre recovery attitudes)' and 'When you meet a prospective partner do you have fantasies of . . . being partners? . . . How glad will you be to tell your friends you have a lover or a mate?'[127] Such a comprehensive inventory refers as much to societal dictates as to personal symptoms.

With no shortage of published critiques of the way the self-help industry pushes individual solutions for social problems, it is still difficult to dismiss it outright. The bottom line is that these books, meetings and support groups have helped women – and they are no more submerged in false consciousness than I'm in denial (which is of course the pop psychologist's equivalent). These constructs and the accompanying lan- guage provide much-needed reality checks for many, a means of getting one's life witnessed, a label for a problem, which allows a solution to be sought. There is also great overlap with the 'survivor movement' – those recovering from physical, emotional and sexual abuses. The problem with the momentum of such movements is that we become defined by pain: habits and actions are seen purely as being determined by our histories. A balance is needed between getting support for what hurts and allowing it to take over our lives. Recovery is in danger of becoming yet another goal, like 'perfect sex', a lifelong process of ever closer approximations, but ultimately unobtainable.

While many of us may be content with reading our armchair analysis, the appeal of therapy is widespread amongst those acclimatized to its ethos and in the privileged position to access it. This trend invokes the political argument that 'privatization' of such issues distracts from wider social analysis. It has been suggested that lesbians abandon their support groups and therapy sessions in favour of 1970s style consciousness raising groups: talking, sharing and supporting in an environment conducive to making the personal political. However, in communities where we are still torn over struggles of race, class, disability politics and sexual practice, this idea has the makings of little more than a feminist fairytale. There are times in our communities when the very idea of a unified subculture is the most alien concept of all.

ISD/HSD, addiction and codependency provide hooks on which we can hang our experience, rendering it intelligible. They have emerged in an era of great social change, reflecting the fluidity of social codes, norms and diagnostic practice, while providing new anchors to imply fixity. These labels function to validate personal experience while simultaneously issuing licence for social control. The debate is ongoing as to whether, in their absence, we would suffer in silence or not at all. But the widespread adoption of these performative pathologies is testimony to the level of anxiety concerning sex in contemporary society. Throwing ourselves into the arms of experts, in search of comfort if not cure, when our romanticized expectations do not match up with reality, begs the question of whether we are suffering dysfunction, disorder or merely disappointment. If sex were knocked off its carefully sculptured pedestal, this modern-day malaise might be seen less as a sexual sickness and more as a socially produced dis-ease.

NOTES

1.   Alan P. Bell and Martin S. Weinberg, *Homosexualities: A Study of Diversity Among Men and Women*, London, Mitchell Beazley, 1978, inside cover.
2.   Kaye Wellings, Julia Field, Anne M. Johnson, and Jane Wadsworth, *Sexual Behaviour in Britain: The National Survey of Sexual Attitudes and Lifestyles*, London, Penguin, 1994, p. 1.
3.   Edward O. Laumann, John H. Gagnon, Robert T. Michael, and Stuart Michaels, *The Social Organization of Sexuality: Sexual Practices in the United States*, University of Chicago Press, 1994, p. xxx.
4.   Gregory M. Herek, Douglas C. Kimmel, Hortensia Amaro and Gary B. Melton, 'Avoiding heterosexist bias in psychological research, *American Psychologist*, vol. 46, no. 9, p. 957.
5.   Kaye Wellings et al., op. cit.

6. Edward Laumann et al., op. cit.

7. Philip Blumstein and Pepper Schwartz, *American Couples*, New York, William Morrow, 1983.

8. The Lesbian Sex Survey was the initiative of Deborah James (then Senior Health Adviser at the Alexandra Clinic, King's College Hospital). In the early stages of the project, I became involved, as did a gay men's research organization, then called Project Sigma – the branch now known as Sigma Research. The design produced by Deborah and myself was piloted, modified, and changed again in a meeting with members of Project Sigma (Ford Hixon, Peter Davies, Peter Weatherburn, Andrew Hunt and Michael Stephens) and a lesbian panel consisting of Rosa Benalto, Diane Richardson and Mary McIntosh.

9. The findings from the 278 replies cannot be applied to the lesbian community in general, as the sample was not accessed by a method which would have allowed for such generalizations to be made. The demographics reflect recurring bias in research of this nature – the sample is predominantly white, able-bodied, with an average age of twenty-nine (range seventeen to forty-seven). 22 per cent of the sample identified as lesbian, 44 per cent selecting the combined category of lesbian/dyke, 5 per cent specified dyke, 11 per cent gay, 8 per cent 'other' which included 0.7 per cent (two women) identifying as queer. 47 per cent of the sample lived in London, 33 per cent in 'another large city'. 93 per cent identified as white European (81 per cent) or white other (12 per cent), 5 per cent 'other', 0.3 per cent identified as African, 0.7 per cent Afro Caribbean, 0.3 per cent black other, 0.2 per cent of the sample listed disabilities. Thus, the sample is not representative of the diversity in our community.

10. See Alfred C. Kinsey, Wardell B. Pomeroy and Clyde E. Martin, *Sexual Behaviour in the Human Male*, Philadelphia, W.B. Saunders, 1948; and Alfred C. Kinsey, Wardell B. Pomeroy, Clyde E. Martin and Paul H. Gebhard, *Sexual Behaviour in the Human Female*, Philadelphia, W.B. Saunders, 1953.

11. Alfred Kinsey et al., 1953, ibid., pp. 446–487.

12. See, for example, Julia O'Connel Davidson and Derek Layder, *Methods, Sex, and Madness*, London, Routledge, 1994; and Janice M. Irvine, *Disorders of Desire: Sex and Gender in Modern American Sexology*, Philadelphia, Temple, 1990.

13. Cited in Bennett L. Singer and David Deschamps (eds.), *Gay and Lesbian Statistics*, New Press, 1994, p. 10.

14. Ibid., p. 11.

15. See Shere Hite, *Women as Revolutionary Agents of Change: The Hite Reports 1972–1993*, London, Bloomsbury, 1993.
16. Kaye Wellings et al., op. cit.
17. Edward Laumann et al., op. cit.
18. Jesse Helms led a campaign in 1989 to prevent the National Endowment for the Arts (NEA) funding exhibitions thought to be indecent or obscene, or more accurately, homoerotic. Although the amendment failed, Helms's display of homophobic hostility had been particularly virulent, and was to continue to be so. His amendment to a bill on funding for the National Institution of Health prevented any bid for funding ever being made for the study of adult sexual practices. See Laumann et al., op. cit.
19. Kaye Wellings et al., op. cit., p. 11.
20. Ibid.
21. Edward Laumann et al., op. cit.
22. See Julia Field, Ann Johnson, Jane Wadsworth and Kaye Wellings, 'The facts of homosexual life: The sex survey part two', *Independent on Sunday*, 23 January 1994, pp. 8–11.
23. Peter Wilby, 'Research team defends 1-in-90 gay sex claim', *Independent on Sunday*, 23 January 1994, p. 1.
24. Kaye Wellings et al., op. cit., pp. 183–188.
25. Edward Laumann et al., op. cit., p. 29.
26. Kaye Wellings et al., op. cit.
27. Edward Laumann et al., op. cit., p. 293. The numbers of those identifying either as lesbian or bisexual were so small that the categories were combined for analysis. The ratio of lesbian to bisexual women was approximately two to one.
28. Ibid., p. 294.
29. Kaye Wellings et al., op. cit., p. 88.
30. Edward Laumann et al., op. cit., p. 294.
31. See, for example, Julia Heiman, 'Women's sexual arousal', *Psychology Today*, April 1975, pp. 91–94; or Margaret Nichols, 'Lesbian sexuality: Issues and developing theory', in Boston Lesbian Psychologies Collective (eds.), *Lesbian Psychologies*, Urbana, University of Illinois Press, 1987.
32. Kaye Wellings et al., op. cit., p. 253.
33. See Jeffrey Weeks, 'Pretended family relationships', in *Against Nature: Essays on History, Sexuality and Identity*, London, Rivers Oram Press, 1991, p. 139.

34. In probability sampling, all members of the population have an equal chance of being selected (a random selection is produced by statistical techniques). In non-probability or purposive sampling, the chance of selection is unknown. Much of the research cited in this chapter, with the exception of the National Survey, is based on non-probability sampling techniques. It is especially difficult to access lesbian and gay samples which are representative, as discussed by John C. Gonsiorek, 'The empirical basis for the demise of the illness model of homosexuality', in John C. Gonsiorek and James D. Weinrich (eds.), *Homosexuality: Research Implications For Public Policy*, Newbury Park, Sage, 1991. The Wellings study used a probability sample, accessed via the sampling frame (list of all available elements for selection) of the Post Office Small Users Postcode Address File (PAF). This is more up to date than the Electoral Register, as it is upgraded quarterly by the Post Office. However, it does not specify the number of residents or households at each delivery point and it excludes the homeless and the majority of institutionalized populations.
35. Kaye Wellings et al., op. cit., p. 193.
36. Ibid., p. 179.
37. Robert T. Michael, John H. Gagnon, Edward O. Laumann and Gina Kolata, *Sex in America: A Definitive Study*, London, Little, Brown, 1994, p. 170.
38. Letitia Anne Peplau, 'What homosexuals want in relationships', *Psychology Today*, March 1981, p. 28.
39. Suzanna Rose, 'Sexual pride and shame in lesbians', in Beverly Greene and Gregory M. Herek (eds.), *Lesbian and Gay Psychology: Theory, Research and Clinical Applications*. Thousand Oaks, Sage, 1994.
40. Kaye Wellings et al., op. cit., pp. 178–227.
41. Ibid. Data on lesbian sex are generated by the questions: 'Any sexual experience/contact with a female?', followed by questions pertaining to age and frequency. A broad question asks about sex involving 'genital/vaginal contact', including oral sex and 'Any other form of sex with a woman that involved genital contact but not also oral sex? (for example, stimulating sex organs by hand)'. See pp. 427–9.
42. See, for example, Kinsey, 1953, op. cit., Bell and Weinberg, op. cit., and JoAnn Loulan, *Lesbian Passion: Loving Ourselves and Each Other*, San Francisco, spinsters/aunt lute, 1987.
43. Kaye Wellings et al., op. cit., pp. 224–225.
44. Edward Laumann et al., op. cit., p. 319.

45. Philip Blumstein and Pepper Schwartz, op. cit., p. 196.
46. See Alan P. Bell and Martin S.Weinberg, op. cit., p. 110.
47. Philip Blumstein and Pepper Schwartz, op. cit., p. 237.
48. Kaye Wellings et al., op. cit., pp. 178–227.
49. Philip Blumstein and Pepper Schwartz, op. cit., p. 226.
50. See, for example, Alfred Kinsey et al., 1953, op. cit., Alan P. Bell and Martin S. Weinberg, op. cit., and JoAnn Loulan, 1987, op. cit. note 42.
51. See 'Lurid lexicons and sexual semantics' in Chapter 3 for the descriptive statistics related to SM role adoption.
52. See Project Sigma and City Limits, 'The final score', City Limits, June 20–27, pp. 14–17.
53. See 'Life and loves of a London lesbian: Survey results – part two: Sex', Lesbian London, issue 10, Sept/Oct 1992, p. 4.
54. Marcel T. Saghir and Eli Robins, 'Clinical aspects of female homosexuality', in Judd Marmor (ed.), Homosexual Behaviour: A Modern Reappraisal, New York, Basic Books, 1980, p. 284.
55. See Barbara Ponse, Identities in the Lesbian World: The Social Construction of Self, Westport, Greenwood Press, 1978, pp. 148–9. Also cited in the same text is a study by Delores Klaich, Woman and Woman: Attitudes towards Lesbianism, New York, William Morrow, 1974. However, both authors stress that their lesbian subjects (or 'women related women', as they were called), avoided graphic descriptions about sexual activities. The language Ponse uses to describe dildos – 'artificial penis substitutes' – reflects a tenacious association between toys and practice, which is still quite prevalent today. While both commentaries endorse the socio-emotional aspects of mutual pleasure, it is of interest that Klaich acknowledges the anus as one of the areas which responds readily to the fingertips and tongue.
56. See Robert T. Michael et al., op. cit., p. 174.
57. See Edward Laumann et al., op. cit.
58. Six casual compared to four regular. The mode, however (that is, the most frequently occurring value in the data) is one in both cases.
59. See Edward O. Laumann and John H. Gagnon, 'A sociological perspective on sexual action', in Richard G. Parker and John H. Gagnon (eds.), Conceiving Sexuality: Approaches to Sex Research in the Postmodern World, New York, Routledge, 1995, pp. 183–214.
60. Quote from Armistead Maupin, Further Tales of the City, cited in Peter M. Davies, Ford C.L. Hickson, Peter Weatherburn and Andrew J. Hunt, Sex, Gay Men and AIDS, London, Falmer, 1993, p. 147.

61. Rita Mae Brown, cited in Neil Miller, *Out of the Past: Gay and Lesbian History from 1869 to the Present*, Vintage, 1995, p. 467.
62. See Margaret Nichols, op. cit., p. 102.
63. Ibid., p. 103.
64. See, for example, Shere Hite, *The Hite Report on Love, Passion and Emotional Violence*, London, Optima, 1991; *Lesbian London*, op. cit., and Philip Blumstein and Pepper Schwartz, op. cit.
65. Elizabeth Kasoff, 'Non monogamy in the lesbian community,' in Esther D. Rothblum and Ellen Cole (eds.), *Loving Boldly: Issues Facing Lesbians*, New York, Harrington Park Press, 1989, pp. 167–182.
66. Philip Blumstein and Pepper Schwartz, op. cit.
67. See for example, Letitia Anne Peplau and Hortensia Amaro, 'Understanding lesbian relationships', in William Paul, James D. Weinrich, John C. Gonsiorek and Mary Hotvedt (eds.), *Homosexuality: Social, Psychological and Biological Issues*, New York, Sage, 1982. See also Project Sigma and *City Limits*, op. cit.
68. Philip Blumstein and Pepper Schwartz found in their follow-up study that the lesbian couples reported the highest incidence of relationship breakdown, op. cit.
69. As can be seen when looking at psychological theories of love and attraction. In addition, see the work of Letitia Anne Peplau on lesbian and gay couples.
70. Deaux and Hanna, cited in Esther D. Rothblum, 'Lesbians and physical appearance: Which model applies?', in Beverly Greene and Gregory Herek (eds.), op. cit.
71. See, for example, Philip Blumstein and Pepper Schwartz, op. cit.
72. Project Sigma and *City Limits*, op. cit.
73. Philip Blumstein and Pepper Schwartz, op. cit.
74. Ibid., p. 196.
75. Jane Alexander, 'Sex: The results of our survey,' *Elle*, April 1992, pp. 29–37.
76. Ibid., p. 34.
77. See Edward Laumann, op. cit.
78. Emily L. Sisley and Bertha Harris, *The Joy of Lesbian Sex*, New York, Pocket Books, 1977, p. 137.
79. JoAnn Loulan, *Lesbian Sex*, San Francisco, Spinsters/aunt lute, 1984.
80. Alfred Kinsey et al., 1953, op. cit., p. 468.
81. Letitia Anne Peplau and Hortensia Amaro, op. cit., p. 244.
82. See Shere Hite, op. cit., 'The Hite Report on female sexuality', p. 35.

83. Jane Alexander, op. cit. p. 34.
84. Project Sigma and *City Limits*, op. cit.
85. See Kaye Wellings et al., op. cit., p. 211.
86. Mode: three, median: five. Average number of female partners: eight, mode: two, median: six.
87. See Jeffrey Weeks, 'History, desire and identities', in Richard G. Parker and John H. Gagnon (eds.), op. cit., pp. 33–50.
88. Kaye Wellings et al., op. cit., p. 211.
89. Ibid., p. 218.
90. Quoted in Patricia Stevens, 'HIV prevention education for lesbians and bisexual women: A cultural analysis of a community intervention', *Social Science And Medicine*, vol. 39, no. 11, 1994, p. 1569.
91. Ibid.
92. See, for example: Michael Marmor, Lee R. Weiss, Margaret Lyden, Stanley H. Weiss, W. Carl Saxinger, Thomas J. Spira and Paul M. Feorino, 'Possible female to female transmission of human immunodeficiency virus', *Annals of Internal Medicine*, 105(6), December 1986, p. 969; and Ofelia T. Monzon and Jose M. B. Capellan, 'Female to female transmission of HIV', *Lancet*, vol. 2, no. 40, 4 July 1987. Stephens, op. cit., Susan Y. Chu, Lisa Conti, Barbara A. Schable and Theresa Diaz, 'Female-to-female sexual contact and HIV transmission,' *JAMA*, 10 August 1994, vol. 272, no. 6, p. 433; Susan Y. Chu, James W. Buehler, Patricia L. Flemming, and Ruth L. Berkelman, 'Epidemiology of reported cases of AIDS in lesbians, United States 1980–89', *AJPH*, November 1990, vol. 80, no. 11, pp. 1380–1. See also the San Francisco studies, by the San Francisco Department of Public Health, 1993, reported in both Stevens, 1994, and Anna Poppa, 'Lesbians and HIV', *Body Positive*, no. 167, 5 April 1994.
93. Michael Marmor et al., op. cit.
94. Ofelia Monzon et al., op. cit.
95. Susan Y. Chu et al., 1994, op. cit.
96. Cited in Patricia Stevens, op. cit., p. 1566.
97. Ibid.
98. Heather Findlay (ed.), *On Our Backs*, vol. 10, no. 3, Jan/Feb, 1994, p. 21.
99. R. Raiteri, R. Fora, P. Gioannini, R. Russo, A. Lucchini, M. G. Terzi, D. Giacobbi and A. Sinicco, 'Seroprevalence, risk factors and attitude change to HIV-1 in a representative sample of lesbians in Turin', *Genitourinary Medicine*, vol. 70, 1994, pp. 200–205.

100. 'Lesbian sex low risk for HIV, says study', *Pink Paper*, 338, 29 July 1994, and 'Study queries need for dyke safer sex', *Capital Gay*, 655, 29 July 1994.
101. See Patricia Stevens, op. cit.
102. Community Health Councils were established in 1974, in every local authority, to monitor NHS services on behalf of their local populations. We do not have to wait for an adverse experience before we get involved with CHCs. Each individual council sets its own objectives, which can be influenced to include lesbian health needs, if lesbian participation draws attention to those needs.
103. Kaye Wellings et al., op. cit., p. 367.
104. Ibid., p. 370.
105. The Sandra Bernhard Clinic at London's Charing Cross Hospital opened in April 1992. The Audre Lorde clinic opened in October 1993, at the Royal London Hospital.
106. The two most common strains of HIV are labelled HIV 1 and HIV 2.
107. JoAnn Loulan, 'Research on the sex practices of 1566 lesbians and the clinical applications', in Ellen Cole and Esther Rothblums, *Women and Sex Therapy: Closing the Circle of Knowledge*, New York, Harrington Park Press, 1988, p. 233.
108. Margaret Nichols, op. cit., p. 100.
109. Alan P. Bell and Martin S. Weinberg, op. cit., p. 119.
110. Cathy Winks and Anne Semans, *The Good Vibrations Guide to Sex*, San Francisco, Cleis Press, 1994, p. 11.
111. See World Health Organization, *The ICD-10 Classification of Mental and Behavioural Disorders: Clinical Descriptions and Guidelines*, Switzerland, WHO, 1992, and American Psychiatric Association, DSM-IV: *Diagnostic and Statistical Manual of Mental Disorders*, (4th edition), Washington, American Psychiatric Association, 1994.
112. See Janice Irvine, 'Regulated passions: The invention of inhibited sexual desire and sex addiction', in Ann McClintock (ed.), *Social Text*, 37, Winter 1993, pp. 203–226.
113. Discussed in more detail later in the text, see Chapter 5.
114. Betty Berzon, *Permanent Partners: Building Gay and Lesbian Relationships That Last*, New York, E.P. Dutton, 1988, pp. 217–225.
115. Marney Hall, 'Sex therapy with lesbian couples: A four stage approach', in Eli Coleman (ed.), *Integrated Identity for Gay Men and Lesbians: Psychotherapeutic Approaches for Emotional Wellbeing*, New York, Harrington Park Press, p. 138.
116. Cited in Janice Irvine, 1993, op. cit., p. 205.

117. Edward Laumann et. al., op. cit.
118. Robert T. Michael et. al., op. cit., p. 170.
119. 'Hot Monogamy' has been authored by Helen Singer Kaplan, cited in Ted Polhemus and Housk Randall, *Rituals of Love: Sexual Experiments and Erotic Possibilities*, Picador, 1994.
120. See Anthony Giddens, *The Transformation of Intimacy: Sexuality, Love and Eroticism in Modern Societies*, Cambridge, Polity Press, 1993.
121. Helen Singer Kaplan, quoted in Janice Irvine, 1993, op. cit.
122. JoAnn Loulan, *Lesbian Sex*, San Francisco, Spinsters/aunt lute, 1984.
123. See, for example, Ann Wilson Shaef, *When Society Becomes An Addict*, San Francisco, Harper and Row, 1987.
124. Alcoholism was primarily considered a male problem; codependency, stereotypically, a female one.
125. Charlotte Davis Kasl, *Women, Sex and Addiction: A Search For Love and Power*, Cedar, 1992.
126. Ibid., pp. 176–181.
127. Ibid., pp. 182–192.

5 butch and femme I: dressed to thrill

The following chapter outlines the persistent debates surrounding the femme/butch tradition in lesbian subcultures. Beginning with a personal narrative, the complexity of identity and its gendered meanings are introduced via the tensions and contradictions inherent in the process of an evolving sense of self. The history of femme/butch roles and their contemporary meanings are discussed. As engendered codes, detailed attention is given to notions, meanings and performances of gender throughout the chapter. Going beyond much of the existing literature to reflect current counter-cultural shifts, the chapter concludes with a look at the distance (if any) between transgression and transgender.

'Me, Myself, I'

As I stood on the Castro, the lesbian and gay nerve centre in San Francisco, I paid less attention to my friends, and more to the diversity of lesbian appearance that paraded past us. Call me intuitive, but I just knew most of the women I looked at were lesbians! It was like watching the dispersing crowd of a k.d. lang concert!

But *how* did I know? The first reason for my assumption was purely geographical. The gay ghettoization of the Castro provides a safe and popular scene with an international reputation. But at least 10 per cent of the people around me could have been heterosexual! Searching for signals, I drew my own conclusions. But what signals? Dress code, hair length, body language, symbolic jewellery? Did these women radiate lesbian attitude? Was I so intoxicated by the atmosphere that I simply couldn't see straight?

Membership of the counter-culture could only prime my perception up to a point. Much as I pride myself as being able to spot a dyke at fifty feet, the reality is, of course, that all lesbians do not look the same. So, was I operating on a subculturally socialized lesbian sonar, or merely subscribing to a homophobic ideology that assumes lesbians can be identified by appearance?

Prompted by my interest and running commentary, a friend categorized me, my ex-lover and herself along the butch/femme continuum. I was described as a lesbian/dyke boy, my ex-lover, despite her androgynous appearance, was pronounced femme, and the aspiring taxonomist declared herself femme top. In other words, two femmes and a butch, 1990s style. The language she used to place us along the continuum had become all the more colourful as she employed the vernacular of contemporary sexual genres and sexiopolitical movements. I had not been told anything I didn't know already. I knew my ex-lover was femme. Over the years I had watched her appearance change from undeniably feminine (in terms of stereotypical visual cues) to 'androgynous' dyke. The surface transformation did not alter what lurked in the depths – the remodelling of an image had not altered the way we related. We had not become incompatible. Nor had it altered the very slight division of labour that contaminated our relationship: I continued to spend hours in the kitchen and she repaired the bikes, her knowing fingers demonstrating the type of skill and dexterity I was more intimately familiar with. And so what about the femme top? She was emphatic in her definition, ensuring we would harbour no illusion of potential sexual passivity. A woman who knew exactly what she wanted and how to get it, and – unless she wanted it otherwise – she was totally in control.

So by what trick of classification was I a lesbian/dyke boy as opposed to butch? Was I not as butch as a butch is supposed to be? Or was the shift merely a contemporary reflection of a genre, with a touch of queer? Was it based on my age, as I had not experienced the 1950s, when butch/femme was in its heyday? Was it contingent upon some form of sexual mastery, potentially lacking, in her opinion, since my failed attempt to seduce her, years ago? Or was it a definition determined by style and dress code? (Dressed casually, in a fashion more masculine, though not traditionally butch formal, my present-day style was met with an equally *en vogue* label.) Or had she, with perceptive sensitivity, detected my ambiguous feelings around being labelled butch? It was an ambiguity arising not only from my college-acquired lesbian feminist consciousness, but also from a pained awareness of early parental disappointment and disapproval.

As a young lesbian, the word butch did not inspire me with pride and courage, but shame and guilt. For when it became obvious to my family that my tomboy phase was overrunning into my scheduled feminine pubescent years, what had previously been tolerated now provoked worry and persistent comment. I could not go from tomboy to 'tomman' – societal dictates of puberty removed the relative freedom and flexibility I had known as a child. Here was my last chance to step into the sextyped line before sanctions would be enforced. The gender-based script I had chosen to ignore for so long became a social imperative, the watershed of my adolescent maturity. But my uninvited womanhood left me without a socially acceptable category in which to place myself, with a body in which I was not totally happy. Every now and then that little 'b' word would just slip out, as my family tried to encourage gender conformity and forewarn me of the messages my appearance and mannerisms would convey to the world at large. I reeled from the word, sensing their shame, unwilling to change, despite an increasing sense of isolation. A self-induced gender exile.

Familial disapproval paralleled the harsher and more punitive sanctions imposed by my peers, as they all too readily recognized the lesbianism my family were reluctant to name. For they automatically assumed that my gender transgression could only mean one thing: that I was a dyke. As is the experience of many young lesbians, the extra-curricular lessons in the price of nonconformity were provided by other students.

Moving to London, I found the bright lights provided me with other equally unchosen names – Sonny and Sir. It is likely that, with my athletic build and 'masculine' attire, many really did assume I was male. For those who looked a little closer, realizing their mistake and yet continuing to misassign my gender, this, no doubt, was my punishment for such defiant gender transgression.

This apparent ability to pass prevented my (then) lover and me from getting 'queerbashed': after heckling us as dykes, they apologized, thinking I was 'one of the boys'. Thinking that such erroneous perceptions had been abandoned with my bad-taste haircut, it came as something of a surprise to me when a locum doctor made the same misattribution in a recent consultation. Coming from a doctor, the assault seemed all the more painful. My body had lost the muscularity it once had – so what was she reading? There I was, kitted out in loose-fitting shorts, a shirt and short hair. She, like anyone reared in a culture where gender is afforded great significance, processed the information in an androcentric way. Her view of the world could not accommodate my identity with its obvious ambiguity – indeed she did not process the ambiguity until I drew her attention to it. Her designation of gender had resulted from her hasty interpretation of accepted signifiers of dress code, hair length and cosmetic law and order. So it seems that in the 1990s, despite the challenges of unisex, androgyny, feminism and long-haired men, it would still take the presence of at least four female cues to outweigh the visibility of one male one.[1] I did not want to be taken for a man, but what can I expect if I play around with the codes?

I knew that I was not the only butch-looking woman in that part of London. Familiarity with the lesbian subculture would have lessened the doctor's dependence on such stereotypical processing. I wondered afterwards if I would have been happier if she had looked up and said 'butch dyke', leaving my gender intact. The probability is that this was her next, albeit unspoken, assumption.

Is being butch or a lesbian/dyke boy central to my identity and my desire? Does it influence my choice of sexual partner? Do I look for complementary femininity in a lover, or for another butch, on the grounds that she is a 'proper lesbian'? Is my look what draws a woman to me? Do I need a partner who can read my appropriated masculinity and reflect it back to me, or is it irrelevant in a one-on-one situation, being more of a political statement of gender subversion? Indeed is it subversive at all considering the associations readily made between gender inversion and lesbianism? When I pick up my lover and put her on the bed, the chain of events which follow tell me that her pleasure in who I am seems endless. I'm happy, she's happy. Does this make me butch? Or does it make me a victim of pulp novel romanticism or, worse still, stereotypical masculine socialization? Am I a product of patriarchal sexist reality, trapped in seeing from a heterosexual perspective? Am I oblivious to lesbian diversity and desire? A prefeminist waiting for my 'false' consciousness to be raised on a crash course of political correction?

From the late 1980s, the terms butch and femme re-emerged in our language – that is, if they had ever gone away. Their meanings carried forth both the negative and positive connotations of earlier eras. Butch is still a pejorative term, used not only by straights who feel threatened by such a flagrant manipulation of the gendered scripts, but also by lesbians who equate the symbolic with heteropatriarchal masculinity. It is an insult deployed to remind the guilty of her crime.

Femmes do not escape the vitriol. They are commonly assumed to be 'straight women really'. So what are we colluding with here – notions that only men or their second-rate imitations can really love a woman?

Likewise, what is the message we give when 'femme' is used as a playful putdown to denote a lack of some kind?

The butch/femme revival may be more aptly described as the neo-femme renaissance, as it is doubtful whether the butch look ever went away. Even in contemporary styles it reflects the 1950s rebel: jeans, white T-shirt, leather jacket ... and, of course, an athletic, able-bodied white male. Where is our identity left when we cannot begin to approximate the icon? Our chosen identities integrate race, ethnicity, and disability in the absence of representative iconography. When we do see other components of identity reflected in butch and femme imagery, all too frequently they embody the ubiquitous stereotypes. Black women appear as butch, Asian women as femme, and disabled women are largely invisible as they are not considered sexual people.

The scripting of this chapter has taken many months as I have grappled with the issues and meanings surrounding identity, politics and sexual practice. Reconciling my desires with my politically correct super-ego has often proved an arduous task, as I struggled to balance the complexity of the subject in hand while walking the sexuality tightrope. Yet my mission to detail the pleasures and pains of the butch and femme dynamic is rendered less formidable by those whose words precede my own.

There has probably never been a better time to address the 'role' of butch and femme within our communities. In an era of post-feminism, post-gay-liberation and the postmodern, the harness which held together sexual identity and erotic practice is, in some circles, seductively undone. As early as the 1950s, Kinsey demonstrated that identity labels do not necessarily correlate with sexual practice. While America reeled in horror at the 'immoral behaviour' of the population, every effort was made to gag the messenger by pulling his funding. Decades later, HIV/AIDS began to devastate populations. Western bureaucracies, happy to blame isolated groups like gay men and populations in developing countries, clung to the myth that labels concurred with sexual practice. While the scapegoating continued, institutions were forced to recognize that it was not how you described yourself but what you did that was important. Moving into the 1990s, with the abatement of the initial panic of the crisis (due to the rapid response of the lesbian and gay community), identity and gender occupy the foreground of sexual politics debate.

As lesbians, we have not been forced to scrutinize our identities and sexual practices; our realities and our experiences are different from those of gay men. As we are often ignored by the law, historians cannot refer to a rich source of historical records of our illegal sexual acts, with which to chart the evolution of the lesbian identity. However, we are able to access evidence of cross-dressing and sexological case studies of gender inversion. Thus, one of the most tangible aspects of our history is the 'butch/femme' debate. Just as gender ideology assumes a direct relationship between the feminine and a passive sexuality, we find butch and femme roles overwritten with assumptions of activity and passivity – with all the attendant problems this produces. Nowadays, to assume that our chosen identities are indicative of who we have sex with, and how we perform sex itself, is to be distinctly passé and unqueer. But have we really let go of such predictable associations? Do we not continue to respond to others on the grounds of their gender? Is our sexual psyche not shaped and informed by dominant ideologies? Are butch and femme codes not real signals?

Just how extensive is the butch/femme identity – and how are we to recognize it, in view of shifting fashions? Studies suggest that the celebrated dynamics of butch and femme identities are more the property of lesbian mythology than everyday realities.[2] While we could emphasize the political climates in which these studies were conducted, more recent research also reflects a low incidence of butch/femme role-play.[3] Two such projects, investigating specific butch or femme identities, have found that roles are definitely a minority within a minority practice. Loulan found that 18 per cent of her sample identified as femme and 15 per cent as butch (48 per cent identified themselves as androgynous, while 19 per cent declined to identify with any of the provided labels). Only 5 per cent of the 'role' players felt this was important to their identity. What is even more interesting is that, while 95 per cent responded that they had either rated other women, or been rated themselves in terms of butch or femme, the same percentage also felt that butch and femme had little real meaning in their lives.[4] This seems to be a lesbian language which practically everyone speaks, yet no one listens to. In the Pride study, 6 per cent described themselves as butch, 7 per cent as femme. These figures raise some questions, such as why America seems to have more butches and femmes than we do. But they show clearly that lesbian liaisons occur in the absence of such gendered magnetism.

Loulan's research affirms that most of us equate butch and femme with masculinity and femininity. In her study, butches were commonly described as masculine, athletic and dominant, with femininity, gentleness and affection attributed as femme characteristics. These attitudes were documented not at the height of the politically correcting 1970s, but in a time when neo-butch/femme was becoming a marketable fashion accessory. Still, few embrace the labels and fewer still hold them with any seriousness. Walking around the Pride festival (where the Pride survey was circulated), I would have said butch and femme dykes constituted more than 13 per cent of the population. But that is because, to me, certain codes and personal styles had particular meaning.

Anchored in lesbian reality by time-honoured statistics, the question becomes: is butch/femme a convenient shorthand, with no real-life application? Or perhaps many of us shy away from the identity in the same way that we shied away from lesbianism, fearful of the consequences. Some may be put off by the gender border patrol or the dyke police; others by the limitations of identifying with such polarized extremities. Loulan describes the roles as archetypes: a collective unconscious; something we've never had to talk about yet we all know. Nobody taught us about butch/femme, yet some of us live it and the rest of us recognize it. It can also be seen as a stereotype, a mental template, with all the attendant dangers of such lazy information processing. We see only what we want to see and ignore all information which contradicts such swiftly assigned categorizations. And in doing so, we fail to appreciate the diversity of lesbian looks, desires and sexual signals.

The butch/femme debates are based on the transformation of basic psychological and sociological concepts. While for some, they have intimate meaning, for others they provide a general but less significant counter-cultural reality. Live it or loathe it, it is like a stormy love affair that keeps us apart. Such polarization can be seen in the juxtaposition of text from two influential writers in the field, JoAnn Loulan and Sheila Jeffreys.

> There was no love lost between them, everybody knew that, but she had to try, to explain how she felt, how these women made her feel inside. She reached deep inside and found these words – 'It's the erotic dance. It can be a rhythm ... The women you pass by, the ones that you cannot leave, the ones you must leave: What is it that makes you want to dance with one and not another? What is the erotic craving that draws you to her?'[5]

> Her response was abrupt and to the point, no attempt was made to answer the questions she had been asked, for they were not worthy of an answer. When would this woman understand this was about more than sex – it was politics. She chose her words carefully so she would be left in no doubt of how she felt, 'The erotic dance of role playing, the rhythm that Loulan

rhapsodises about is the rhythm of slavery, of male dominance and female submission, an old rhythm indeed but not very natural.'[6]

A cultural continuity

When we recognize a 'man' or a 'woman' it is not just their biological sex[7] we are reading but the cultural meanings assigned to it – their gender. The roles prescribed in western cultures, for women/men and girls/boys, create the illusion that there are far more differences between them than there really are. Because gender has become harnessed to biological sex, all manifestations of gendered difference become naturalized. We believe that they are the direct product of some biological blueprint. But masculinity and femininity are not inevitable behavioural patterns and psychological experiences – they are socially defined characteristics, acquired through socialization. Any deviations from the prescribed norms then become individualized problems instead of reflecting the limitations and inequalities of the sex-role system which prompt such acts of resistance. Within the dominant discourse, there is assumed to be an inflexible relationship between sex, gender and sexual identity. Thus, born female, we will become suitably feminine, conforming to social expectations of dress and behaviour and becoming heterosexual – and will happily identify as such. It is within this ideological context that lesbian experience is mediated and that our own stereotypes evolve. So ubiquitous is the dominant reality that it becomes difficult, if not impossible, to conceive of identities and power relations beyond the existing binaries: male/female, active/passive, masculine/feminine, homosexual/heterosexual. Such beliefs, acting in continuing service of sexism, heterosexism and homophobia, also ensure that white heterosexual masculinity is the norm from which all other experiences differ. It is from such a frame of reference that butch and femme are defined.

Lesbian desire and sexual practice break this natural chain of events and as such constitute a quintessential challenge to the sexual and gender hierarchies. By loving women 'we fell off the biologically charted maps'[8] – maps drawn by sexological cartographers who could not conceive of the world of sexuality as anything but flat, where the opposite poles were female and male and the centre of erotic gravity was heterosexual attraction. To reconcile the dislocation of gender identity (woman) and love object/object choice (also woman), lesbian sexuality was colonized and rewritten as a substandard heterosexual copy. No attempts were ever made to explain lesbian desire, beyond those based on ideas of gender inversion. By assimilating 'alien phenomena' into the dominant perspectives, the threat of sexual plurality was contained. Lesbian desires and identities were heterosexualized.

The idea that we simply imitated an inferior version of Mr and Mrs caught the popular imagination. Counter-arguments are difficult in view of the fact that butch and femme women did/do endorse the prevailing binary of masculinity and femininity, by deploying some of the most gender-typed codes of dress and mannerisms. However, to suggest that a significant aspect of our heritage is mere imitation is to ignore the fact that, although subcultural realities are influenced by the parent culture, the process is less replication than transformation. The vernacular itself shows a departure from the sexological constructs: 'mannish lesbian', 'invert' or 'pervert' are not the same words as butch and femme. We created these names. And so we see in the lesbian-written literature:

> these are not the voices of Havelock Ellis, Sigmund Freud ... these are our own women expressing their need to create another category of women's gender to explain their view of their bodies and their way of loving, their search for erotic dignity and pleasure.[9]

Butch and femme are not properties of the ill-fitting binary. To deny this fact is testimony to how pervasive the delusions of the dichotomy are. Butch and femme can be considered a lesbian rebellion to break free of the ties that bind lesbian desires to a system which will forever render our actions illegitimate and invalid.

The need for additional gender categories is becoming increasingly clear, as it is not only the sexual deviants who are painfully aware of the limitations of established traditions. The women's liberation movement and the recent theoretical interest in 'masculinities', document the oppressive consequences faced by western society and its constituents. Overspill from the narrowly defined categories is treated differently depending on the cultural and historical context. While it remains apparent that, as a society, we cannot squeeze people's identities, behaviours and desires into one of two mutually exclusive categories, we continue to try. Yet, even at the very building block of humankind, the genes, there are more combinations of the sex chromosomes than xx (female) and xy (male). Variations include Turner's syndrome (xo), Klinefelter's syndrome (xxy) with variants, xxxy, xxyy, and poly x females, xxx. The effects differ among individuals, from little effect to degrees of learning difficulties.

Theories of ultra males are especially common in the psychological literature, most frequently around the role of genetics in the manifestation of male aggression. Male-to-female transsexual Caroline Cossey (see later in the chapter), is additionally unusual in that her genetic fingerprint is that of a Klinefelter Variant mosaic, xxxy. She personally, along with many willing scientists, refers to this as evidence for the biological basis of transsexualism,[10] genetic coding, resulting in prenatal feminization of the brain. It is estimated that fifteen out of every 5000[11] births involve 'abnormality' of the gendered chromosomes. Rare, but probably not as rare as people think. Science promptly medicalizes such differences, to protect the binary. The further away we move from genetic and biological realities, the greater the diversity becomes. By the time we reach the subjective experiences of gender identities, sexual identities and the content of desires, it is a wonder the binary has any relevance at all.

Retreat and revival

During the Second World War, it was vital that traditional sex roles were abandoned to ensure the success of the war effort, With so many men fighting on the front lines, women moved into industry, *en masse*, performing what had formerly been considered male tasks. The blurring of gendered norms was also reflected in the suspension of rigid dress codes. With the cessation of the war, resurrection of the traditional sex roles became imperative for social and economic recovery. The restoration of prescribed norms also fulfilled the covert function of discouraging the extensive same-sex bonding which had occurred (which, it is suggested, was the reason for the exaggerated frequencies of same-sex attraction documented in the Kinsey studies). Yet, despite the reign of McCarthyism in the USA, with all its attendant horrors, including police harassment of lesbians who were not wearing more than three items of women's clothing, and similar conservative repercussions in Britain, butch and femme dykes became both the private and the public face of lesbianism. Sexual difference, as communicated through styles and overt behaviours, was no longer the prerogative of artistic eccentricity or the bohemian aristocracy. It was becoming increasingly obvious: women were not only competing for education and jobs, but for the love of other women.

As an organizing principle, such difference not only shaped the identity of individual women, by encouraging conformity to butch or femme scripts, but dictated laws of attraction. At the height of the butch/femme era, to be without a role – 'kiki' – or to move between the two – a 'switch hitter' – was strongly discouraged.[12] In the absence of a firm categorical commitment, a woman's lesbian loyalties were subject to question. Attraction was sanctioned between opposite roles only. Mutual attraction between two of the same 'kind' was often met with the same abhorrence and incomprehensibility that the general public displayed when confronted with lesbianism itself. It seems we had our own brand of essentialism – our own natural laws to be broken. Thus, the lesbian genders of butch and femme were just as limiting as the prescriptions of femininity and masculinity.

Few would contest the surface similarities between the gendered scripts of the parent culture and those of the counter-culture. But, as will be stressed throughout the chapter, detailed comparison exposes a number of contradictions. For instance, in times of recession, when the flagrant transgressions of butch women rendered them virtually unemployable (unless they passed as men), it was the femme's ability to 'blend in' that secured her job, and thus the economic survival of the couple. Her sexuality was only illuminated by the presence of her butch: 'butches were known by their appearances, fems by their choices.'[13] In a time before feminism and gay liberation, butch/femme dykes were undoubtedly a prepolitical form of resistance. Walking to and from the bars, surviving the outpourings of verbal and often physical aggression from those unable to see beyond their own bigotry, and living a life unsupported and unlegitimated by men: these were acts of courage and defiance. In the absence of a politicized collective consciousness, they were individual statements with political meaning.

The honeymoon of the butch/femme lifestyle was not to last very long. The erosion begun by the homophile organizations was replaced by an upfront attack from emerging political movements. The critique launched by groups like Daughters of Bilitis (DOB) was primarily motivated by an attempt to win tolerance and acceptance for lesbians. Role-play was detrimental to such an assimilationist stance, as it alienated and offended the heterosexual majority; hence one of the goals of DOB was to encourage 'a mode of behaviour and dress acceptable to society'.[14] Early lesbian groups, meeting in the backrooms of London pubs (not gay bars), also frequently discussed the impression given to the straight community by butch dykes:

> I remember we had a very bitter debate on whether women should come
> dressed as men. A lot of women would ... brylcream their hair and get into

gents' natty suitings, but their friends would dress in an exaggeratedly female way ... I preferred people not to look too extremely masculine because we had to go through the public bar.[15]

Later research validated such fears, showing that butch/femme styles were disliked by heterosexual onlookers.[16] It is likely that even more unpopular than gender transgressions was the sexual practice that they so blatantly advertised.

With the advent of second-wave feminism and the gay liberation movement, 'role-play' came under a more orchestrated critique. Built on generations of experiences of oppression, these movements identified the sex-role system as the cause of women's subordination and the containment of sexual identities. It became apparent that the liberation of women and sexual minorities would never be achieved while society continued to prescribe masculine and feminine scripts, which restricted the expression of diversity and sustained a male-dominated, stratified society. As long as gender remained a prime organizing principle, sexism, heterosexism and homophobia would prevail in service of it. While they were seemingly united in cause, however, the routes taken by GLF (Gay Liberation Front, London) and the WLM (Women's Liberation Movement) were somewhat different, ironically influenced by the very reality they set out to attack – gendered difference.

The GLF determinedly vowed in its manifesto 'to rid society of the gender role system which is at the root of oppression',[17] and claimed the battle was under way as, by the expression of our desires, we had 'already in part at least rejected the masculine or feminine roles society has defined for us.'[18] But its actual impact was limited. While some in the movement were critical of lesbian roles and gay camp, others recognized the wider implications and advocated their adoption as a national strategy. In the throes of all the activism, however, the different experiences of women and men were becoming divisive. Lesbians, discouraged by what appeared to be an unscalable wall of misogyny and sexism, defected to a movement united by gender rather than sexual identity.

Because GLF operated from the position of promoting sexual plurality (as well as fighting gender oppression), butch/femme roles were not the heinous crime against the sisterhood that radical feminists considered them to be. Role-play did have its opponents within the gay movement, but radical feminists considered it a prime target for attack. Because sex roles were considered vital for the survival of heteropatriarchy, butch/femme identities were seen as an equally oppressive replication. And, as such, they had to go. There were to be no excuses – once the deeper truths of feminism were realized, roles were to have no place in the new regime, unnecessary for the newly politicized lesbian identity. They were to be cast off with the ease with which some had thrown aside their heterosexuality when the personal became political. Our own communities became the training ground for sex-role destruction, as radical feminists set out to put our own house in order. The dynamic of monogamous cohabitation based on roles was seen to emulate the marriage machine upon which the parent culture relied to sustain sex roles and consequently women's subordination.

The assault on this particular sexual style, albeit shortlived, was quite effective in brow-beating its exponents back into the closet. But not all women could access feminist theory. And when they put their own beliefs into practice, many did so without relinquishing their identities. For many, it was about a way of being, loving and feeling; 'living a butch femme lifestyle was not an intellectual exercise or set of theories',[19] it was the only way they knew, the only way they ever wanted to know. 'I can't not be a femme, just as I can't not be a lesbian, because with butches I really do know what it is like to be a woman.'[20] We can write off such passionate declarations as statements of essentialism, or we can choose to recognize the early feminist goals of sexual agency and autonomy – issues submerged in an era when the 'sex' fell from the agenda of sexual politics.

The anti-role sentiments are embodied in the literature of the time: 'the minority of lesbians who still cling to traditional male-female or husband–wife patterns in their partnerships are more likely old timers, gay bar habituees and working class women.'[21] The ageism and classism is a recurring theme in critiques of butch and femme. The authors of this text will allow for no other interpretation than their own. While negating the experience of many women, they ignore the asylum these bars provided, the opportunities for friendship, romance, and sexual discovery. It was through these bars that a sense of community began to evolve. It was a raid on one of these bars that sparked a new force in lesbian and gay liberation.

It is not uncommon to find that the bar culture and butch roles are blamed for many of the problems and unpleasant realities in our communities. The high incidence of alcoholism is associated with both, in lesbian folklore and in the work of the social scientist. Domestic violence, in popular mythology, is seen to be perpetrated by butch dykes. But adoption of male styles is not synonymous with male identification in the political sense. There is no evidence to suggest that butch dykes abuse power in a characteristic 'male' fashion. While the butch and femme dykes of the 1950s bar culture, especially, were no strangers to violence, it is wrong to scapegoat butches as the likely aggressors. Much as we might want to distance ourselves from the reality that lesbians abuse each other verbally, emotionally and physically, butch-blaming colludes with the conspiracy of silence already prevalent in our communities.

Butch and femme are common lesbian colloquialisms. In the 1970s, 'androgyny' was added to our subcultural vocabulary. Emerging from several strands of feminist thought, the term was popularized by psychologist Sandra Bem.[22] She came up with the idea that femininity and masculinity were not mutually exclusive categories, but learned traits which both women and men could possess. It was hardly a new idea, reminiscent of Jungian concepts of the anima and animus and of eastern philosophies of yin and yang. Based on the questionnaire she designed to demonstrate this, it became the mentally healthy norm to be androgynous. However, as an answer to the real problems, it rapidly fell from favour. The adding of a third category reinforced the prevailing binary rather than destabilizing it. By assuming androgyny and the other gendered traits were measurable properties, the meanings of gender became individualized, distracting from much-needed institutional analysis. The much-complained-of phallocentricity of the word itself, with the male 'andro' preceding the female 'gyny', is ironically a recurring problem with the *butch/femme* debate itself.

While abandoned as a unitary strategy for change, the androgynous ideal did impact upon the lesbian community, becoming commonly associated with a non-objectifying natural look and egalitarian sexual practice.

Orgasm was no longer the goal, the new model being based on mutual appreciation, devoid of such male-identified activities as penetration, gender fetishism and tribadism (with its similarity to the missionary position). For those lesbians already part of the communities, and for those coming out in the decades between the 1950s and the 1980s, there were very clear guidelines – not only on how to dress and behave but, equally, how not to. The level of conformity and compliance was high. To those who were literate in the codes, there were very definite cues to sexual status and style: in the 1950s, if you didn't want to lie on your back, you didn't go for a dyke in men's trousers. Likewise, in the 1970s, if you wanted to play the 'old-fashioned way', you avoided a woman who called you sister on the grounds that she would make you roll over after the regulation forty minutes. Butch/femme might have been pushed out of the spotlight but, even in the throes of the androygnous takeover bid, it did not disappear altogether.

Considering the role which such identities play in individual histories and in that of the evolving community, are they a facet of the much-documented 'coming out model'? Applied to individuals, the idea that women over-identify with stereotypes, in order to gain recognition and access to the community, fails to explain those women who have always avoided such identities or those who live them for life. The implication for this latter group is that they are suffering from arrested development.[23] At the level of the community, it is possible that with the expansion of lesbian and gay services, and the evolution of a politicized and visible subculture, such blatant signals are no longer necessary. But many of us still scrutinize others for visible signs.

Throughout the demise of the butch/femme imperative and the reign of androgyny, radical feminists seemed as oblivious to the endemic and internalized misogyny amongst women, as they were to alternative meanings of the much-despised roles. Again, butch-blaming ignored the complexity of all this – much as she may not have liked femininity in herself, the butch has historically been the one to fully appreciate it in another. This does not mean her male identification included collusions with inequality, exploitation and oppression. The appropriation of masculine codes by butch women is undeniable, indeed proudly flaunted. 1970s activism exposed many oppressive practices and belief systems, such as how the fashion industry dictated norms of femininity and beauty, setting goals few could reach or maintain. Many myths were exposed, even if the mountains themselves were not moved. But, with lesbian feminism, women found themselves denied the right to construct gendered identities or to explore their sexual freedom. Little opportunity was provided to transform femininity from a form of social control into a chosen style, redefined by women themselves. This was itself misogynistic. 'Dressing for the enemy' is one way of looking at it, but what about dressing for ourselves – or with the explicit intention of finding someone to remove the carefully chosen outfit?

In the late 1980s, after a decade of political correctness which had imposed non-negotiable constraints on lesbian identity and sexual practice, neo-butch/femme appeared on the scene. The play with masculine and feminine signification was there, but the 'neo' was testimony to the fact that identities are not static, but constantly transforming. 1980s chic was more of a 'self conscious aesthetic'.[24] History was not being repeated, a new chapter was about to be written. The neo genre was stylized, commodified and commercialized – glamorizing and objectification became the name of the game, in a frenzy of fashion. This was a bad-girl rebellion: no longer were women prepared to have their identities contained, and this was one way to kick against the vanilla vogue.

Neo-butch/femme was evolving in communities where the realities of the HIV/AIDS pandemic left few untouched. Even in the designated safe zone of lesbianism, few could fail to notice the urgency with which identity and sexual practice had to be wrenched apart. In the throes of a crisis around sexuality, and as the war cry of the right wing rang out, direct-action politics re-emerged. These activists overshadowed the assimilationists in their anger, public profile, and their adoption of gender play as a subversive strategy. Such a ploy was not new; like the queer label itself, it was recycled from our history. While such politics remained a challenge to the system, the impact – mediated through a much-changed society – was different. The regulatory function of the gendered and sexuality labelling systems, which shaped our ability to define ourselves and others – 'identity is what you can say you are according to what you can be'[25] – was exposed. Adoption of the word queer is part of this strategy, as it does not rely on the gendered difference of lesbian and gay. The inevitable neglect of other dimensions along which people can be oppressed is discussed elsewhere in the text. The theory was one thing, the practice was another – many still saw 'queer' as a white middle-class gay men's plaything, with theatrical subversion displayed from the secure position of their privilege. As has also been stressed elsewhere, many dykes did not believe lesbians and gay men could work around issues of gender, without the experiences of gay liberation repeating themselves. Those who would not engage at all with the new politics were also those most hostile to butch/femme in our communities – which suggests the direction of the alliances made.

Queer aimed to accommodate all diversity. Drag queens, dyke daddies, neo-butch/femme, lesbian boys, drag kings, he-shes, transgender and camp – these were all included under the auspices of queer. (The principle around which queer's identity politic revolved was not gender *per se*, but the subversion of it.) The movement promoted the previously alienated and marginalized to the perverted frontline – becoming the emblem of queer. While groups identified with the cause, many resisted a takeover bid – transgender and transsexual politics kept their names. In contrast to earlier generations, in this new era of gender challenge there is a collective confidence, which renders the exercise of social control by shaming tactics all the more difficult. With counter-cultural language being deployed with renewed vigour, the meanings of 'queerspeak' demonstrate both the continuities and discontinuities with our history, and between the experiences of lesbians and gay men.

Lesbian roles functioned as an organizing principle – those reluctant to be 'sextyped' were marginalized. If such divisions existed among gay men, they were not articulated in the same way. Unlike butch prowess, male effeminacy was to be avoided at all costs. In Newton's documentary of camp,[26] she differentiates between the 'drag queens' (female impersonators, stage performers) whose 'staged' masquerades were legitimized by their professional status, and the 'street fairies'. Traditionally, the drag queens limited their performances to working hours. The street fairies lived their masquerades all day – every day. It was these effeminate fairies who battled alongside the butch dykes and the other bar patrons the night of the Stonewall riot, not the performance artists. Newton's distinction is no longer common; contemporary vernacular is that men in drag are drag queens, whether or not this is how they make their living. (We have our drag queens in the Newtonian sense: Lily Savage and RuPaul, to name two whose commercial success has taken them into the mainstream media. But equally so, in the clubs and on the marches we see many more men in drag, whose stage is life in general.) The attributes she identified have survived the inevitable changes in 'ladies' fashions'; drag continues to thrive on incongruity, theatricality and humour. Another difference between the butch/femme dynamic and drag is that while the former is largely associated with working-class women (although there is a historic tradition amongst the bohemian aristocracy), drag has more associations with high culture.

The criticisms against camp and butch/femme are as current today as they ever were. As are the contradictions. While re-enacting accepted codes of the binary, the belief that there are only two alternatives is further endorsed. But such performances demonstrate the ease with which gender identities can be constructed, no longer on the map of genital geography – showing that all gender is a performance, a masquerade.[27] The drag queens were even more unpopular with lesbian feminists than those ill-informed patrons of the sex-role system, butch and femme. The misyogyny of these 'phallic women' was greater, a parody of heterosexual femininity that had little resonance with lesbian reality. Proponents of drag counter that a queen's style has little to do with anyone's reality, except that perhaps of a Hollywood make-up artist. 'When people say "You dress like a woman," I say I don't think I do, because women don't really dress like this. I dress like our cultural made-up version of what femininity is, which isn't real.'[28]

Many in our communities seek distance from gender play, seeing it as a theatrical compliance with medicalized assumptions. But cross-dressing is a challenge to the homophobia which suppresses femininity in men and masculinity in women. Neo-butch and -femme dykes, with their stylistic subversions, are key players in this camp critique. The fact that camp and drag remain widely used symbols of gay and lesbian life is testimony to our continued defiance of the laws of gender. And as long as the binary prevails, with all its attendant oppressions, this will remain a prime strategy of our community: 'a way of poking fun at the whole cosmology of restrictive sex roles and sexual identifications which our society uses to oppress its women and its men.'[29]

In this new camp, a woman's desire is not policed as it once was. While neo-butch/femme remains a mutual appreciation society, it allows for all possible 'laws' of attraction. Opposites do not necessarily attract, in 1990s narcissism. Like can be with like – butch on butch, lifestyle or lipstick lesbians sharing beds and bad behaviours. The new glam girls who sleep with girls – an *en vogue* fad, as reflected in the glossy magazines – epitomize the fact that there is more to attraction than either politics or the mystery of gendered difference, be it genital, textual or otherwise. The neo-butch also reflects fashionable shifts like never before, highlighting the homoeroticism of gay masculinity as opposed to its straight master. The niche which gay masculinity has carved for itself not only penetrates representation in popular culture, but in the psyches of designer dykes with the purchasing power to shore up every postmodern masquerade.

The work of Della Grace reflects this. She takes her photography to the ever-shifting demarcation line of acceptability and promptly crosses over it. Images of the conventional butch have become almost passé, as the shirt and tie have lost the potency they once had when worn by women. More is needed in order to shock and Grace creates it: textual suggestion is replaced by a more visible phallic usurpation, the dildo. And when accompanied by tattoos, leather and piercings, it screams outlaw and is read as Sexual Minority. The coded gender fetishism may resonate with a genre typical of gay iconography, but it is evidence that the boys have lost the monopoly. She jerks phallic power out of the hands of men and proudly catalogues her stolen goods.

Schulman describes one particular photo of a butch/femme couple:

> their positioning and relationship to the camera are gender-role prescribed.
> The femme is standing behind her butch ... she lays claim. It is a stance of
> honour, respect and sexual possession. The butch sits in front of her, legs
> spread to reveal her large leather encased dildo. Her muscles are tensed in a
> masculine pose and she avoids the camera altogether.[30]

Minus the dildo, the scenario sounds familiar, incorporating the same celebratory language, but the visuals might leave Beebo Brinker (a classic butch character featured in a series of novels by Ann Bannon) somewhat horrified and with a second wave of penis envy. To some, Grace's representations epitomize the outlaw culture and are daringly refreshing, to others the work smacks of the pornographic and is a generation away from their experience.

Grace's work is often the point of discussion in the rapidly expanding lesbian and gay publications. The tone of such commentary, in its celebration of the 'postmodern', is dismissive of the past:

> unlike the butch-femme dynamic which borrows from the heterosexual
> model, the butch daddy dyke and the lesbian boy, for example, appropriate
> masculine codes without denying the femaleness of their protagonists ... the
> image boasts of the fun of a butch on butch dyke style camp that doesn't need
> to bind its breasts to impress.[31]

It is progressive in the flaunting of an identity unleashed from sexual practice. But surely the dildo serves the same function of anatomical disguise as did breast-binding? Without those dykes who so religiously bound their breasts, butch daddy dykes and lesbian boys would have no image to boast of. What differs in Grace's work, perhaps, is the sense of play – those moustaches are obviously not for real. Camp on camera remains 'a leading edge in the deconstruction of gender because camp wrests social control from the hands of the fanatics and reshapes it as a consensual game'.[32]

The 'determined' butch and 'essential' femme

[W]hat makes a feminine girl like that gay? Why does she love other girls, when she's just as womanly and perfumed as the girl who goes for men? I used to think that all homosexual girls were three-quarters boy ... Like me, I guess. And that they were all doomed to love feminine girls who could never love them back.

Beebo Brinker[33]

Butch/femme certainly seems to epitomize early sexological notions of the 'mannish' lesbian with her feminine complement, described in the works of Havelock Ellis and Sigmund Freud. These polarized caricatures were portrayed with even more clarity when the psycho-medical discourses were reframed in the fictional narratives of writers like Radclyffe Hall, in 1928, and Ann Bannon, in the 1950s. Not only are questions of causality debated through the dialogue of the characters, but their personae typify stereotypes of the time. Stephen and Mary in *The Well of Loneliness* fit the criteria of Ellis's invert/pervert as perfectly as if he scripted them with Hall's literary intentions in mind. While accepting on a surface level that butch/femme may endorse the sexological assumptions, I would suggest that, far from being our weakest link in the battle against such ideologies, butch/femme symbolizes the strongest line of resistance.

The essentialist theories appear feasible enough, because they are based on the heterosexualization of our desires. Thus, lesbianism is understood from the heterosexual perspective, which itself is a product of dominant discourses that there are only two sexes, two genders, and one natural way to love. As a result of these basic beliefs, lesbianism is tied to gender expression or, more specifically, an 'inversion' of this expression. The logic is that lesbian desires stem from a position of maleness and masculinity (be it biological, psychological or both), symbolized by 'mannish' appearance. Such a woman will therefore seek a feminine lover – because that is what a man would do. And it is at that juncture that the story becomes less than convincing. Because when our hero finds her sweetheart, the reciprocal attraction of the femme is never really discussed. The very fact that essentialists could not explain all lesbianism from their deterministic perspectives is testimony to the limitations of such a theoretical approach. The femme, as Beebo articulates in the above passage, defies explanation. With her feminine style, she does not threaten the law of the father in the same way, and is thus ignored in the literature.

A popular folklore to account for the difference between 'born that way' lesbians (read, butch) and 'made that way' (read, femme) is the hormone tale. The first misplaced building block of this myth is the labelling of the hormones as 'male' or 'female'. As we all have both, it is something of a misnomer. What differs is the ratio of circulating hormones. As women, we have higher levels of the oestrogenic hormones (oestrogen and progesterone) while men have more of the androgenic hormones (mainly testosterone).[34] Accepting that hormones do affect our behaviour, is not to say we are driven by a chemical cocktail. During puberty we experience the surge of the sex hormones responsible for the secondary sexual characteristics which signal reproductive maturity. It is commonly accepted that we cannot pass through this stage without trauma, as a result of the internal storm. And again we must confront the interface of biological realities and cultural interpretation.[35] I would attribute my own admirably theatrical displays of the 'teenage temper tantrum' less to the onset of physical maturity and socially sanctioned psychosexual awakening, and more to the wall of prejudice I came up against trying to explore these ... as a lesbian.

The idea that butch lesbians are the 'proper' lesbians, born with some congenital blueprint, and that 'femmes' are those women who defected later in life, is too simple. As is the idea that butch dykes are driven by the 'curse' of male hormone, by having excessive levels of testosterone. Of the little research done into the hormone profiles of lesbian and heterosexual women, or between those labelled primary lesbians (lifelong lesbians) and secondary lesbians (previously heterosexual), no differences were found, beyond those expected for individual variation.[36] (Science has not recruited self-identified butch or femme women to its experiments, probably because they know the answer and do not want to destroy the myth.) So, if butches take sexual agency without a testosterone trip, then the answers lie beyond body chemistry. This fact is best remembered when assumptions of the male biological imperative are bandied about, because such reasoning leads us up some very dubious pathways when it comes to explaining male sexual violence. It is not necessarily that hormones have no part in the process of our sexuality. Lesbians, like other little girls, are made of sugar and spice and all things nice – including testosterone – and a brain which mediates a lifetime of experience, which the essentialists all too readily forget.

That lesbians have higher levels of circulating male hormones is only one theory. Other biological approaches focus on the role of these hormones at a much earlier stage, when the foetus is developing in the womb. As with essentialist explanations of male–female difference, these theories are based on the fact that hormones play a crucial role in the development of basic sexual anatomy. It is reasoned that the same chemicals which produce (usually) either female or male forms, may 'sex' the brain as well as the body.[37] Thus, boys will have boys' brains, and girls will have girls' brains, and both will behave accordingly. Hence, it is believed that, if a male foetus is exposed to low levels of male hormone, or a female is exposed to high levels, adult homosexuality will result, because the brain has been wrongly sexed. According to this approach, sexual and gender behaviours are the same thing, yet such a theory could not explain the macho gay male nor the femme. Contradictory evidence can also be drawn from studies of girls born with adrenogenital syndrome. In such cases, excessive levels of androgen during foetal development have caused, among other things, ambiguous looking genitalia, which is usually 'corrected' by surgery. If brain sexing theories were correct, all these girls would be acting on 'male desire' or, more accurately, lesbian desire, but this is known not to be the case.[38]

Brain theories are seductively simple and difficult to dismiss outright, not only because so little is known about the brain, but because, at one level, the brain does play a role in sexual behaviour. The idea of the 'gay brain' has gained yet more support over recent years, as a result of the work of Simon LeVay.[39] Drawing on evidence based on rodent and monkey studies, and his own limited investigations, he too has suggested that differences can be identified in the brain structures of homosexuals and heterosexuals. Focusing on an area of the brain known to be involved in sexual behaviour, the hypothalamus, LeVay suggests that a section of this region, known as INAH-3, differs with orientation. This area, he suggests, is bigger in those oriented towards women – that is, straight men and lesbians – and smaller in those oriented to men – that is, heterosexual women and gay men. While extreme in its determinism and politically dangerous (though it can also be used in our favour, depending on the argument), the theory's development is stunted by the limitations of brain research on living people. The same cannot be said about advances in human genetics. As with the gay brain research, genetic studies have focused largely on men,[40] with any findings then simply applied to lesbians. Again, the evidence is far from conclusive. But the implications of the search and of whatever may be found are far more sinister than the brain research, in view of the possible misuses of genetic engineering.

Despite the obvious limitations of the biological theories, they remain pervasive and influential. The fact that they all fail to explain the femme is a reflection of the lower status femininity is afforded in our patriarchal culture, and is compatible with the belief that femininity will always remain an enigma. The association between lesbianism and the necessary adoption of a masculine modus operandum, is prevalent not only in our coming out stories (feelings of difference, tomboy status), but also in social science research. When cross-cultural studies[41] emphasize that early cross-gender preferences are common to many lesbian women, this tells us as much about the gendered meanings in that cultural context, as about biological destiny. In many cultures where masculinity is valued more highly, many girls become tomboys.[42] It is expected that we should aspire to such greater 'traits'. Of course, many of these behaviours are merely reflecting the energized vitality of a child, but such physical activity is labelled male. It is somewhat ironic that the male child, destined for such gender privilege in later life, is denied the same flexibility as girls. Femininity in boys is not greeted with the same tolerance. Someone whispers 'sissy boy syndrome' and activates a homosexual panic. He is seen as letting the side down, and his transgression can mean only one thing – that he is gay.

Saskia Wieringa, in her review of cross-cultural data,[43] suggests that the roles which we label as butch and femme occur throughout lesbian cultures, although the westernized vernacular may be inappropriate elsewhere. Her preferred terms are dominant and non-dominant and coincide with the cultural prescriptions of masculinity and femininity. So it would seem that what we readily see as butch/femme is a universal inevitability. Although found in lesbian couples, Wieringa emphasizes the economic functions of role division as opposed to the erotic implications. This necessitates a reading from the wider constructionist perspective of the organization of power relations and child-rearing practice; a contradiction to her conclusion that such divisions result from 'a constitutional temperament which is determined individually by psychobiological factors'.[44] The diversity of experience, subjectivity, desire and wardrobe preference which we squeeze into bipolar categories is phenomenal. Roles, like every other construct of the social sciences we can label, 'are constituted in society and history, not biologically ordained. This does not mean that biological capacities are not prerequisites for human sexuality. It does mean that biological capacities are not comprehensible in purely biological terms.'[45]

The biological is only one aspect of determinism – the psychological is another. While the Freudian legacy is at times problematic, its contribution is useful to lesbian and gay theorizing, and valuable to the elucidation of butch and femme roles. While the inconsistencies and ambiguities in Freud's own thinking, as evidenced in his writing, have allowed for pathological interpretations of 'homosexuality', his emphasis on the delicate psychic construction of our sexualities and the role of the unconscious is invaluable.

A quote from Audre Lorde is our point of departure, and it will also act as the point of frequent return, for it portrays the complexity which even Freud could not negotiate. With the model of the 'family romance', she embraces her fantasy yet never relinquishes activity, passivity, identification with either parent, masculinity or femininity. And this constitutes the Freudian nightmare – because Freudian sexual maturity involves surrender of half the whole. We give up masculinity, because we will resume completeness when we find it in a man.

> I have always wanted to be both man and woman, to incorporate the strongest and richest parts of my mother and father within/into me ... I would like to enter a woman the way any man can, and to be entered – to leave and to be left – to be hot and hard and soft all at the same time in the cause of our loving ... I love to feel the deep inside parts of me ... other times I like to fantasize the core of it, my pearl, a protruding part of me, hard and sensitive and vulnerable in a different way.[46]

A vastly oversimplified version of Freudian theory is that we pass through five stages of psychosexual development.[47] The third phase, the 'phallic stage', is central to the development of our gender and sexual identities, which result from our adequate resolution of the 'Oedipal crisis'. The story for girls is thus: we notice that like our mothers we *lack* a penis, and we suspect her of castrating us. In the absence of the phallus we are overcome with 'penis envy'. This is resolved by a more realistic wish – sexual desire for a penis, a male lover. Our first port of call is our fathers – and in this establishment of heterosexual attraction we replace the desire to possess the penis with a desire for a baby. In the depths of our unconscious we want to bear our father's child. Since this is taboo and such a union would cost us the love of our mothers, we transfer this latent desire onto other men. The process is visibly completed when we identify with our mothers, that is, become like her, an appropriately feminine heterosexual. At the same time we relinquish our active clitoral sexuality and relocate the pleasure zone from the clitoris (an inferior version of the penis, in this story) to the vagina – becomingly 'passively receptive'.

Up until this stage we were all bisexual and prone to all sensations of pleasure (polymorphous perversity). If we negotiate the Oedipal conflict effectively, we emerge as normal young feminine heterosexuals, who are by definition inferior and sexually passive. Freud reasoned that this goal was not easy to reach, but a must for social order. As we ramble through the psychic jungle there are many pitfalls of regression or fixation which can result in the emergence of taboo and illicit desires and sexual practice. Female homosexuality is one such example. Aware of the complex nature of unconscious desire, Freud's own view of homosexuality was one of non-judgementalism, as in his letter to the mother of a (male) homosexual:

> homosexuality is assuredly no advantage; but it is nothing to be ashamed of, no vice, no degradation; it cannot be classified as an illness; we consider it to be a variation of the sexual function produced by a certain *arrest of development* (italics added).[48]

Unfortunately this arrest of development left the pathological floodgates open.

In the one case in which Freud knowingly dealt with a lesbian, his tolerance seemed to diminish, his sexism expanded and his fragile male ego took centre stage. In this instance, the 'girl' (whose lack of an identity is interesting in itself, as she is the only case study he failed to name), resolves her Oedipal crisis on schedule, but her lesbianism becomes manifest in an adolescent reactivation of (return to) it. The Oedipal revival was triggered when her mother gave birth to a son, which should have been her baby (according to Freud). The inevitable and equally unconscious disappointment resulted in the subtle rejection of men, and of the roles of feminine heterosexuality and motherhood; 'she changed into a man and took her mother in place of her father as her love object'.[49] Freud forgets his earlier assertions that cross-gender characteristics do not always accompany homosexuality (which are difficult to reconcile with the central role given to the phallic stage in homosexual histories) and diagnoses a masculinity complex. The 'girl' is unwilling to accept her secondary status or relinquish her active sexuality, and is thus driven by penis envy.

His interpretation goes on to a full-blown heterosexualization of her desires, reflecting his own inability to conceive of a woman's proclivities beyond the gendered binary. 'She had thus not only chosen a feminine love object, but had developed a masculine attitude toward that object'[50] – and in doing so usurped the ultimate male privilege, that of a woman's erotic love. He writes his own version of the butch/femme debate: 'The active inverts exhibit masculine characteristics both physical and mental, with particular frequency and look for femininity in their sexual objects though here again knowledge of the facts might reveal greater variety.'[51] Pre-empting the revelation of a greater diversity, his writing is deficient as he tenders no explanation for the motivation of the feminine object. Like Beebo, he finds no answer; but unlike our insatiable young butch, he does not even pose the question. Throughout the course of the brief analysis with the 'girl', he refused to recognize any of her feminine attributes, putting great effort into legitimizing his interpretations of the masculine. He terminated the analysis without resolving any psychic conflicts she may or may not have had or confronting his own. He suggested this 'feminist' sought the interventions of a female analyst.

Culture as seen through lavender-coloured glasses

I'm not sure I like having my sexuality touted as a fad. It makes me feel exposed and grouchy. I resent having my sexuality processed, packaged and fed back to me in the name of fashion. I'm a pervert, not a trend.

Lily Burana[52]

Newsweek's lesbian chic cover girl lovers, say wearing suits makes them feel 'feminine, powerful and sexy'.[53]

In the 1990s, as never before, we can see our realities represented in popular culture. Prior to this, we perceived movies and music through a lesbian filter, changing the words, rewriting the scripts – adjusting our mental sets until we found an acceptable picture. Hungry for images and role models, we adapted the available romantic escapism to fit our everyday dreams and desires. For lesbians, especially those aware of their desires at a younger age, the mental flexibility to transform the dominant reality into something meaningful becomes a survival technique in an otherwise barren and lonely cultural wilderness. Society's obsession with sex, love and romance is apparent in popularized representations, from text to television. Sex and love sell. Playing on basic needs, our expectations and desires are shaped by the dominant ideology and sex-role socialization. We come to believe that sex, love and romance should be experienced in certain ways, meaning certain things. Time after time Hollywood boasts yet another box office hit in which we see the trials and tribulations of a heterosexual couple in love. As a regular diet of escapism, we digest it as usual. As a baby dyke, I too watched, listened and – without ever intending to – I learned. I knew I would eventually find my Doris Day – I had this fantasy and sure enough, I found her and we lived happily ever after, for what must have been all of a month, until it went hideously wrong. She must have lost the script because my failings were not forgiven, and our problems not resolved with a passionate kiss. Continually under bombardment with society's permanent special offer, pleasure,[54] it becomes a major act of resistance for us not to be tempted and seduced by romantic fantasy. Who wouldn't want to live in a perfect world, be stunningly good looking and filthy rich, while dating the girl of your dreams?

A vast amount of the lesbian literature is also based on formula romance. The roles of butch and femme provide a ready-made framework from which to conceptualize romantic encounters and the subjective experiences of love. In a familiar literary convention in the 1950s, pulp fiction, such stories not only reflected the subcultural realities of the time but helped shape them. For those whose introduction into lesbianism was through the works of writers like Ann Bannon, the escapist narratives doubled as a starter course, especially in terms of role rules. The genre was revived in the 1980s when these books came back into print. They were more accurate in their depictions of lesbian life than later critics have allowed for, especially given that the sensationalized love and sex actually occurs in a context of serial monogamy. Lee Lynch departs from the convention of portraying romance through complementary roles, as *The Swashbuckler* is a love story between two butches. Although reflecting a past and present reality, it was not a framework which was commonly adopted, as in the early to mid 1980s writers were avoiding the use of butch/femme roles altogether, immersed in a fog of political correctness.

The proliferation of lesbian erotic literature in the late 1980s began with Nestle's *A Restricted Country*, in which butch and femme roles were eroticized, fictionalized and analysed. Other erotic writing was not often based on the same gendered formula. Moving into the current decade, we have several more femme and butch texts and butch readers. As edited texts, the material ranges from political analysis to the sexual wanderings of healthy dyke imaginations. While being described as stories by which even Mills and Boon would be embarrassed,[55] one thing is clear – they sell, suggesting that if Mills and Boon were not so heterosexist they could cash in on a lucrative market.

Aware of the debates bouncing off the academy walls as to the wider implications of such literature, I find myself questioning my own right to enjoy these books. Yet again, my enquiry reveals a quagmire of contradictions – an increasingly familiar experience as I toil with the never-ending debates of butch/femme roles. Memories of my teenage years consist of a peer group preoccupied with the mutual appreciation society of boys and girls, as they began the first of many practice runs to find the perfect heterosexual partner. Their liaisons were sanctioned, legitimized and encouraged. My own were illicit. These books provide us with the accolade which is unforthcoming from the parent culture. The celebratory narrative is not merely a deference to masculinity, where the butch replaces the man as the icon of hero worship – it provides affirmation for readers who have previously had no such reinforcement, because they stood beyond the pale of gendered conformity. However, in the current wave of books of this kind, the femme is still under-represented.

Romantic narratives, whether in the form of the mass-produced hetero-sexual fictions or lesbian stories employing the same artistic conventions, have been subject to analysis and criticism. Yet it remains apparent that the genre of romance in literature (and on the small and large screens) is a constant. What constitutes the difference between two characters may alter in line with social change, but there will always be barriers to overcome, for they are the essence of the tension. Will they overcome the obstacles of geography, class, the fact that she's with another . . . ? And thus we are suspended in delayed gratification, our interest is sustained – and the distinction between fantasy and reality all too easily become blurred.

The radical/revolutionary feminist line is that by reading (or viewing) such predictable storylines – of which, I stress, we seemingly never tire – we are being sold a false consciousness, from which we will never break free, thereby remaining deluded and forever oppressed. Romance and the notion of romantic love is nothing more than a 'monolithically pernicious and disabling ideology'.[56] This is as true of lesbian pulp as it is of the products of the patriarchal publishing houses. Implicit in such reasoning is that we are as intellectually passive as the early sexologists purported our sexuality to be. It is to assume the function of such literature is unitary. But these books perform many functions – we identify with characters, change our expectations, yearn for something different, we escape from the reality of daily life. The romantic storylines also offer the thinly veiled excuse for detailed descriptions of sex and desire. In the lesbian narrative, declarations of love legitimize sex, in the absence of marriage. Butch and femme provide the gendered difference, backs arch and eyes close in wild abandon and, with hands and tongues trading places of active and passive, the exchange culminates in the climax which it has taken 111 pages to reach. And as is the nature of such graphic commentary, one woman's pleasure becomes another's pornography.[57]

As the number of lesbian books grows steadily, lifestyle lesbians are becoming regular fashion accessories in the glossy magazines that escort the transforming teen into womanhood, and in those with a regular twenty-something, thirty-something readership. The emphasis is less on sexual style and more on commodifiable chic. These lipstick lifestylers have the bodies, the hair, the wardrobe, which fit the fashion guru's specifications. The look is reflected in the material girls who play the lesbian characters in the sapphic soap wars. As with any fashion, the sensationalism will fade and the novelty of this titillating representation will wear off. The gay girls will go when interest expires.

None of the characters in the soaps fits the butch/femme mould. And indeed, why should they? This way, cliched stereotypes are avoided and diversity is appreciated. But is the message then, 'we're no different except we fancy each other'? Does the lesbian character's ability to blend in rob her of political clout? In the absence of gender, the audience is provided with other avenues of difference through which to mediate their under-standing of lesbian desire. Channel 4's *Brookside* relied on the institution-alized inequality of academic roles – lecturer/student – playing on a regular stereotype without due consideration of the implications. The power difference was eroticized and the thrill magnified by the taboo of a common schoolgirl fantasy. The BBC's *EastEnders* depends on the viewer looking at its lesbian relationship through a filter of racialized inequal-ities. This operates as 'a form of differentiation between people of the same gender'.[58] While putting inter-racial relationships on the agenda, the opportunity to explore the other meanings is missed. It is beyond escapist requirements to represent the experiences of these dykes: the clashing of cultures, the realities of social power, identity politics, the effects of multiple oppression and of facing racism, sexism, heterosexism and homophobia. Sadly, the script-writers ignore the fact that 'when gender inevitably combines with other social relations of power in fluid exchange, it can no longer be maintained as the primary or exclusive term of analysis.'[59]

1994 was not only the year when lesbians appeared on prime-time TV, but when a lesbian movie went mainstream, without the central protagon-ists having sex with or killing men! Through the characters in *Go Fish*,[60] many contemporary realities are depicted and controversies debated. The cast include a sexual hedonist with a high turnover of partners (including a man), the monogamous couple who end up living together (with bed death nowhere in sight – still, they have *just* moved in) and the central protagonists – the predator and her prey. It is between these two that the sexual tension is generated in a 'will they won't they' fashion. If read as butch/femme at all, it subverts assumptions with a cleverly coded twist. Max (whose real name, we find out later, is Camille) looks like your average lesbian boy at the beginning of the story, right down to the jeans and the baseball cap. It is ten months since she last had sex and she yearns for a romantic interlude. Her friends try to find her a mate. Their selected match, Ely, enters the story embodying the style of the 1970s folksy stereotype. As the plot progresses, Ely's image is transformed, as she is tailored to an almost 1960s-style masculinity ('but don't call her butch because she's sensitive about it!'). What began with an exchange of phone numbers then signalled an exchange of roles and culminated in an exchange of body fluids. If Max visually embodies the hungry femme, the sex scene shatters any illusion of gendered division. The difference is dissolved in mutual desire and exploration. As with any good lesbian love story, from that night on they were not divided.

What about our real-life cultural icons – those women who admit to real-life choices and are left to face the music? Madonna and her flirtation with the sexual *en vogue*, staged boundary violations and homoeroticism, commands a high media profile. Initially an icon of sexual agency, her exploits now seem little more than fashionable acts to shock – good girls go to heaven and bad girls go everywhere else, at least when videotape is running. Amidst speculation about some of Hollywood's leading names, our 'out' icons, the golden girls, are in fact golden boy/girls. If we were forced to place lang and Navratilova on a butch/femme scale, it would require little effort: they're both on the butch side. Would we have put them on pedestals otherwise? Where are our femme role models? Where is Lois Weaver when you need her?[61]

While rumours ran rampant about both Navratilova and lang prior to their coming out, both the press and dyke communities had a field day. Hearsay about Navratilova's love life became as traditional to the Wimbledon fortnight as rain delaying play. With strength and stamina surpassing that expected of female athletes, her every performance both on and off the courts was read as masculine. Her relationship with former Texan beauty queen Judy Nelson became a real-life Barbie and Ken marriage to an inquiring press. The ending of which was televised, as Navratilova found herself in a court with which she was less familiar, settling monies and property rights. Meanwhile, back at the tennis, did anyone notice she had broken with convention and was wearing shorts, or did the first three rows of suspiciously short-haired women just dwell on her forehand?

lang's butch persona is not so much married with her occupation but a privilege of it – the music industry has traditionally tolerated eccentric gender transgressions, as one performance leads to another. Her masculine attire is part of the k.d. image. Lang's audiences leave her in no doubt as to their adoration and dishonourable intentions. Gone are the 1970s-style concerts where idolizing and objectifying were lesbian heresy. Here is a girl willing to show her inner child – but when she does, he's a boy. With lang modelling on the cover of *Vanity Fair* with a scantily clad Cindy Crawford, the butch/femme erotica takes shape as lang assumes the classic masculine subject position and Crawford, the feminine object. lang's body can remain hidden while Crawford is exposed to the 'male' gaze. In the cutting-edge image, Crawford is about to shave lang: 'It was all done in a fun tongue in cheek piece of Americana with a sexy modern-day twist.'[62] Lesbianism and gender play have always been sexy, the twist is that this is now a commercialized gimmick. It may be tongue in cheek, but how many will realize that the tongue could be elsewhere? After years of lesbians being defined by sexual object choice, the erotic codes which signalled that identity are now advertised as a stylistic fashion accessory.[63]

The photographs are accompanied by an interview with the singer – documenting her vegetarianism, inability to sustain long-term relationships, therapy (yep, she's a lesbian), and her career. Her preference for practical clothing and boots that could 'carry you for miles' prevents objectification by the music industry, while simultaneously reducing her discomfort with her womanly body. Despite the emphasis on her boyish stance and penchant for cross-dressing, counter-cultural vernacular is mostly absent from the interview. When such language appears in the piece, it is in other people's descriptions of lang: 'Ms gender bender, who's not afraid to let her butch side out',[64] who appeared in 'drag' 'when she actually dressed as a woman'.[65] To k.d. there is no contradiction – while priding herself on being 100 per cent woman, she has penis envy and a problematic connection to her femininity.

> I don't know how to use my femininity as a powerful tool. I use my sexuality but I eliminate the gender from it. I hesitate to use the word androgynous because it is overused and misunderstood, but androgyny to me is making your sexuality available to your art, to everyone.[66]

k.d. is not genderless, but her performance is better located in the lesbian gender of butch, than in the categories of the ill-fitting binary. She knew from the time she played Batman and Robin with the other boys that she wanted a wife. She is a commercial success, accepted in her gender trespass. An article in the British broadsheet press suggests the nature of this tolerance: 'She stopped acting like a masculine woman, and became like a *feminine man*. It looked much better'[67] (their italics). By realigning her masquerade within the accepted framework, the reality of her being a mannish woman and a visible lesbian was renegotiated. This redefinition allowed for any threat to be negated.

The changer and the changed

Sexualities keep marching out of the Diagnostic and Statistical Manual *and on to the pages of social history. At present, several other groups are trying to emulate the successes of homosexuals . . . transsexuals, and transvestites are all in various states of community formation and identity acquisition. The perversions are not proliferating as much as they are attempting to acquire social space . . . and a measure of relief from the penalties of sexual heresy.*

Gayle Rubin[68]

The primacy of biology as the basis of gender is sustained when all the challenges to this system are assimilated as second-rate imitations. Such a reading of butch/femme, as has already been suggested, contains its challenge to the binary of masculine–feminine. Functioning also as third and fourth genders, they are not legitimized by the wider culture and hence remain marginalized. The binary is preserved and stratification remains supported.

In precolonial indigenous American cultures (also in Asia and Africa) gender was not so polarized. Although men and women fulfilled different roles, for those who wanted to adopt the role of the other gender,[69] a socially legitimate route was available. Although considered by many western writers to be an example of institutionalized homosexuality, there is strong evidence to suggest this was not the case. When same-sex behaviour occurred, role transfer was neither encouraged nor deemed necessary. Erotic preferences were not linked to gender roles, in the way we readily associate the two today. Such desires were only a contributory component to a more complex identity, defined by task specificity, productivity and other displays of the prescribed masculine or feminine roles. This was true to the extent that those who did adopt 'opposite-sex' roles could still have someone who was their biological opposite as a sexual partner, even if their genders were similar, without compromising their gendered position. A woman could adopt the masculine role without sanction. The labels assigned to members of these additional genders were originally tribally specific, as for example the 'Alyha' and 'Hwame' of the Mohave. Typically, however, through western eyes much of the diversity was lost, and 'female berdache'[70] became the generic name for women living as men.

Controversy prevails over how extensive a cultural practice this was for women.[71] What is uncontested is that there were legitimate social channels for women who wanted to live as men and vice versa. Rituals signalled the transformations and validated the social fiction. In some societies these individuals were afforded higher status; in others, lower. The ridicule and sanction documented by so many in this field was both exaggerated and largely introduced by the colonizers. The changes imposed were not only to the gender system but to the structure of the economy, which the gendered labour divisions would be shaped to serve. With the demise of diversity, the last cross-gender female of the Mohave was raped by the former husband of 'his' wife. After relinquishing the role she was later burned as a witch.[72]

Adoption of the male role is not an artefact of anthropology. In the UK women have always passed as men, albeit without the blessing of the parent culture. Such cross-dressing, usually shrouded in secrecy in the absence of social legitimization, provided women with the socio-economic and career opportunities they would have otherwise been denied, as well as an avenue to same-sex attachments. However, if caught, women could be charged with engaging in homosexual acts, carrying punishments ranging from flogging to the death penalty. In 1929, 'Colonel Barker', who had been married for over three years before deserting 'his' wife, was arrested, having passed successfully for over a decade.[73] Onto such phenomena we impose our current subcultural reality and lesbian meanings. Rightly or wrongly, we claim these women as our own. Although there is a wealth of evidence to suggest that many of them did pass in order to marry their lovers, such historical masquerades need to be set in the context of the time.[74] Across cultures and throughout the generations, women persist in flaunting their appropriated masculinity, in breaking gendered norms. The subcultural gender of butch is one example – allowing for masculine role enactment and erotic rewards. What it means to be butch, how the role is read, negotiated and reflected, depends on its location on the continuum: butchness varies in degree. Some women are perceived as or feel 'butcher' than others. It is a term which embraces a diversity of lesbian experience, from a soft-focus approach to tomboyishness to a degree of dysphoria which causes physical discomfort and psychological distress.

The word 'dysphoric' in its clinical context refers to the experience of individuals who are so unhappy with their assigned gender that they seek sex reassignment surgery (SRS). The feelings are often that of a 'man trapped in a woman's' body. The 'core gender identity' or 'subjectivity' is at odds with the anatomical realities. However, the term is also being used within our own literature, not in its literal clinical sense, but to describe a range of butch experiences which, while not requiring medical intervention, also depart from conventional norms of gender identification. Many butch dykes have fantasies about being boys or men – daddies not mummies. To disregard such desires as 'male identification' in the political sense – claiming that these women are essentially sexist, misogynist and colluding with patriarchy – is to foreclose on the issue before it has come out into the open. Such an argument underestimates the complexity of sexual identity and its erotic potentialities. Even though the parameters of acceptable femininity have broadened, some of us still have difficulty locating ourselves within such a category. Lesbian, yes; woman? well, not exactly . . .

Our communities 'harbour a great deal of gender dysphoria – Drag, cross-dressing, passing, transvestism and transsexualism are all common in lesbian populations, particularly those not attempting to meet constricted standards of political virtue.'[75] The first categories are fairly easy to digest, describing an established heritage with which we are familiar if not always comfortable. But transvestism and transsexualism are a little more difficult to swallow. Transsexuals (TS) and transvestites (TV) have a long association with the lesbian and gay community; united in gender outlawry, often seen as synonymous by an obtuse parent culture, yet in reality separated by differences in identity and desire. There are differences in desiring another woman as a woman (lesbian), believing oneself is really a man trapped in a woman's body (TS), and wearing male clothes as a turn-on (TV). The question of whether they were differences in degree or in kind would be a non-starter if sexual identity were not so tenaciously bound to gender. These differences are often pointed out in our own communities with the same kind of gender- and erotophobia[76] and bigoted ignorance which we usually associate with the rest of society. Asylum within the larger and politicized lesbian and gay community is by no means guaranteed.

Many in our deviant enclaves think 'fetishism' and the other paraphilias, along with gender dysphoria, are problematic desires worthy of investigation and intervention. The psychiatric literature (which can be seen as a barometer of morality) reflects popular beliefs that gender transgression is a psychiatric problem. It is interesting to note that the category of 'gender identity disorders' including transsexuality was introduced in 1980, after psychiatry had been forced to surrender the diagnosis of homosexuality. Members of the newly diagnosed populations, lacking the political clout of the lesbian and gay community, could only show limited resistance. But opposition is not always desirable. Assumptions of the 'sick' role can allow for greater societal assimilation. In the USA, for instance, the 'pathological' status of transsexuality may allow for financial assistance from insurance companies, enabling the expansive surgery and treatments necessary for gender reassignment.

For some lesbians, a butch identity is not enough, because ultimately the facade has its limits. Underneath the costume lies a woman's body. Indeed, it is this incongruity between style and anatomy that is one of the celebrated characteristics of butch. But for some dykes, the breasts and curves which excite are the feminine contours of another woman's body, not her own. Her body is a physical betrayal of how she wants to be, a departure from her narcissistic aesthetic. As a result of our consumerist and technological age, gender can now be surgically reassigned. Thus, western society has its own initiation ceremony for those who wish to live beyond the roles assigned to them: medicalization and psychiatrization; with psychological, hormonal and surgical treatments being the recognized rites of passage.

To qualify for sex reassignment surgery (SRS), it is necessary to conform to orthodox expectations. Thus, if a dyke desires reassignment to become male, she must endorse and emulate heterosexual masculinity. Her behaviour, mannerisms and psyche must reflect an 'inherent maleness' – a core male gender identity – and object choice must be female. (This becomes heterosexual virility, as opposed to lesbianism.) Any digressions from prescribed paths, especially in terms of object choice, make it unlikely that the gatekeepers will co-operate in allowing access to surgical transformation. In these instances, less 'official' and more expensive channels are used. Before SRS is performed, the 'patient' must live as their target sex for anything from one to three years, dressing, acting and performing a masculine masquerade twenty-four hours a day. During this time hormones will be used to start the process. Female to males (FTMs) have biweekly injections of testosterone. The changes begin within a month, as periods stop and the body begins to undergo a manufactured transformative adolescence. The emergence of the secondary sexual characteristics, like deepening of the voice, growth of body and facial hair, and the accompanying physical changes like muscle development, take a little longer. While the elongation of the clitoris is welcome, some of the other side effects can constitute quite serious health risks.

Surgeons go on to create the parts hormones cannot reach. The breasts, womb and ovaries are removed (mastectomy, hysterectomy, oophorectomy). Approximations of male genitalia are reached by releasing the clitoris and injecting the labia with silicone to simulate testicles (despite any shrinkage which may have occurred due to the testosterone), a technique known as genitoplasty. Phalloplasy (penis construction) is less successful and not so aesthetically pleasing or functional, because of the lack of sensation it affords. A roll of tissue is made from unhairy areas of the body, grafted on to the pubic region and the abdomen, like a suitcase handle, for several months to let circulation settle, then released from the abdomen and left to hang down. Although attempts have been made to extend the urethra through this phallus to enable urination, the procedure has yet to be perfected. Phalloplasty is not encouraged at the moment – the grafted phallus needs splints to become erect and lacks the neural connections to stimulate powerful sexual sensations. The original urethral and vaginal openings are left intact, although the vagina can be sewn up on request. Clinical reports detail how, in one case, the constructed phallus 'fell off', necessitating further reconstructive surgery. There is a certain contradiction in the clinicians' reports in this instance. While they stress the seeming impossibility of creating an artificial penis, the implicit message is that one can never be a real man without it, yet the attendant distress is read as the quintessential masculine fear, 'castration anxiety'.[77]

Seemingly, despite advances in technological and surgical procedures in cosmetic surgery, the perfect penis is still impossible to construct. Perhaps they are scared – if penises rolled off production lines, everyone might want them, and where would that leave the phallic economy? Looking at the effectiveness of surgical procedures, it is clear that SRS was perfected with men in mind. One of the usual routes of vaginal and clitoral construction uses the original penile tissue, facilitating almost full sensation – we're talking vaginal orgasms Freud would have died for.

Like butch/femme and camp, transsexuals simultaneously legitimize the binary while demonstrating its very constructedness. The polarities are validated because we are led to believe that if we are not women then we must be men. In fact, we can become those women or men and defy biological givens. By offering surgical reassignment, dysphoria is individualized: 'by substituting medical terminology for political discourse, the medical profession has directly tamed and transformed a potential wildcat strike at the gender factory.'[78] The encouragement of reconstruction ensures that genital configurations remain firmly harnessed to gendered identities. However we view people who have surgically reassigned their sex, we struggle to keep them in one of two categories: either women remain women no matter how many hours they spend under the surgeon's knife, or they are manufactured men. Yet the prefix 'transsexual' woman implies an otherness which is, in effect, open to the interpretation of third and fourth genders.

Male to females (MTFs) have, in the past, outnumbered FTMs, but the gap is now closing. In an era when constructionist theories challenge ideas of the fixity of gender, some dykes still feel like 'men' and reassign to become those men, or to enter the land of she-hes, the territory of the transgender. Although numbers are still small, they are increasing. Predictions that such gender benders are another witch-hunt waiting to happen[79] echo experiences already familiar to men in the FTM community. Seeing them as patriarchal pawns, traitors to feminism or simply pathological, women mobilize to exclude them. MTFs are subject to more virulent rejection. Regarded as rapists of our biology, these women are accused of retaining male privilege and being a threat to the 'true biologically ordained female'. Ironically, some feminists – the infantry of the movement that initiated gender-role terrorism – retreat behind 'woman born woman' arguments and notions of women's innate biological superiority, ignoring the contradiction of having battled long and hard against the oppressive repercussions of biological rhetoric.

Another equally oppressive argument stems not directly from biology *per se*, but relies on the homosexual–heterosexual divide. Transsexuals are accused of merely exploring their same-sex desires through the licence of gender reassignment, to allow for a reading of heterosexuality. Problems with such reasoning lie in the reality that the stigma of transsexuality is greater than that of lesbianism. It also underestimates the complexity of desire and the body's role in mediating the experience. Such analysis remains anchored to dominant discourse. A departure from such ideologies is vital to explain those transsexuals who adopt a lesbian or gay identity after reassignment. Such realities should compel theorists to contemplate the feasibility of competing narratives.

The transsexual landscape has included high profile and heterosexual MTFs including Jan Morris (formerly James), Renee Richards (formerly Dr Richard Raskind), a tennis coach to our own Martina, and Caroline Cossey, also known as Tula (formerly Barry).[80] As a professional model, Tula markets her femininity in a style unlikely to endear her to most feminists.

She was 'exposed' as a transsexual after being a 'decorative extra' in a film where she revealed her scantily clad body *For Your Eyes Only*. Her conventional beauty and sex appeal had won her a place on the set with that quintessential icon of masculinity, James Bond. Her punishment for the convincing 'masquerade' was a press invasion, humiliation and a great deal of personal distress. Like FTM, Mark Rees, Cossey also appealed to the European Commission on Human Rights to change British laws which prevent alteration of birth certificates and thus marriage. They were both unsuccessful in their challenges. In a bureaucratic twilight zone fraught with contradictions, Mark Rees may not be able to marry but, equally, he probably won't get his pension until he is sixty-five.

Why discuss transsexuality in a chapter on butch/femme? In addition to demonstrating the constructedness and flexibility of gender, not to mention the complexity of desire, the fact remains that of the women who explore these avenues, many begin the journey as butch dykes and may wish to remain so, or become so again. With increasing frequency, many of these women enter 'no gender land', identifying neither as woman nor man. The term transgender may be the identity of choice, to further distance from the clutches of the medical profession. About 25 per cent of MTFs and as yet, an undocumented number of FTMs, adopt a lesbian/gay identity after reassignment. The founder of San Francisco's FTM organization, Louis Sullivan, did just that.[81] Such a transformation is not uncommon amongst lesbians who have changed their genders. As women, they desired women, as men, men. To assume 'they were heterosexual all along' is to ignore the meanings of the body through which that desire is communicated. To love a woman as a woman is different to loving as a man – if it were not, why should so many of our taboo cross-gender fantasies be so arousing? Gay sex is a different erotic script from lesbian sex. And, like female same-sex desire, it is the ultimate endorsement of gender role. What could be more validating to an acquired masculinity than having it verified by another man in an act of sexual bonding? Becoming a gay man may ensure continued membership of the gay subculture, but this in itself is an inadequate explanation. For the partners of TS lesbians and gay men, there is no contradiction, no threat to identity, no limit to desire. They have no problem in reading and responding to appropriated gender. As the TV and TS community become increasingly active and politicized, they are hosting their own sociosexual challenge.

Kate Bornstein, 'the only lesbian to have castrated a man and gone on television to laugh about it', describes her own transsexual journey in her book *Gender Outlaw: On Men, Women and the Rest of Us*. She underwent surgery not because she always felt like a woman, but because she did not feel like a man. She wanted to love women as a woman? Why? Well, of course, because the sex is better! If only it were that simple. Her new (improved?) sex life involves a range of performances, including dildo play. It does not return her to her former gender, no matter how nostalgic it seems. But some would argue that she remains a man whatever. In the week after the Pink Paper published an interview with Kate Bornstein,[82] community hostility was embodied in a letter describing her as 'a man who sacrificed his balls but continues screwing women'.[83] She sacrificed far more than her phallic pride, although it may be suggested that she continues to act out male privilege by becoming a public figure, while her former lesbian lover, who now identifies as a gay man, has a relatively low profile. Socialized difference, biological birthright or personal choice? Ironically, before the breakdown of their relationship they could assume the facade of the ultimate in acceptability, the heterosexual couple.

To deny others the right to explore as they see fit is a sad indictment of just how insidiously pervasive the dominant discourses really are. Despite the challenge posed by our own erotic choices, some move little beyond them.

NOTES

1. Suzanne J. Kessler and Wendy McKenna, quoted in Kate Bornstein, *Gender Outlaw: On Men, Women and the Rest of Us*, London, Routledge, 1994, p. 26.
2. See, for example: Philip Blumstein and Pepper Schwartz, *American Couples: Money, Work, Sex*, New York, William Morrow, 1983; Alan P. Bell and Martin S. Weinberg, *Homosexualities: A Study of Diversity among Men and Women*, London, Mitchell Beazley, 1978; Letitia A. Peplau, Christine Pedesky and Mykol Hamilton, 'Satisfaction in lesbian relationships', *Journal of Homosexuality*, vol. 8 (2), 1982; Julie M. Rosenweig and Wendy C. Lebow, 'Femme on the streets, butch in the sheets? Lesbian sex-roles, dyadic adjustment and sexual satisfaction', *Journal of Homosexuality*, vol. 23 (3), 1992; Jean Lynch and Mary E. Reilly, 'Role relationships: Lesbian perspectives', *Journal of Homosexuality*, vol. 12 (2), 1985/6.
3. JoAnn Loulan, *The Lesbian Erotic Dance: Butch, Femme, Androgyny and Other Rhythms*, San Francisco, Spinsters, 1990; and Pride Survey, see Chapter 4.
4. JoAnn Loulan, ibid., p. 239.

5. Ibid., pp. 3–4.
6. Sheila Jeffreys, *The Lesbian Heresy*, London, Women's Press, 1993, p. 94.
7. Biological sex can be determined by anatomical and physiological characteristics: chromosomes, gonads (ovaries in women, testes in men), hormones, internal accessory organs (the embryonic fore-runners of the reproductive structures), external genitalia, and secondary sexual characterises.
8. Joan Nestle, *A Restricted Country*, London, Sheba, 1988, p. 108.
9. Joan Nestle, 'Flamboyance and fortitude: An introduction', in Joan Nestle (ed.), *The Persistent Desire: A Femme Butch Reader*, Boston, Alyson, 1992, p. 16.
10. Caroline Cossey, *My Story*, London, Faber and Faber, 1992.
11. See Suzanne J. Kessler and Wendy McKenna, *Gender: An Ethnomethodo-logical Approach*, University of Chicago Press, 1978.
12. For a more detailed discussion, see either: Lillian Faderman, *Odd Girls and Twilight Lovers: A History of Lesbian Life in Twentieth Century America*, Harmondsworth, Penguin, 1991; or Elizabeth L. Kennedy and Made-line D. Davis, *Boots of Leather, Slippers of Gold: The History of a Lesbian Community*, Harmondsworth, Penguin, 1993.
13. Joan Nestle, 'The fem question', in Carole S. Vance (ed.), *Pleasure and Danger: Exploring Female Sexuality*, London, Pandora, 1992, p. 233.
14. Quoted in Sheila Jeffreys, 'Butch and femme: Now and then', in Lesbian History Group, *Not A Passing Phase: Reclaiming Lesbians in History 1840–1985*, London, Women's Press, 1989, p. 172.
15. Margot Farnham, 'Diana Chapman' (interview) in Hall Carpenter Archives Oral History Group, *Inventing Ourselves: Lesbian Life Stories*, London, Routledge, 1991, p. 55.
16. Mary Riege Laner and Roy H. Laner, 'Sexual preference or personal style? Why lesbians are disliked,' *Journal of Homosexuality*, vol. 5 (4), 1980, pp. 339–357.
17. Cited in Lynne Segal, *Slow Motion: Changing Masculinities, Changing Men*, London, Virago, 1990, p. 146.
18. Ibid., p. 148.
19. Joan Nestle, 'The fem question', op. cit., p. 232.
20. Amber Hollibaugh, in Madeline Davis, Amber Hollibaugh and Joan Nestle, 'The femme tapes', in Joan Nestle (ed.), *The Persistent Desire: A Femme Butch Reader*, op. cit., p. 266.
21. Del Martin and Phyllis Lyon, quoted in Sue Ellen Case, 'Butch-femme aesthetic', *Discourse*, 9.11.1, 1988, p. 58.

22. Sandra L. Bem, *The Lenses of Gender: Transforming the Debate on Sexual Inequality*, New Haven, Yale University Press, 1993.

23. There are a number of different coming out models, all of which are based on the idea that the coming out 'process' occurs in stages. If butch/femme is to be viewed from this perspective, as an identity adopted as part of a 'process', then by implication we should abandon it at a later stage.

24. See Arlene Stein, 'All dressed up, but no place to go? Style wars and the new lesbianism', in Joan Nestle (ed.), *The Persistent Desire: A Femme Butch Reader*, op. cit., pp. 431–439.

25. Jill Johnston, quoted in Celia Kitzinger, 'Liberal humanism as ideology of social control: The regulation of lesbian identities', in John Shotter and Kenneth Gergen (eds.), *Texts Of Identity*, London, Sage, 1989, p. 82.

26. Esther Newton, *Mother Camp: Female Impersonators in America*, University of Chicago Press, 1972.

27. See Judith Butler, *Gender Trouble: Feminism and the Subversion of Identity*, London, Routledge, 1990.

28. RuPaul, quoted in Mary Harron, 'A hero for our times', *Independent on Sunday Review*, 29 January 1995.

29. Richard Dyer, quoted in Lynne Segal, op. cit., p. 146.

30. Sarah Schulman, 'Della Grace: Photos on the margin of the lesbian community', in Della Grace, *Love Bites*, GMP, 1991, p. 6.

31. Cherry Smyth, *Lesbians Talk Queer Notions*, London, Scarlet Press, 1992, p. 43.

32. Kate Bornstein, op. cit., p. 158.

33. Ann Bannon, *Beebo Brinker*, Tallahassee, Naiad Press, 1986 edition, p. 56.

34. While the gonads in both sexes produce androgens and oestrogens, the adrenal glands in women also produce androgen.

35. Adolescence is a social invention to provide the young adult with a moratorium before officially entering the adult world. While creating a time for identity development it is also fraught with contradictions as to societal expectations and legal constraints, especially in terms of sexuality and its expression.

36. See, for example: Natette K. Gartrell, D. Lynn Loriaux and Thomas Chase, 'Plasma testosterone in homosexual and heterosexual women', *American Journal of Psychiatry*, 134, 10, 1977, pp. 1117–1118; M. MacCulloch and J. Waddington, 'Neuroendocrine mechanisms and

the aetiology of male and female homosexuals', *British Journal of Psychiatry*, 139, pp. 341–45; C.P. Dancey, 'Sexual orientation in women: An investigation of hormonal and personality variables', *Biological Psychology*, 30, 1990, pp. 251–264; Jennifer Downey, Anke A. Ehrhardt, Mindy Schiffman, Inge Dyrenfurth and J. Becker, 'Sex hormones in lesbian and heterosexual women', *Hormones and Behaviour*, 21, 1987, 347–357.

37. See, for example, John Archer and Barbara Lloyd, *Sex and Gender*, Cambridge University Press, 1985.

38. Anke A. Ehrhardt, Ralph Epstein and John Money, 'Fetal androgens and female gender identity in the early treated adrenogenital syndrome', *John Hopkins Medical Journal*, 122, 1968, pp. 160–167.

39. See Simon LeVay, *The Sexual Brain*, Cambridge, Mass., MIT Press, 1994. His work must be viewed with caution as all his gay subjects had died from AIDS, which may have caused or contributed to the phenomena LeVay was observing.

40. Dean Hamer and Peter Copeland, *The Science of Desire: The Search for the Gay Gene and Biology of Behaviour*, New York, Simon and Schuster, 1994.

41. Frederick L. Whitam and Robin M. Mathy, 'Childhood cross-gender behaviour of homosexual females in Brazil, Peru, the Philippines, and the United States', *Archives of Sexual Behaviour*, 20, 2, 1991, pp. 151–170.

42. 'Tomboy' in the Philippines is a common word for lesbian.

43. Saskia Wieringa, 'An anthropological critique of constructionism: Berdaches and butches', in Dennis Altman (ed.), *Homosexuality, Which Homosexuality?*, London, GMP, 1989.

44. Ibid., p. 231.

45. Gayle Rubin, 'Thinking sex: Notes for a radical theory of the politics of sexuality', in Carole Vance (ed.), op. cit., pp. 267–319.

46. Audre Lorde, *Zami: A New Spelling of My Name*, London, Sheba, 1982, p. 7.

47. Freud's theory of psychological development replaced his earlier idea of infantile seduction, in which he suggested his patients' neuroses were the result of early childhood abuse. His later theory of development allowed for a rewriting of these events as being the inevitable product of the unconscious fantasy life of a child.

48. Freud, quoted in Jeffrey Weeks, *Sexuality and Its Discontents*, London, Routledge, p. 155.

49. Sigmund Freud, 'The psychogenesis of a case of homosexuality in a woman' in Sigmund Freud, *Collected Papers Vol.* II, London, Hogarth Press and Institute of Psychoanalysis, 1957, p. 215.
50. Ibid., p. 211.
51. Freud, quoted in Noreen O'Connor and Joanna Ryan, *Wild Desires and Mistaken Identities: Lesbianism and Psychoanalysis*, London, Virago, 1993, pp. 37 and 38.
52. Lily Burana, quoted in Kiss and Tell, *Her Tongue on My Theory: Images, Essays and Fantasies*, Vancouver, Press Gang, 1994, p. 45.
53. 'Suit yourself', *Deneuve*, October 1994, vol. 4 and 5, p. 34.
54. See Rosalind Coward, *Female Desire: Women's Sexuality Today*, London, Paladin, 1984.
55. Sheila Jeffreys, *Lesbian Heresy*, op. cit., p. 80.
56. See Jackie Stacey and Lynne Pearce, 'The heart of the matter: feminists revisit romance', in Stacey and Pearce (eds.), *Romance Revisited*, London, Lawrence and Wishart, 1995, p. 13.
57. See, for example, Ann Barr Snitow, 'Mass market romance: pornography for women is different', in Ann Snitow, C. Stansell and S. Thompson (eds.), *Desire: The Politics of Sexuality*, London, Virago, 1984.
58. See Teresa de Lauretis, 'Film and the visible', in Bad Object Choices, *How Do I Look: Queer Film and Video*, Seattle, Bay Press, 1991, p. 275.
59. Inge Blackman and Kathryn Perry, 'Skirting the issue: Lesbian fashion in the 1990s', *Feminist Review*, no. 34, p. 72.
60. *Go Fish*, directed by Rose Troche, written by Troche and Guinevere Turner (Max, in the film), launched the London Lesbian and Gay Film Festival in 1994. By this time, the film's potential had been recognized, as the Samuel Goldwyn Co. had bought the world rights.
61. Lois Weaver, actress, is part of Split Britches theatre group, and starred in the controversial film, *She Must Be Seeing Things*.
62. Herb Ritts, quoted in Leslie Bennetts, 'k.d. lang cuts it close', *Vanity Fair*, August 1993, p. 4.
63. As evidenced by the fact that we can also read about the brand names of the clothing worn by both lang and Crawford.
64. Tori Osborne, quoted in Bennetts, op. cit., pp. 95–6.
65. Dan Mathews, ibid., p. 96.
66. Lang, ibid., p. 94.
67. Rosa Ainley and Sarah Cooper, 'She thinks I still care: Lesbians and country music', in Diane Hamer and Belinda Budge (eds.), *The Good, The Bad and The Gorgeous: Popular Culture's Romance with Lesbianism*, London, Pandora, 1994, p. 51.

68. Gayle Rubin, in Carol Vance (ed.), op. cit., p. 287.
69. Such cross-gender characteristics were usually signalled in childhood by dreams and general cross-gender preferences.
70. The term 'Berdache' was originally applied to men.
71. See: Evelyn Blackwood, 'Sexuality and gender in certain native American tribes: The case of cross gender females', *SIGNS*, 1984, vol. 10, 11, pp. 27–42; and Harriet Whitehead, 'The bow and the burden strap: A new look at institutionalized homosexuality in native North America', in Sherry B. Ortner and Harriet Whitehead (eds.), *Sexual Meanings: The Cultural Construction of Gender and Sexuality*, Cambridge, Cambridge University Press, 1991.
72. Evelyn Blackwood, ibid.
73. See Martha Vinicus, 'They wonder to which sex I belong: The historical roots of modern lesbian identity', in Dennis Altman (ed.), op. cit.
74. Ibid.
75. Gayle Rubin, 'Of catamites and kings: Reflections on butch, gender and boundaries', in Joan Nestle (ed.), *The Persistent Desire*, op. cit., p. 468.
76. Erotophobia as defined by Patton is 'the terrifying, irrational reaction to the erotic which makes individuals and society vulnerable to psychological and social control in cultures where pleasure is strictly categorised and regulated'. Cindy Patton, *Sex and Germs: The Politics of AIDS*, Boston, South End Press, 1985, p. 103.
77. Marjorie Garber, '*Spare parts: The surgical construction of gender*', in Henry Abelove, Michèle Aina Barale and David M. Halperin (eds.), *The Lesbian and Gay Studies Reader*, New York, Routledge, 1993, pp. 321–336.
78. Dwight B. Billings and Thomas Urban, 'The socio-medical construction of transsexualism: An interpretation and critique', *Social Problems*, vol. 29, no. 3, 1982, pp. 266–282.
79. Gayle Rubin, in Nestle, op. cit., p. 474.
80. Caroline Cossey, *My Story*, London, Faber and Faber, 1991.
81. Louis Sullivan died of an AIDS-related illness.
82. Vicky Powell, 'Growing pains', *Pink Paper*, issue 346, 23 October 1994, p. 15.
83. Jan Aram and Soreh Levy, 'When a man is a man' (letter), *Pink Paper*, issue 347, 30 October 1994, p. 8.

butch and femme 2: public performance and private practice

As demonstrated in the last chapter, the associations made between gender and behaviour are tenacious. Central to our self-perception and interactions with others, our subjective experiences of gendered identity will inevitably have some impact upon our sexual and erotic desires and their manifestations. And it is these private dimensions of a public performance that are the focus of the following enquiry and commentary.

But we do not yet know enough at all about what women – any women – desire.

Joan Nestle[1]

You can tell she's butch because
She lies on top of her woman
And puts her thigh up against
Her mount . . .
And rubs, pushes, watches . . .

You can tell she's a femme because
She slips her leg up
Between her butch's thighs
Spreads her knees wide
And groans, 'oh, that's good, stay right there'.

Pat Califia[2]

I think by focusing on roles in lesbian relationships, we can begin to unravel who we really are in bed. When you hide how profoundly roles can shape your sexuality, you can use that as an example of other things that get hidden.

Amber Hollibaugh[3]

Do butch and femme really have a role to play in sex? As an erotic dictate does it really mean anything? In the 1950s how you identified was definitely a sign of how you wanted it to be or how you thought it had to be. Clothes were the first page of a detailed sexual script, the costume directing the continuing role of the cast once they disrobed. In the absence of such clearly defined textual cues, others were left uncertain as to the nature of a woman's desire: 'you can't tell the players without a program ... look at those two – when they go home they'll toss a coin to see who will be on top.'[4] In an era preceding the 1960s sexual revolution and women's liberation, articulation of desires via the dress code was the public statement of an otherwise private erotic conversation. Prevailing norms ensured behavioural roles from the bar to the bedroom.

The classic sexual scenario of the 1950s was thus: the butch held all the erotic responsibility, she 'ran the scene' from start to finish, allowing for little mutual exploration of her own body beyond reciprocal holding. The femme's 'duty' was literally to lie back and enjoy it, it was her pleasure that was the butch's goal, her orgasm was testimony to the butch's sexual mastery. As with the popular notion of men's masculinity, butchness was also confirmed through sexual performance. But such similarities hardly constitute an importation of heterosexual norms. While sex may have been initiated by the woman wearing the trousers, the beginning of 'sex' was not signalled by an erect penis, nor was it concluded with the organ's inevitable downfall. What butch/femme dynamics of the 1950s did, in effect, was to reverse the 'sex' roles prescribed by masculinity and femininity. The butch's nurturing and attentive style is more readily associated with femininity, while the femme, by ensuring her own gratification and caretaking, is coming from a traditionally masculine position. This behaviour may have been influenced by the popularized sexual fashions at the time, which instructed men to please women as much as themselves while perpetuating ideas that men did not need tactile comfort; but I would argue that this does not in itself explain the uniqueness of the butch/femme dynamic. To rely on such sexual scripture is also further collusion with the idea that women lack sexual agency.

Being a modern-day butch genital hedonist (if I must identify within the framework), I have spent a great deal of time researching this unselfish butch trait. And it was indeed a pervasive dictate. Although tribadism provided stimulation and sometimes orgasm, it seems that generally, especially for inflexible stone butches, orgasm was more of a mental experience. To surrender to a femme (to 'roll over for', to be 'flipped' or 'pancaked') was a violation of the stone code. If such indiscretions became common knowledge, it was butch identity suicide. These rigid scripts left many women frustrated, either because they wanted to be caressed and be responsive to their lovers, or because they wanted to reciprocate in an active way. Due to the combination of personal discontent and the ascendancy of feminist philosophies, butch/femme roles and their particular erotic connotations became the focus of a community critique.

The 'stone code' in particular came under close scrutiny. Functioning as more than simply a consensual sexual script, its role as protective barrier was not the initial line of enquiry. Stone behaviours such as remaining partially clothed (in men's underwear) and preventing reciprocal touch maintained the masquerade. To allow for breast appreciation or penetration would have necessitated acceptance of the female physique and thus terminated the phallic fiction. For some butches, the extent of their masculine identification was such that their own female bodies afforded them little pleasure. The erotic wiring was different and the butch exterior reflected this. Removal of the mask would expose a vulnerable side. Many stones traded the pleasures and attendant vulnerabilities of wild sexual abandon for the security of predictable encounters. Beyond the individual psychology (which cannot really be segregated from the forces which shape it) is the fact that to submit to the femme was frowned upon, inviting social sanction.

As feminist activism placed the issue of sexual abuse firmly on the agenda, psychologizing the code gained popular currency. Lesbian feminist Julia Penelope bravely subjects her own sexual history to such analysis:

> When I was a stone butch, I believed I was in control; now I know I was being controlled by my past ... naming myself butch enabled me to misdescribe the reasons for my emotional and sexual coldness and to ignore, even trivialise, my utter inability (indeed my fear of intimacy).[5]

As a survival tactic it needs no further interrogation. She is neither alone in her experience nor in her analysis of it. Many survivors of incest/abuse may 'automatically' perform to 'please' their partners. A product of early learning, sex becomes a currency traded for affection or love. The early messages often leave us with confused boundaries and expectations. Such violations of trust and touch have a tremendous impact on our

sexual personae. The environment created in our communities and relationships has provided the safety for many to give voice to their
experiences. Lesbian survivors are just that – surviving, functioning and
recovering from earlier hurts. Our damage is not our destiny, we are not
eternal victims of violation. For those women who have experienced abuse
and who identify as butch, there need not be link between the two. Neither
the experience of sexual abuse nor butch control is synonymous with
being emotionally vacant. The assumption that the stone code is a
product of sexual abuse in all women for whom both are realities, is in
itself a perpetuation of disempowerment and abusive practice.   The
configuration of our sexual identities takes shape from many influences; it
is often ill founded to make such linear assumptions. A further effect is to
return our sexualities to the hands of the eagerly waiting pathologizers,
who then debate our dysfunctions without any mention of the perpetrators of abuse and their motivations.

Sex as an act is exciting and extremely pleasurable. It is also fraught
with terror, consciously or unconsciously returning us to an infantile state
of neediness, dependency, and fear of loss. Women, men, butch, femme,
androdyke ... allowing for individual histories, the experiences are
similar, if we trust enough to feel them. The diverse careers dictated by the
gendered scripts are not ordained by biology, they are masks. Butch and
femme and their straight copies, masculinity and femininity, are only as
real as we want them to be.

In the urban ghettos of today's lesbian populus, the stone butch as a
species appears just about extinct. Hence it came as something of a
surprise when my tendencies to control were relabelled as stone, during
an intimate conversation. Since losing an extremely significant partner, I
had sought to protect myself against the reactivation of my basic emo-
tions. To protect myself from further hurt, my own way of dealing with the
shattered trust and an almost infantile separation anxiety was to contain
my emotional investment, by being in sexual command. To a woman
familiar with our heritage and with my own personal style, it was a small
step farther to transform my identity to stone butch. Within a context of
androcentric definitions of what constitutes sex, it seems I was not having
sex at all. She used the pervasive social norms of sexology along with a
lesbian colloquialism. Her analysis was necessitated by our understandings of how it ought to be. Was it me, was it her, was it us, or was I just
frigid? Is such interrogation useful as a route to self-discovery, when
conducted in straitjackets of definition? The stone code has been
subject to so much investigation primarily because it does not fit the

sexual scripts labelled feminine or masculine, and we have been led to believe that all behaviour must fit somewhere. If we let go of this notion, perhaps the stone butch would be less of an enigma.

Over the years, the labels we have adopted have changed, and sexual practice continues to evolve in line with social transformation. This allows for both continuity and discontinuity. The rules may have changed as to who does what to whom, but what is actually done is not a radical departure. Queer lesbian boys may like to think they single-handedly fathered the dildo, but it certainly precedes contemporary photographic penis-posturing. Leaving aside the imagination of Havelock Ellis, our own commentaries document the dildo's role. Unlike today, there were definite rules as to who was at which end of it. Phallic appropriation was harnessed to the butch identity. In *Stone Butch Blues* (the baby butch apprenticeship manual) the coming-of-age butch, Jess, finds herself being tutored on sex by an older butch role model. The knowledge is handed down not only with the emotional illiteracy associated with stereotypical masculinity, but with the assumption that sex is fundamentally natural and thus requires little instruction – as if butches are endowed with some basic instinct. The femme partner to the 'mentor' reassures the novice after her partner has departed:

> You know, you could make a woman feel really good with this thing. Maybe better than she's ever felt in her life. Or you could really hurt her and remind her of all the ways she's ever been hurt in her life. You got to think about that every time you strap this on. Then you'll be a good lover.[6]

Jess is educated in the most valuable instruction of all, sensitivity to another's needs, while (true to its time) responsibility is placed firmly, if not literally, in the lap of the butch.

But, of course, phallic acquisition was not necessary to be a 'good lover':

> when penetration was wanted they used their hands. Their confidence in their own hands and their ability to please did not dispose them to think that a dildo would improve lovemaking ... fem narrators did not mention desire for the use of a dildo.[7]

This is as true now as it was in the 1950s to which these oral histories refer. Many of us feel real sexual skill lies in the ability to use our hands and our tongues, not in the bravado of brandishing a rubber object. We're lesbians; who wants to imitate men and heterosexual sex? Butch and femme dykes are accused of doing just this, with or without a dildo. The doctrines of the lesbian feminists were far-reaching, as reflected in one of the first lesbian sex texts, *The Joy of Lesbian Sex*. If you were butch or femme, there was to be no 'joy' at all. Such gendered identities are berated amidst accusations of being stuck in a time-warp, and we are reassuringly informed that role-play usually stops at the bedroom door. Even the misguided, it would seem, defer to their true womanly essence in the sack. I find it fascinating that, in an era which grew out of the sexual division of labour, the authors simply ignored the wider sexual meanings. Their definition of lesbianism was a political one, not a sexual one. And so in a book which, if it were true to the messages of lesbian feminism, we should not have been looking in anyway, we are instructed:

> a kiss should never start mouth to mouth. You are not engaged in the resuscitation of the half drowned ... The problem with a lot of mouth-to-mouth kissing is too much too soon. And unfortunately, many lesbians are guilty. Maybe it's one of those macho notions left over from olden days when lesbians felt they had to emulate male behaviour.[8]

A generation apart, the text is a stark contrast to Bright's later claim, that dildo-play is as heterosexual as kissing. It seems that the lesbian feminists had decided that, given the inevitability that women would read books of this genre, better they write them and define the true nature of lesbian desire.

Modern-day butch/femme style has broken some of the chains of sexual practice. In yet another example of the lack of fit between identity and sex, analysis of available data suggest there is no relation between label and practice. Loulan, reviewing individual cases, suggests that femmes are more likely to penetrate their lovers – it looks like the girls are out to make up for lost time.[9] How we describe our 'global' sex-role perceptions of how we act on a daily basis may differ from how we see ourselves sexually. As self-supporting lesbians, we inevitably have to enter male arenas and exhibit traits which are commonly labelled 'male', to survive. One study[10] suggests that – irrespective of whether our everyday self-perceptions are feminine, masculine, androgynous or undifferentiated – in our most intimate behaviour, many lean toward the feminine (with androgynous a close second). Although nearly a third of the sample rated their global sex-role as masculine, sexually, only 5 per cent considered themselves as such. This contrasts to global perceptions of 15 per cent as femme, increasing to 45 per cent as an adopted sexual style.

Reluctance to enact 'male sexual traits' is a popular explanation for the seeming low frequency of lesbian sex. Since femininity is, by definition, reactive not active, the result is that no one takes the initiative. Blumstein and Schwartz's much-quoted survey[11] throws in an interesting contradiction. In lesbian samples, the proactive partner also tends to be the emotionally expressive partner, prone to more public and spontaneous acts of affection. Surely this is classically the prerogative of a woman (read, femininity). This study and the previous one cited produce evidence suggesting that those who identify sexually as more feminine or androgynous report higher levels of satisfaction. With the demise of stone, why is this?

In another study detailing the pervasiveness of egalitarian dynamics in lesbian relationships, 70%[12] of respondents report inequalities around initiation. However, in the absence of further information, it is not clear whether or not this is indicative of who is in control. Several conclusions are made by the authors that equality in sex may be neither 'possible' nor 'desirable' – issues we shall return to. In a culture where challenges to the segregation of behaviour into masculine/feminine and active/passive are constant, it may be that the categories of butch/femme are no longer necessary. And although the lesbian and gay community do not shy from reclaiming language that is harshly used by the parent culture, butch/femme may pose a more difficult task, as the attack came primarily from within.

We have our own sexual styles – they are not inflexible and they vary from day to day, influenced by factors of mood, health and physicality. They vary with partners, confidence and sexual knowledge. It is not uncommon in relationships, however, for patterns to become habitual until, all too quickly, one or other is landed with the role of initiator. Despite years of feminist struggle, sexual agency is still seen as a male trait. As women we have had to overcome a lifetime of conditioning of sexual passivity and stories that our libido is reactive as opposed to proactive. Butch/femme has always allowed for the perpetuation of this myth; because of its dependence on the past and what many regard as archaic sexual styles, the words may now be unpopular – inadequate in their conveyance of wider issues. Is there a style of physical posturing from which we can read difference, active/passive, dominant/submissive or butch/femme? Is there a butch and femme way to hold hands? For example, do arms around the neck or waist really mean anything? In popular representation there is a very definite gendered way to hold. Is it inevitable that we have a sensual lead and follow for this particular erotic dance?

In neo-butch/femme there are no hard and fast rules as to sexual style. Yet Susie Bright, combining erotic butch/femme dialogue with just a hint of product pushing,[13] suggests there is a difference in skill where dildo dexterity is concerned. Toys for the girl/boys? Her reasoning is informed by her own personal experience:

> The first person who got fucked by me with a dildo probably felt like she was in some kind of anthropological experiment with a teenager, because I kept laughing . . . I was bad . . . it never occurred to me to have something between my legs.

The advantage which butches have, she claims, is that 'they usually had cock fantasies, so would have imagined doing it before'[14] and thus are endowed with a natural rhythm. Many women do have cock fantasises, but is this solely a butch experience? Probably not. I suspect that Bright is far from alone in her early dildo experiences. The embarrassment of putting on something which, in the cold light of day, does look pretty silly, often produces giggles. As do fears that, if we want it this bad, we are probably wannabe men, heterosexual women, or a confusing combination of the two. Then there is dildo anxiety: what if it's too big or too small? What if a member of the dyke police jumps out of the wardrobe, or even worse, your mother phones while you're wearing it? And there is the question of what to do with it: after all, the instructions which come with it tell you how to clean the little darlings, not how to get them dirty.

Notions of instinctive sexual expertise are amongst the most damaging of the butch/femme myths. Assuming that any woman – whether butch, femme, daddy dyke, or Miss tweed skirt and sensible shoes – is going to be perfect first time around with an inanimate object which affords the wearer little immediate sensation, is misleading to say the least. The experience can be pleasurable for the wearer as well, if not by clever positioning of the dildo base to stimulate the clitoris, then by letting the psyche compensate for the absence of neural connections. Yet entering, coming out and rhythmical motion take some practice. As does receptive positioning to maximize pleasure and minimize the risk of an untimely exit (as is common in the standing position).

Bright, on the cutting edge of sexual commodification, introduces a new angle – the thigh harness. Just as it sounds, it is a harness worn on the upper thigh. A starter toy for femmes? Susie seems to think so . . . 'because it mounts on your thigh, which we're accustomed to rubbing. If I could have started with that I'm sure I would have been better.'[15] The thigh harness, although not easily available in the UK, is a popular variation in North America. Wearing of the harness by many a practised tribadist allows for penetration of the partner while she gets off as usual. The advantage of the thigh harness, for those who want the sensations of dildo penetration but feel uncomfortable with the aesthetic associations with men, is that it allows for dislocation of the phallus away from the genital region, reaffirming the difference of lesbian sex.

'Objectify my love'

Butchness, for me is a form of transgender on a continuum that is as wide as the heterosexual – homosexual continuum. I think butches are feeling a lot of traditionally masculine erotic feelings with this sense of erotic identity that's very powerful to them because it is so focused on other women. They stand out because what they're doing is so unconventional. My desires are not so easily detected in a crowd except when I'm with a woman . . . it would be easy to say that I've had relationships with women because I get all the sexy part of masculinity without the oppression of dealing with a real man. But it's not that easy. I've found that my love and lust are never that rational.

Susie Bright[16]

Transgender is becoming the ever-expanding transgressive territory in which we can find many of our identities and desires. With the constraints of normative masculinity and femininity, many may feel more comfortable locating themselves in the realms of transgender. Not just butches, but femmes, with their deviant desires and potentially exaggerated feminine signification. As the transgender movement gains momentum, I suspect we will see more defections into it, because hostile resistance to gender bending is not only the prerogative of the parent culture. If it were, there would be no butch/femme debate. It is amazing how many join the moral majority when fetishistic practice is on the menu.

'Gender fetishism' in popular understanding implies a practice which is explicitly sexual, definitely taboo, traditionally naughty and definitely weird. Much of fetishistic practice remains the property of psychiatry – reflecting how institutions like medicine continue to codify social mores.

It is only recently that women's activities have been brought under this medical gaze. It was originally believed, for example, that women could not become transvestites, because they could not have erections. (This visible marker, along with orgasm, was the proof of male arousal from the wearing of women's clothes.) Clinicians were eventually forced to acknowledge that some women did orgasm simply by wearing men's clothes and in the absence of any other form of stimulation. They still maintain that this is more typically a man's game – hardly surprising, as men's bodies have not been commercially objectified in the same way. Their clothing, and especially their underwear, has not been marketed in ways which capitalize on the explicitly sexual. Transvestism satisfies a sexual desire, the erotic aim is focused on objects (in this case clothing) as opposed to a sexual partner. And as such, it is generally accepted as high intensity or orthodox fetish.[17]

Butch and femme are less intense fetishes (if we choose to place them in this paradigm at all). The costume and styles of relating become vital for arousal in the presence of a partner who reaffirms the titillating scenario. As if wanting our girls to be girls were not bad enough, to want a boy in a girl goes beyond the confines of established order. For such preferences to dictate attraction, they rely on the unprincipled indulgence of objectification. To recognize, respond and reciprocate to these identities, is to become a player in the game. And thus, this type of politically incorrect mutual appreciation meets with lesbian feminist censorship. Another reason is that the commodification of butch/femme feeds the coffers of the heteropatriarchal sex industry. Having bought false consciousness along with our other accessories, we are pawns to our patriarchal masters, fetishizing our own oppression.

Nowhere is this patriarchal psyche more apparent than in the act of packing – wearing a dildo under the clothing. Whether this is done as a defiant cock-shock tactic, a daring act of eroticism, an act to authenticate 'passing', or playtime for the wearer and the woman she wears it for, the practice is not as rare as some like to think. In *The Good Vibrations Guide to Sex*,[18] the sexual recipe book guaranteed to stimulate any flagging appetite, packing can be found in a list of tantalizing suggestions.

The book was produced by the San Francisco sex shop. (Catalogues produced by manufacturers in Britain have yet to adopt this user-friendly commercial approach, giving instead a basic list of ingredients, in terms of height, width and whether or not it clashes with your duvet cover). The motivation is more than purely profit. There is advice on the more flaccid types – the stiffer versions are not suitable for 'evening wear' as they tend to cause bruising as well being uncomfortable. For the packing prince-less], it's possible she has just made another girl's dream come true: what she's always been looking for, a dyke with a dick. As she falls to her knees to give that much desired blow-job, she can rest assured that her date is probably not lying when she promises not to come in her mouth.

Another aspect of the commercial value of transgender is the advent of 'drag king' workshops, which at the time of writing seem to be fashionable 'passing' playdays for any aspiring chick with a dick. We're talking false facial hair – the lot. The finale is to go out on the town as a man, to see how convincing the masquerade really is. However, long after such theatrical novelties wear off, transgender dykes will remain.

From Role-Play to Power Games

I think the reason butch stuff got hidden within lesbian feminism is because people are afraid of questions of power in bed . . . The question of power affects who and how you eroticize your sexual need. And it is absolutely at the bottom of all sexual enquiry.
Amber Hollibaugh[19]

Butch/femme is commonly associated with another sexual style, SM. This is partly due to the convergence of fashions as reflected in the contemporary iconography. Although we can no longer confidently iden-tify erotic preferences, some dress codes and signals are less subtle: the leather look, body decorations like piercing and tattoos. The association between butch/femme and SM goes beyond surface similarity. Both sexual styles are based on the eroticization of power and different roles. These become psychic props in the elaborate sexual games. In SM this involves explicit negotiation and articulation of boundaries. For butch/femme, such arrangements rely more on inherited cultural practice.

Power is a constant companion in any sexual exchange. Sex, by its very nature, can never be power-free. Such a reality does not inevitably result in oppression or psychic and emotional damage. In fact, it is the recognition of this power and often the attendant inequalities which can safeguard against such negative consequences. Power stems from the differences between people – this is part of the 'otherness' that attracts. It is for this reason that sex therapists recommend styles of relating which rely on 'difference'. It is argued that the denial or attempted elimination of inequality, as well as being politically correct, will have an erotic price in terms of compromising our desires – as evidenced by the low frequency of our sexual activity. Popular explanations for this phenomenon include passive feminine socialization and – terms coined more recently by lesbian psychology – 'merging' or 'fusion'. This occurs when a couple get so close emotionally that their individual boundaries blur and mutual dependency is exaggerated. In the absence of any sense of separateness or 'otherness', we lose the desire to have sex. There are no barriers left. The therapeutic answer to this 'inhibited sexual desire' (ISD)/'hypoactive sexual desire disorder' (HSDD) or 'bed death', is libidinal resuscitation through role-play. On the basis of observations that gay men and hetero-sexuals are not plagued by the death of desire on the same scale, we are encouraged to introduce similar dynamics into our own relationships. Egalitarian principles may grease the wheels of everyday living but they bring passion grinding to a halt.

However, we have yet to see any statistical evidence showing that those choosing butch/femme or SM have more sex. If they do, this could be a facet of role-play, or just the unique sexual personae that lead them to that point anyway. The bottom line remains that many of us perceive another as different, and that is part of the attraction. Power is ubiquitous throughout. In terms of butch and femme, both have power. To write off a femme as disempowered is to define lesbian sexuality by the male heterosexualized yardstick. 'Femmechismo' is not a product of the patri-archal culture:

> femme is active, not passive. It's saying to my partner 'love me enough to let me go where I need to go and take me there' ... I want to give up power in response to her need. This can feel profoundly powerful and unpassive ... my power is that I know how to read her inside her own passion ... there are femme ways to orchestrate sexuality ... I'll simply seduce her ... but it's seduction as a femme.[20]

Again, the interpretation of butch and femme as active and passive continues to be inadequate. Such femme power remains while we are seeing a definite butch shift. A modern-day butch response to Holli-baugh's passionate declaration might be: 'I love you enough to take you where you need to go ... but I want to *come* with you.' Equally so, a contemporary femme request may be more of a direct demand as she asserts equitable if not total control.

It may be that the words we have to describe our sexual styles are inadequate in conveying the meanings of the experience. Equating butch/femme with masculine/active and feminine/passive is a semantic short-cut which excludes much of the complexity. Reluctance to use our own vernacular may stem from the associations with parent models. Or, despite identity construction based on reverse discourse, reclamation of butch/femme may be difficult because the greatest hostility and denigration came from (and continues to be) within our own culture. Newton and Walton [21] document the need for a more inclusive language in a paper motivated by their failure to have a successful sexual liaison. Years later, the reason became apparent: despite their mutually attracting butch and femme identities, they both wanted to be in control and, at the time, there was no way of articulating this. To circumvent these dilemmas they recommend that 'top' and 'bottom' are taken out of the SM arena and redeployed with wider meaning.

Many of our desires, both realized and imagined, revolve around issues of power. It is hardly surprising that the inequalities which make up the fabric of our society should be reflected in the psyche. Getting lesbians to talk about sexual activity is one thing, getting them to talk about the realm of fantasy is practically impossible. Mirroring the women's movement generally, we remain relatively silent around sex. Nancy Friday[22] publishes the popularized versions of the fantasies which we seem so reticent to discuss. We need to see more of our fantasies mapped out, without the demarcation lines of preference, which of course is one of the finer themes of fantasy. From both popular texts and discussion groups, common themes emerge: power, domination, submission and the 'pornographic'. The functions of mental life are wide-ranging: from a mechanism to relieve boredom, to well-rehearsed psychological aphrodisiacs. Some we may want to enact, others we will always see as fantasy, aware that literal translation in reality is not wanted.

The butch/femme and SM scripts of fantasy are one reason we remain silent about them. As are the anatomical incongruities and mythical transformations which both ourselves and others undergo in the imagination. As for those who break the implicit vow of silence, this is how a few of them have described their fantasies: thinking she's inside you with a real penis and when she comes, you're pregnant or vice versa; she's that woman at the bus stop and she obeys every word; he's that guy from the library and you obey his every word; she's not the only one touching you and that's not including the camera crew; she's paying for sex or vice versa; she's that woman you wake up with every morning, who has suddenly learned to read your mind and she becomes your every fantasy. Whether real in our beds or our heads, the forces that keep us silent are psychological censorship, as we feel guilt, shame and embarrassment. Denying women the freedom to discuss their fantasies is not in service of wider liberation. But the arms of lesbian sex law remain far-reaching.

Some lesbian feminists are so opposed to the eroticization of inequality and gender fetish that, according to their analysis, our desires are not 'homosexual' at all. Sheila Jeffreys, in her book *Anticlimax*, describes two types of desire, differentiated by the role which power plays.[23] Heterosexual desire is based on the erotic manipulation of inequalities. It is within this framework that most of us operate, irrespective of object choice. True homosexual desire, the lesbian nirvana, is based on harmonious balance and total equality. Those of us who wallow in the cesspit of gender fetish are probably beyond political correction.

> Role playing in the eighties is the soft pornography compared to the hard pornography of S/M, it provides the thrill of eroticised power difference without the extremes of violence and vulgarity ... The new role playing is the fundamentalism of lesbianism. As fundamentalism in all patriarchal religions is founded upon and designed to maintain the oppression of women through the enforcement of male dominance and female submission, so too is lesbian role playing.[24]

The message is clear: stop it and stop it now!

There are both similarities and differences between the gradations of role-play and SM. United in the manipulation of symbolic power, it has been suggested that femme/butch dykes should mobilize along the lines of the SM model. This would involve claiming to be another minority within a minority, and would provide a power-base from which to organize resistance to the hostile onslaught which is communicated in loaded and emotive language. When Jeffreys describes Nestle as a leading propagandist,[25] she relies on the negative associations such words carry, and equates Nestle's philosophies with regimes with which there is simply no comparison. This is the modern-day vernacular of the moral right and does no justice to a woman who is undoubtedly controversial and possibly even pornographic (depending on definition) in her writing, but whose words empower and are pleasurable to many women. As one of the women responsible for opening the floodgates of the summer of sex in 1988, Nestle will forever remain a target to her opponents: women who seek to silence much-needed debate around sex; whose politically correcting style at times appears a lot more oppressive than donning a dildo and calling yourself John Thomas.

The words and labels we have not only shape and reflect our realities but sculpt our very identities. Consequently, we need to expand the vocabulary we have available. Not only in the creation of new words but the expansion of the definitions we have. Nowhere is this needed more than in the arena of butch/femme. The meaning is not singular, for this is what the war of words is about, as disagreements over its meaning have forced artificially polarized definitions. On whichever side of the sex wall we sit, fighting among ourselves is not going to change the meanings of gender in the world. While we continue to direct our collective anger against each other, who challenges the oppressors? Horizontal hostility makes us all pawns of the dominant order and ultimately ensures its unaccommodating survival.

NOTES

1. Joan Nestle, 'The fem question', in Carole S. Vance (ed.), *Pleasure and Danger: Exploring Female Sexuality*, London, Pandora, 1992, p. 234.
2. Pat Califia, 'Diagnostic tests', in Joan Nestle (ed.), *The Persistent Desire*, Boston, Alyson, 1992, p. 483.
3. Amber Hollibaugh and Cherríe Moraga, 'What we're rollin' around in bed with: Sexual silences in feminism: A conversation toward ending them', in Joan Nestle (ed.), ibid., p. 244.
4. Elizabeth Lapovsky Kennedy and Madeline D. Davis, *Boots of Leather, Slippers of Gold: The History of a Lesbian Community*, Harmondsworth, Penguin, 1994.
5. Julia Penelope, 'Whose past are we reclaiming?', in *Call me Lesbian: Lesbian Lives, Theory*, Freedom, Crossing Press, 1992, p. 14.
6. Leslie Feinberg, *Stone Butch Blues*, Ithaca, Firebrand Books, 1993, p. 31.
7. Elizabeth Lapovsky Kennedy and Madeline D. Davis, op. cit., p. 228.
8. Dr Emily Sisley and Bertha Harris, *The Joy of Lesbian Sex: A Tender and Liberated Guide to the Pleasures and Problems of a Lesbian Lifestyle*, New York, Pocket Books, 1977, p. 96–7.
9. JoAnn Loulan, *The Lesbian Erotic Dance*, San Francisco, Spinsters, 1990, p. 247.
10. Julie Rosenweig and Wendy Lebow, 'Femme on the streets, butch in the sheets?', *Journal of Homosexuality*, vol. 23 (3), 1992, p. 11.

11. Philip Blumstein and Pepper Schwartz, *American Couples: Money, Work, Sex*, New York, William Morrow, 1983, p. 219.
12. Mary Ellen Reilly and Jean M. Lynch, 'Role relationships: Lesbian perspectives', *Journal of Homosexuality*, vol. 12 (2), 1985/6, p. 65.
13. Susie Bright has worked in San Francisco's sex shop, Good Vibrations..
14. Susie Bright and Shar Rednour, 'The joys of butch', in Lily Burana, Roxxie, and Linnea Due (eds.), *Dagger: On Butch Women*, San Francisco, Cleis Press, 1994, p. 145.
15. Ibid., p. 145.
16. Ibid., p. 141.
17. See Lorraine Gamman and Merja Makinen, *Female Fetishism: A New Look*, London, Lawrence and Wishart, 1994; and Marjorie Garber, *Vested Interests: Cross Dressing and Cultural Anxiety*, Harmondsworth, Penguin, 1992.
18. Cathy Winks and Anne Semans, *The Good Vibrations Guide To Sex*, Pittsburgh, Cleis Press, 1994.
19. Amber Hollibaugh and Cherríe Moraga, op. cit., p. 246.
20. Ibid., p. 246–7.
21. Esther Newton and Shirley Walton, 'The misunderstanding: toward a more precise sexual vocabulary', in Carol Vance (ed.) *Pleasure and Danger: Exploring Female Sexuality*. London: Pandora, 1989.
22. Nancy Friday, *My Secret Garden*, London, Arrow Books, 1973.
23. Sheila Jeffreys, *Anticlimax: A Feminist Perspective on the Sexual Revolution*, London, Women's Press, 1990.
24. Sheila Jeffreys, *The Lesbian Heresy: A Feminist Perspective on the Lesbian Sexual Revolution*, London, Women's Press, 1994, p. 94.
25. Ibid., p. 77.

epilogue

Lesbian sex is not as simple as how many times the tongue enters the vagina compared to the slow linger on the clitoris. Nor is it as straightforward as right or wrong, private or public, ethical or unethical, lesbian feminist or heteropatriarchal imitation. Neither leather, lace nor latex precludes an ethical approach to living. Sex has fewer forms, either in language, visual representation or behaviour, than it has functions – both deeply personal and publicly or privately political. And it is the utilitarian aspect and its wider meanings to which we now need to turn our attention. This extends the remit beyond the pragmatics of sexual practice, embracing all the levels at which sex operates, opening our minds and bringing the nature of desire and love into our field of vision. Chapter 3 detailed understandings of what sex is; any other enquiry should take up where this left off, asking, what does this mean to you? Looking at the links, tensions and contradictions between practice and politics. Exploring the gender conventions and language, in both its symbolic codes and spoken and scripted words. Sex can mean practically everything between two people or more, or almost nothing in conventional terms. Sex means many things, not just and not always, 'I love you.' It can signal a need for pure physical release, comfort, escapism, power struggles and an expression of anger or hate. The more willing lesbians are to recognize the numerous functions and manifestations of sex, the broader our minds will become.

The only certainty in sexual theory is that we will constantly seek such ideas and explanations, through which to understand what we believe to be the most fundamental aspect of human nature and need. The history of the lesbian in such notions, is one in which we have not only been described by others, but in which we have defined ourselves. We continue to do so. The resurgence of sexuality as a focus is not a signal of the demise of politics but a sign of changing style. And while the debates which monopolized the 1980s have yielded a rich harvest, they are fast becoming circular arguments from which we need to break out and move on. We cannot maintain that sexuality *per se* is contingent upon an historical moment and social context, if progressive politics remain chained to what is fast becoming the past. The issues themselves are not redundant – representation, censorship, civil rights and ethical private practices are still central – but the climate is changing, and lesbian sex needs an outfit befitting the transition of season. The personal is still political. If anything, this becomes more apparent as sex is being pushed centre stage – what could be more personal or political than that?

In contemporary British society, the recession continues, class divisions deepen and the welfare state is being dismantled before our eyes. The shared sense of community and social belonging beyond insular dimensions continues to dwindle. The philosophies of individualism are nurtured, those of collectivism, neglected. Social citizens and sexual aliens, we, like everyone else, turn increasingly to our lovers – excited by their presence, aroused by their touch, transported by their passion, and secure in their love. And no matter what the law says, one of the few times we pretend is when fantasy enters the bedroom. Lesbian sex operates on this level and at all others where power resides, from pillow talk onwards. Desire is little understood and love and human bonds are underrated. These are issues we need to develop, while living ethically, establishing a wider community and valuing difference. Having undressed lesbian sex, it is time to accept that fashions change, and we must move with such change. This is a beginning as opposed to a conclusion. The strands of new perspectives and approaches in the text need to be developed. Effective strategies for working together need to take a working form other than the textual. Lesbian sex is a private act with public consequences. It can be a route to resistance or a road for the reactionaries. It is the lesbian and gay community who, collectively, must work to ensure it remains a practice of freedom.

At last, the first explicit lesbian sex questionnaire. This is a questionnaire about lesbian sex – about what we do when we have sex. It is totally anonymous and should take you about ten minutes to complete. It is written by a team of lesbians who aim to publish the results in various forms, including the lesbian and gay press.

Circle one response per question unless asked to do otherwise.

Background

1 What term would you usually use to describe yourself sexually?

lesbian	1
lesbian/dyke	2
dyke	3
gay	4
homosexual	5
bisexual	6
heterosexual	7
Other	8*

*(please specify_____)

2 How old are you? ____years

3 Where do you live?

London	1
Another large city	2
A town	3
A village	4
Other	5*

*(please specify_____)

4 How would you describe/define your ethnic origin?

African	1
Afro-caribbean	2
Asian	3
South East Asian	4
Black other	5
White European	6
White other	7
Other	8*

*(please specify_____)

5 Are you differently abled/disabled in any way?

No	0
Yes	1*

*(please specify_____)

Sexual Behaviour

6 At what age did you first have a sexual experience with . . .
another woman or girl?____ years old
a man or boy? ____ years old

7 How many female sexual partners have you had in your . . .

	REGULAR	CASUAL
Whole life	[ ]	[ ]

Last year   [   ]   [   ]   [   ]   [   ]

8 Have you *ever* had a relationship with a man?
No   0
Yes, but no sex   1
Yes, with sex but not penetrative   2
Yes, with sexual intercourse   3

9 How many male sexual partners have you had in your . . .

	REGULAR		CASUAL	
Whole life	[	]	[	]
Last year	[	]	[	]

10 How would you describe your current sexual relationship status with women?
Single, no 1 to 1 relationship (sexual or not)   1
In a non-sexual relationship   2
In a monogamous relationship (1 partner only)   3
More than one regular partner (no casuals)   4
One or more regular partner and casuals   5
Only casual partners   7
Celibate   6
Other   *8
*(please specify_____)

11 How often do you have sex with . . . (circle one in each column)

	A Regular Female Partner	A Casual Female Partner
Every day	1	1
2–3 times a week	2	2
Once a week	3	3
2–3 times a month	4	4
Once a month	5	5
Every 2–3 months	6	6
Every 6 months	7	7
Less often	8	8
Never	9	9

12 How often would you like to have sex with . . .

	A Regular Female Partner	A Casual Female Partner
Every day	1	1
2–3 times a week	2	2
Once a week	3	3
2–3 times a month	4	4
Once a month	5	5
Every 2–3 months	6	6
Every 6 months	7	7
Less often	8	8
Never	9	9

13 Have you ever had group sex?
Yes, with women only   1
Yes, with men only   2
Yes, with men and women   3
No, never   0

14 During sex, do you and your partner/s discuss what you are doing and/or want to do?
Always   3
Usually   2
Sometimes   1
Never   0

15 In the next three questions, answer:

Very important	3
Important	2
Not very important	1
Not at all important	0

1 How important is sex in your life?
[   ]

2 How important is it that you orgasm (come) when having sex?   [   ]

3 How important is it to you that your partner orgasms (comes) during sex?
[   ]

4 How satisfied are you with your sex life at the moment?

Very satisfied	3
Quite satisfied	2
Not very satisfied	1
Not at all satisfied	0

Sex and Money

1 Have you been paid for sex?

	ever	last year
Yes, by a man or men	1	1
Yes, by a woman or women	2	2
Yes, by both men and women	3	3
No, never ☞ **go to question 17**	0	0

2 When you have been paid for sex, in the last year, did you practise safer sex?
(circle as many as apply)

No, never	0
Yes, always	1
Sometimes, depending on the client's wishes	2
Sometimes, depending on the fee	3

17 Has the risk of HIV/AIDS changed your sexual behaviour in any way at all?

No, never	0

Yes . . . **(circle as many as apply)**

Reduced number of male sexual partners	1
Reduced number of female sexual partners	2
Asked partners about their sexual history	3
Monogamy (staying with one sexual partner)	4
Avoided certain sexual acts	5
Used dental dams	6
Used latex gloves or finger cots	7
Washed hands/sex toys	8
Using condoms on sex toys	9
Used condoms for penetrative sex with males	10
Abstinence/celibacy (no sex)	11
Stopped sharing works/needles/syringes	12
Used diaphragm/cervical cap to prevent menstrual blood entering vagina	13
Worn underwear with latex gussets	14
Other forms of safer sex	*15

*(please specify)

_____

18 Do you consider yourself

butch	1
femme	2
neither	3

19 What would have to happen between you and another woman for you to call it sex?

20 When having sex with a **female** in the **last year**, have you … **(answer 1 for YES or 0 for NO)**	Regular Partners	Casual Partners
Deep kissed		
Massaged		
Showered or bathed together		
Given oral sex/gone down on/licked sucked		
Received oral sex/she went down on you		
Done tribadism/body rubbing/humping		
Stimulated her clitoris		
Had your clitoris stimulated by her		
Talked explicitly about sex (dirty talk)		
Licked or sucked her breasts		
Had your breasts licked or sucked by her		
Stroked/caressed parts of her body other than genitals		
Masturbated (wanked) in front of your partner		
Had your partner masturbated (wank) in front of you		
Fantasized		
Talked about fantasies		
Acted out fantasies		
Dressed up		
Done water sports (played with piss, urine)		
Done SM as top		
Done SM as bottom		
Restraint		
CP/Spanking		

Abuse and Rape

21 Have you ever been sexually abused by a man?
No   0
Yes   1
Don't know   2

22 Have you ever been sexually abused by a woman?
No   0
Yes   1
Don't know   2

23 Have you ever been raped by a man?
No   0
Yes   1
Don't know   2

24 When having sex with a female in the last year... **(answer I for YES or 0 for NO).**

	...have you penetrated her vagina with...		...have you penetrated her anus with...		...has she penetrated your vagina with...		...has she penetrated your anus with...	
	With regular partners	With casual partners	With regular partners	With casual partners	With regular partners	With casual partners	With regular partners	With casual partners
Fingers								
Fist								
Tongue								
Fruit or vegetables								
Vibrator								
Dildo								
Strap-on								

...AND FINALLY

Issues like sexual abuse, sexual health, disability, and the sex industry are important – we know this but we do not have the space to investigate them in depth here.

Obviously in a survey like this things have been missed out. Is there anything you think should have been included?

glossary of terms

Note: this glossary is not intended to be a comprehensive list of terms used in this book, and refers in particular to Chapter 3.

Analingus: oral–anal contact. Licking and or penetrating anus with the tongue. Also known as rimming or tonguing.

Anal sex: Includes acts of penetration with fingers/fists/tongues/objects and may be referred to with words used for vaginal penetration, e.g. fucking, intercourse.

Anatomy: because anal sex has an unhygienic reputation, it is rarely discussed, which is partly why accidents happen. Both the anal opening and the anus have a rich source of nerve endings, allowing for stimulation to be either extremely pleasurable or painful depending on the care taken. The anal canal is about one to two inches in length, leading into the rectum, which is between five and nine inches, which leads to the colon. It is here that faeces are stored, only being moved along the passageways of the rectum and anus following the rectal reflex (experienced as the feeling that a bowel movement is needed). While the anal passage is straight, the rectum is not – bending sharply toward the front of the body, then to the back, then to the front again – vital knowledge if penetration is practised. For further details, see either the sex texts of Cathy Winks and Anne Semans or, more specifically, Jack Morin.

Body rubbing: close body contact involving rhythmic movement in various positions and involving different pleasure zones. Often involves vulva to vulva contact or vulva to arse or thigh. Also known as tribadism, frottage, humping, grinding or dry fucking.

Butt plug: toy designed for anal penetration.

Dildo: object designed for vaginal/anal stimulation/penetration; made of a variety of different materials, including latex, rubber, silicone, leather and wood.

Fingering: penetration with fingers.

Fisting: insertion/thrusting of hand into vagina or anus and rectum.

G-spot: the urethral sponge on the front wall of the vagina. Called the G-spot after Ernst Grafenberg, a gynaecologist who detailed its erotic potential in the 1940s and 50s. Rich in nerve endings, it is extremely sensitive, and on stimulation some women may ejaculate fluid from the urethra.

Harness: straps to be worn round the torso, whole body, pelvis or thigh, to hold a dildo/butt plug in place.

Open relationship: relationship where the partners are non-monogamous by arrangement.

Oral sex/cunnilingus: oral-clitoral/vaginal contact. Can involve licking, sucking, biting and penetration with the tongue. Colloquially known as coming down/going down on, sucking off, eating out.

Serial monogamy: if someone is said to practise serial monogamy, it means that when a relationship ends with one partner, she will begin another monogamous relationship with another, and so on.

Strap-on: a harness and dildo.

Vulva: a woman's genitalia. Colloquially referred to as cunt or pussy. Anatomically specific names are vagina, clitoris, outer lips (labia majora) and inner lips (labia minora).

*b*ibliography

Abbott, Sidney and Love, Barbara (1972) *Sappho was a Right-on Woman: A Liberated View of Women*. New York: Stein & Day.

Abelove, Henry, Barale, Michele Aina and Halperin, David M. (eds) (1993) *The Lesbian and Gay Studies Reader*. London: Routledge.

ACT UP/NY Women & AIDs Book Group (1992) *Women, AIDS, and Activism*. Boston: South End Press.

Ainley, Rosa and Cooper, Sarah (1994) 'She thinks I still care: Lesbians and country music', in Diane Hamer and Belinda Budge, *The Good, the Bad and the Gorgeous: Popular Culture's Romance with Lesbianism*. London: Pandora.

Alexander, Jane (1992) 'Sex: The results of our survey', *Elle*, April, pp. 29–37.

Allen, Jeffner (ed.) (1990) *Lesbian Philosophies and Cultures*. New York: State University of New York Press.

Allison, Dorothy (1995) *Skin: Talking About Sex, Class and Literature*. London: Pandora.

Altman, Dennis (1980) 'What changed in the seventies?', in Gay Left Collective, *Homosexuality: Power and Politics*. London: Allison & Busby.

Altman, Dennis, *et al.* (1989) *Homosexuality, Which Homosexuality? : Essays from the International Scientific Conference on Lesbian and Gay Studies*. London: Gay Men's Press.

American Psychiatric Association (APA) (1994) *Diagnostic and Statistical Manual of Mental Disorders*, 4th edn. Washington, DC: APA.

Archer, John and Lloyd, Barbara (1985) *Sex and Gender*. Cambridge: Cambridge University Press.

Ardill, Susan and O'Sullivan, Sue (1990) 'Butch/Femme Obsessions', *Feminist Review*, 34, Spring, pp. 79–85.

Armitage, Gary, Dickey, Julienne and Sharples, Sue (1987) *Out of the Gutter: A Survey of the Treatment of Homosexuality by the Press*. London: Campaign for Press and Broadcasting Freedom.

Bad Object-Choices (1991) *How Do I Look: Queer Film and Video*. Seattle: Bay Press.

Bannon, Ann (1986) *Beebo Brinker*. Florida: Naiad Press.

Barback, Lonnie Garfield (1975) *For Yourself: The Fulfilment of Female Sexuality*. London: Penguin Books.

Barrett, Michele and Phillips, Anne (eds) (1992) *Destabilizing Theory: Contemporary Feminist Debates*. Cambridge: Polity Press.

Barrington, Judith (ed.) (1991) *An Intimate Wilderness: Lesbian Writers on Sexuality*. Oregon: Eighth Mountain Press.

Bass, Ellen and Davis, Laura (1988) *The Courage to Heal: A Guide for Women Survivors of Child Sexual Abuse*. London: Cedar.

Bass, Ellen and Thornton, Louise (eds) (1983) *I Never Told Anyone: Writings by Women Survivors of Child Sexual Abuse*. London: Harper & Row.

Bayer, Ronald (1987) *Homosexuality and American Psychiatry: The Politics of Diagnosis – With a New Afterword on AIDS and Homosexuality*. Surrey: Princeton University Press.

Bechtel, Stefan (1993) *The Sex Encyclopedia: An A to Z Guide to the Latest Information on Sexual Health, Safety, and Technique from the Nation's Top Sex Experts*. London: Fireside/Simon & Schuster.

Becker, Carol S. (1988) *Unbroken Ties: Lesbian Ex-Lovers*. Boston: Alyson Publications.

Becker, Judith V., Skinner, Linda J., Abel, Gene G., Axelrod, Roz and Cichon, Joan (1984) 'Sexual problems of sexual assault survivors', *Women & Health*, vol. 9(4), winter, pp. 5–20.

Bell, Alan P. and Weinberg, Martin S. (1978) *Homosexualities: A Study of Diversity Among Men and Women*. London: Mitchell Beazley.

Bem, Sandra Lipsitz (1993) *The Lenses of Gender: Transforming the Debate on Sexual Inequality*. London: Yale University.

Berzon, Betty (1988) *Permanent Partners: Building Gay and Lesbian Relationships That Last*. New York: E.P. Dutton.

Billings, Dwight B. and Urban, Thomas (1982) 'The socio-medical construction of transsexualism: An interpretation and critique', *Social Problems*, vol. 29, no. 3, February, pp. 226–78.

Blackman, Inge, and Perry, Kathryn (1990) 'Skirting the issue: Lesbian fashion for the 1990s', *Feminist Review*, 34, Spring, pp. 67–78.

Blackman, Inge (1995) 'White girls are easy, black girls are studs', in Lynne Pearce and Jackie Stacey (eds) *Romance Revisited*. London: Lawrence & Wishart.

Blackwood, Evelyn (1984) 'Sexuality and gender in certain Native American tribes: The case of cross-gender females', *Signs: Journal of Women in Culture and Society*, vol. 10, no. 1, pp. 27–42.

Blank, Joani (1989) *Good Vibrations: The Complete Guide to Vibrators*. Burlingame, CA: Down There Press.

Blumstein, P. and Schwartz, P. (1983) *American Couples*. New York: William Morrow.

Boffin, Tessa and Gupta, Sunil (eds) (1990) *Ecstatic Antibodies: Resisting the AIDS Mythology*. London: Rivers Oram Press.

Bornstein, Kate (1994) *Gender Outlaw: On Men, Women and the Rest of Us*. London: Routledge.

Bosche, Susanne (1983) *Jenny Lives with Eric and Martin*. London: Gay Men's Press.

Boston Lesbian Psychologies Collective (ed.) (1987) *Lesbian Psychologies: Explorations and Challenges*. Urbana: University of Illinois Press.

Breakwell, Glynis (1986) *Coping with Threatened Identities*. London: Methuen.

Bressler, Lauren C. and Lavender, Abraham D. (1986), 'Sexual fulfilment of heterosexual, bisexual and homosexual women', in Monika Kehoe (ed.) *Historical, Literary and Erotic Aspects of Lesbianism*. London: Harrington Park Press.

Bright, Susie (1990) *Susie Sexpert's Lesbian Sex World*. San Francisco: Cleis Press.

Bright, Susie (1992) *Susie Bright's Sexual Reality: A Virtual Sex World Reader*. Pittsburgh: Cleis Press.

Bright, Susie and Rednour, Shar (1994) The joys of butch, in L. Burana, Roxxie, And L. Due (eds) *Dagger: On Butch Women*, San Francisco: Cleis Press.

Bristow, Joseph and Wilson, Angelia R. (eds) (1993) *Activating Theory: Lesbian, Gay, Bisexual Politics*. London: Lawrence & Wishart.

Brown, Terry (1994) 'The butch femme fatale', in Laura Doan (ed.) *The Lesbian Postmodern*. New York: Columbia University Press.

Brown, Laura S. (1986) 'Confronting internalized oppression in sex therapy with lesbians', *Journal of Homosexuality*, vol. 12, pp. 99–107.

Brown, Katie, 'Lesbian porn: Friend or foe?', *Deneuve*, vol. 4, no. 4, August 1994, pp. 36–9.

Brunt, Rosalind and Rowan, Caroline (eds) (1982) *Feminism, Culture and Politics*. London: Lawrence and Wishart.

Bullough, Vern L. and Bullough, Bonnie (1993) *Cross Dressing, Sex, and Gender*. Philadelphia: University of Pennsylvania Press.

Burana, Lily, Roxxie and Due, Linnea (eds) (1994) *Dagger: on Butch Women*. San Francisco: Cleis Press.

Burch, Beverly (1993) *On Intimate Terms: The Psychology of Difference in Lesbian Relationships*. Chicago: University of Illinois Press.

Burch, Beverly (1987) 'Barriers to intimacy: Conflicts over power, dependency, and nurturing in lesbian relationships', in Boston Lesbian Psychologies Collective (ed.), *Lesbian Psychologies: Explorations and Challenges*. Urbana: University of Illinois Press.

Burman, Erica and Parker, Ian (eds) (1993) *Discourse Analytic Research: Repertoires and Readings of Texts in Action*. London: Routledge.

Butler, Sandra and Rosenblum, Barbara (1991) *Cancer in Two Voices*. San Francisco: Spinsters Book Company.

Butler, Judith (1990) *Gender Trouble: Feminism and the Subversion of Identity*. London: Routledge.

Califia, Pat (1988) *Sapphistry: The Book of Lesbian Sexuality*. Florida: Naiad Press.

Califia, Pat (1988) *Macho Sluts*. Boston: Alyson Publications.

Califia, Pat (1988) *The Lesbian S/M Safety Manual*. Boston: Alyson Publications.

Califia, Pat (1992) 'Diagnostic tests', in J. Nestle (ed.) *The Persistent Desire: A Femme-Butch Reader*. Boston: Alyson Publications.

Califia, Pat (1993) *Sensuous Magic: A Guide for Adventuring Adults*. New York: Masquerade Books.

Califia, Pat (1994) *Public Sex: The Culture of Radical Sex*. San Francisco: Cleis Press.

Campbell, Beatrix (1987) 'A feminist sexual politics: Now you see it, now you don't' in Feminist Review (eds), *Sexuality: A Reader*. London: Virago.

Campbell, Beatrix (1988) *Unofficial Secrets: Child Sexual Abuse – The Cleveland Case*. London: Virago Press.

Caplan, Pat (ed.) (1987) *The Cultural Construction of Sexuality*. London: Routledge.

Carter, Erica and Watney, Simon (eds) (1989) *Taking Liberties: AIDS and Cultural Politics*. London: Serpent's Tail.

Cartledge, Sue and Ryan, Joanna (eds) (1983) *Sex and Love: New Thoughts on Old Contradictions*. London: Women's Press,

Case, Sue-Ellen (1988–9) 'Towards a butch-femme aesthetic', *Discourse* 11.1, Fall–Winter, pp. 55–73.

Caster, Wendy (1993) *The Lesbian Sex Book*. Boston: Alyson Publications.

Cavin, Susan (1985) *Lesbian Origins*. San Francisco: ISM Press.

Charles, Helen (1995) '(Not) compromising: Inter skin colour relations', in L. Pearce and J. Stacey (eds) *Romance Revisited*. London: Lawrence and Wishart.

Chu, Susan Y., Conti, Lisa, Schable, Barbara A. and Diaz, Theresa (1994) 'Female-to-female sexual contact and HIV transmission', *JAMA*, vol. 2/2, no. 6, 10 August, p. 433.

Chu, Susan Y., Buehler, James W., Fleming, Patricia L, and Berkelman, Ruth L. (1990) 'Epidemiology of reported cases of AIDS in lesbians, United States 1980–1989', *American Journal of Public Health*, vol. 80, no. 11, November, pp. 1380–81.

Clunis, D. Merilee and Green, G. Dorsey (1988) *Lesbian Couples*. Seattle: Seal Press.

Cochran, Jo Whitehorse (1989) 'Guaranteed a story', in Tee Corrinne (ed.), *Intricate Passions*. Austin: Banned Books.

Cole, Ellen and Rothblum, Esther D. (eds) (1988) *Women and Sex Therapy: Closing the Circle of Sexual Knowledge*. London: Harrington Park Press.

Cole, Rebecca and Cooper, Sally (1990–91) 'Lesbian exclusion from HIV/AIDS education: Ten years of low-risk identity and high-risk behaviour', *SIECUS Report*, December/January, pp. 18–23.

Coleman, Eli (ed.) (1988) *Integrated Identity for Gay men and Lesbians: Psychotherapeutic Approaches for Emotional Well-Being*. London: Harrington Park Press.

Colvin, Madeleine (1989) *Section 28: A Practical Guide to the Law and its Implications*. London: National Council for Civil Liberties.

Connell, R. W. (1987) *Gender and Power*. Cambridge: Polity Press.

Connell, R. W. and Dowsett G. W. (eds) (1992) *Rethinking Sex: Social Theory and Sexuality Research*. Melbourne: Melbourne University Press.

Cook, Blanche Wiesen (1979) "Women alone stir my imagination": Lesbianism and the cultural tradition', *Signs: Journal of Women in Culture and Society*, vol. 4, no. 4, pp. 718–39.

Cooper, Davina (1994) *Sexing the City: Lesbian and Gay Politics within the Activist State*. London: Rivers Oram Press.

Cooper, Davina (1989) 'Positive images in Haringey: A struggle for identity', in Carol Jones and Pat Mahoney (eds) *Learning Our Lines: Sexuality and Control in Education*. London: Women's Press.

Corrine, Tee (ed.) (1989) *Intricate Passions*. Austin: Banned Books.

Cossey, Caroline (1991) *My Story*. London: Faber and Faber.

Coveney, L., Jackson, M.,, Jeffreys, S., Kaye, L. and Mahony, P. (1984) *The Sexuality Papers: Male Sexuality and the Social Control of Women*. London: Hutchinson.

Coward, Rosalind (1984) *Female Desire: Women's Sexuality Today*. London: Paladin Books.

Cruikshank, Margaret (1982) *Lesbian Studies: Present and Future*. New York: The Feminist Press.

Cruikshank, Margaret (1992) *The Gay and Lesbian Liberation Movement*. London: Routledge.

D'Emilio, John (1992) *Making Trouble: Essays on Gay History, Politics, and the University*. London: Routledge.

Dailey, Dennis M., 'Adjustment of heterosexual and homosexual couples in pairing relationships: An exploratory study' (1979), *Journal of Sex Research*, vol. 15, no. 2, May, pp. 143–57.

Dancey, C.P., 'Sexual orientation in women: An investigation of hormonal and personality variables'. (1990) *Biological Psychology*, 30, pp. 251–64.

Davidson, Julia O'Connell and Layder, Derek (1994) *Methods, Sex and Madness*. London: Routledge.

Davies, P.M., Hickson, F.C.I., Weatherburn, P. and Hunt, A.J. (1993) *Sex, Gay Men and AIDS: Social Aspects of AIDS*. London: The Falmer Press.

Davis, Laura (1991) *Allies in Healing: When the Person You Love Was Sexually Abused as a Child*. New York: Harper Perennial.

Davis, Madeline, Hollibaugh, Amber and Nestle, Joan (1992) 'The femme tapes, in J. Nestle (ed) *The Persistent Desire: A Femme-Butch Reader*. Boston: Alyson Publications.

Devor, Holly (1989) *Gender Blending: Confronting the Limits of Duality*. Bloomington: Indiana University Press.

Diamond, Deborah L. and Wilsnack, Sharon C. (1978) 'Alcohol abuse among lesbians: A descriptive study', *Journal of Homosexuality*, vol. 4 (2), winter, pp. 123–42.

Doan, Laura (ed.) (1994) *The Lesbian Postmodern*. New York: Columbia University Press.

Doughlas, Carol Anne (1990) *Love and Politics: Radical Feminist and Lesbian Theories*. San Francisco: ISM Press.

Downey, Jennifer, Ehrhard, Anke A., Schiffman, Mindy Dyrenfurth, Inge and Becker, J. (1987) 'Sex hormones in lesbian and heterosexual women', *Hormones and Behavior*, 21, pp. 347–57.

Durham, Martin (1991) *Sex and Politics: The Family and Morality in the Thatcher Years*. London: Macmillan.

Echols, Alice (1984) 'The new feminism of yin and yang', in Ann Barr Snitow *et al.*, *Desire: The Politics of Sexuality*. London: Virago.

Edwards, Tim (1994) *Erotics & Politics: Gay Male Sexuality, Masculinity and Feminism*, London: Routledge.

Edwards, Anne (1990) 'Sexually transmitted diseases in lesbians'. *International Journal of STD and AIDS*, 1, pp. 178–81.

Ehrhardt, Anke A., Epstein, Ralph and Money, John, (1968) 'Fetal androgens and female gender identity in the early-treated adrenogenital syndrome'. *John Hopkins Medical Journal*, 122. pp. 160–67.

Einsiedel, Edne F. (1992) 'The experimental research evidence: Effects of pornography on the "average individual" ', in Catherine Itzin (ed.) *Pornography: Women, Violence and Civil Liberties*. Oxford: Oxford University Press.

English, Deirdre, Hollibaugh, Amber and Rubin, Gayle (1987) 'Talking sex: A conversation in sexuality and feminism', in Feminist Review (eds) *Sexuality: A Reader*. London: Virago.

Ettore, E. M. (1980) *Lesbians, Women and Society*. London: Routledge & Kegan Paul.

Evans, David T. (1993) *Sexual Citizenship: Material Construction of Sexualities*. London: Routledge.

Evans, David T. (1993) 'Trans-citizenship: Transvestism and transsexualism', in David T. Evans, *Sexual Citizenship: Material Construction of Sexualities*. London: Routledge.

Ewles, Linda and Simnett, Ina (1985) *Promoting Health: A Practical Guide to Health Education*. Chichester: John Wiley & Sons.

Faderman, Lillian (1985) *Surpassing the Love of Men: Romantic Friendship and Love Between Women from the Renaissance to the Present*. London: Women's Press.

Faderman, Lillian (1992) *Odd Girls and Twilight Lovers: A History of Lesbian Life in Twentieth-Century America*. London: Penguin Books.

Faderman, Lillian (1993) 'The return of butch and femme: A phenomenon in lesbian sexuality of the 1980s and 1990s', in John C. Fout and Maura Shaw Tantillo (eds), *American Sexual Politics: Sex, Gender, and Race Since the Civil War*. London: University of Chicago Press.

Fausto-Sterling, Anne (1985) *Myths of Gender: Biological Theories About Women and Men*. New York: Basic Books.

Feinberg, Leslie (1993) *Stone Butch Blues*. New York: Firebrand Books.

Ferguson, Ann (1989) *Blood at the Root: Motherhood, Sexuality and Male Dominance*. London: Pandora Press.

Fernbach, David (1993) 'Tight and tighter genes?: Some mothers do 'ave em', IQ Magazine, vol. 2, issue 2, August/September, p. 11.

Fifield, Lillene H., Latham, J. David and Phillips, Christopher (1977) *Alcoholism in the Gay Community: The Pace of Alienation, Isolation and Oppression*. Los Angeles: A Project of The Gay Community Services Centre.

Fleming, Lee (1989) *By Word of Mouth: Lesbians Write the Erotic*. Charlottetown: Gynergy Books.

Foucault, Michel (1978) *The History of Sexuality: An Introduction*. London: Penguin Books.

Fout, John C. and Tantillo, Maura Shaw (eds) (1993) *American Sexual Politics: Sex, Gender, and Race Since the Civil War*. London: University of Chicago Press.

Freud, Sigmund (1957) 'The psychogenesis of a case of homosexuality in a woman (1920)', in J. D. Sutherland (ed.), *Sigmund Freud: Collected Papers: Volume II*. London: Hogarth Press and Institute of Psycho-Analysis.

Friday, Nancy (1973) *My Secret Garden*. London: Arrow Books.

Frye, Marilyn (1990) 'Lesbian "sex" ', in Jeffner Allen (ed.), *Lesbian Philosophies and Cultures*. New York: State University of New York Press.

Fuss, Diana (ed.) (1991) *Inside/Out: Lesbian Theories, Gay Theories*. London: Routledge.

Fuss, Diana (1993) 'Freud's fallen women: identification, desire, and "a case for homosexuality in a woman" ', in Michael Warner (ed.) *Fear of a Queer Planet: Queer Politics and Social Theory*. London: University of Minnesota Press.

Gagnon, J. H. and Simon, William (1973) *Sexual Conduct: The Social Sources of Human Sexuality*. London: Hutchinson & Co.

Gamman, Lorraine and Makinen, Merja (1994) *Female Fetishism: A New Look*. London: Lawrence & Wishart.

Garber, Marjorie (1992) *Vested Interests: Cross-Dressing and Cultural Anxiety*. London: Penguin Books.

Gartrell, Nanette K., Loriaux, D. Lynn and Chase, Thomas N., (1977) 'Plasma testosterone in homosexual and heterosexual women', *American Journal of Psychiatry*, vol. 134 (10), October, pp. 1117–18.

Gay, George R., Newmeyer, John A., Perry, Michael, Johnson, Gregory and Kurland Mark, 'Love and haight: The sensuous hippie revisited. Drug/sex practices in San Francisco, 1980– 81' (1982) *Journal of Psychoactive Drugs*, vol. 4 (1–2), Jan–June, pp. 111–23.

Gay Left Collective (1980) *Homosexuality: Power and Politics*. London: Allison & Busby.

George, Sue (1993) *Women and Bisexuality*. London: Scarlet Press.

Gibson, Pamela Church and Gibson, Roma (1993) *Dirty Looks: Women, Pornography, Power*. London: BFI Publishing.

Giddens, Anthony (1992) *The Transformation of Intimacy: Sexuality, Love and Eroticism in Modern Societies*. Cambridge: Polity Press.

Gilbert, Nigel (ed.) (1993) *Researching Social Life*. London: SAGE Publications.

Gomez, Jewelle (1989) 'White Flowers', in Sheba Collective (ed.), *Serious Pleasure: Lesbian Erotic Stories and Poetry*. London: Sheba Feminist Publishers.

Gonsiorek, John C. and Weinrich, James D. (1991) *Homosexuality: Research Implications for Public Policy*. Newbury Park, CA.: SAGE Publications.

Gonsiorek, John C. and Weinrich, James D. (1991) 'The definition and scope of sexual orientation', in Gonsiorek, John C. and Weinrich, James D. *Homosexuality: Research Implications for Public Policy*. Newbury Park, CA.: SAGE Publications.

Grace, Della (1991) *Love Bites*. London: GMP.

Grahn, Judy (1984) *Another Mother Tongue: Gay Words, Gay Worlds*. Boston: Beacon Press.

Greene, Beverly and Herek, Gregory M. (eds) (1994) *Lesbian and Gay Psychology: Theory, Research and Clinical Applications*. London: SAGE Publications.

Grey, Antony (1993) *Speaking of Sex*. London: Cassell.

Griffin, Gabriele (1993) *Heavenly Love?: Lesbian Images in Twentieth-Century Women's Writing*. Manchester: Manchester University Press.

Griffin, Gabriele (ed.) (1993) *Outwrite: Lesbian and Popular Culture*. Colorado: Pluto Press.

Griffin, Susan (1982) *Made From This Earth: Selections From Her Writing*. London: Women's Press.

Halberstam, Judith (1994) 'F2M: The making of female masculinity', in Laura Doan (ed.) *The Lesbian Postmodern*. New York: Columbia University Press.

Hall, Marny, 'Sex therapy with lesbian couples: A four stage approach', in Eli Coleman (ed.), *Integrated Identity for Gay Men and Lesbians: Psychotherapeutic Approaches for Emotional Well-Being*. London: Harrington Park Press.

Hall Carpenter Archives (1989) *Inventing Ourselves: Lesbian Life Stories*. London: Routledge.

Halliday, Caroline (1990) ' "The Naked Majesty of God": Contemporary Lesbian Erotic Poetry', in Mark Lilly (ed.), *Lesbian and Gay Writing: An Anthology of Critical Essays*. London: Macmillan.

Hamer, Dean and Copeland, Peter (1994) *The Science of Desire: The Search for the Gay Gene and the Biology of Behaviour*. London: Simon & Schuster.

Hamer, Diane and Budge, Belinda (1994) *The Good, the Bad and the Gorgeous: Popular Culture's Romance with Lesbianism*. London: Pandora.

Hamer, Diane (1990), ' "I am a woman": Ann Bannon and the writing of lesbian identity in the 1950s', in Mark Lilly (ed.), *Lesbian and Gay Writing: An Anthology of Critical Essays*. London: Macmillan.

Hare-Mustin, Rachel T. and Marecek, Jeanne (eds) (1990) *Making a Difference: Psychology and the Construction of Gender.* London: Yale University Press.

Harron, Mary (1995) 'A Hero For Our Times', *Independent Sunday Review*: 29 January.

Harwood, Victoria, Oswell, David, Parkinson, Kay and Ward, Anna (eds) (1993) *Pleasure Principles: Politics, Sexuality and Ethics.* London: Lawrence & Wishart.

Haste, Cate (1992) *Rules of Desire: Sex in Britain: World War I to the Present.* London; Pimlico.

Healey, Emma and Mason, Angela (1994) *Stonewall 25: The Making of the Lesbian and Gay Community in Britain.* London: Virago Press.

Heilbrun, Alfred B. and Thompson, Norman L. (1977) 'Sex-role identity and male and female homosexuality', *Sex Roles*, vol. 3, no. 1, pp. 65–79.

Heiman, Julia R. (1975), 'Women's sexual arousal: The physiology of erotica', *Psychology Today*, April, pp. 91–4.

Henderson, Lisa (1992) 'Lesbian pornography: Cultural transgression and sexual demystification', in Sally Munt, *New Lesbian Criticism: Literary and Cultural Readings.* New York: Harvester Wheatsheaf.

Hepburn, Cuca (1988) *Alive and Well.* Freedom, CA.: Crossing Press.

Herek, Gregory M. (1991) 'Stigma, prejudice and violence against lesbians and gay men', in John C. Gonsiorek and James D. Weinrich, *Homosexuality: Research Implications for Public Policy.* Newbury Park, CA.: SAGE Publications.

Herek, Gregory M., Kimmel, Douglas C., Amaro, Hortensia and Melton, Gary B. (1991) 'Avoiding heterosexist bias in psychological research', *American Psychologist*, vol. 46, no. 9, September, pp. 957–63.

Herman, Judith Lewis (1992) *Trauma and Recovery: From Domestic Abuse to Political Terror.* London: Pandora.

Hinds, Hilary (1992) 'Oranges are not the only fruit: Reaching audiences other lesbian texts cannot reach', in Sally Munt, *New Lesbian Criticism: Literary and Cultural Readings.* New York: Harvester Wheatsheaf.

Hite, Shere (1991) *The Hite Report on Love, Passion and Emotional Violence.* London: Macdonald Optima.

Hite, Shere (1993) *Women as Revolutionary Agents of Change: The Hite Reports 1972–1993.* London: Bloomsbury.

Hoagland, Sarah Lucia (1988) *Lesbian Ethics: Toward New Value.* Palo Aito, CA: Institute of Lesbian Studies.

Hollibaugh, Amber and Moraga, Cherrie (1992) 'What we're rollin' around in bed with: Sexual silences in feminism: A conversation toward ending them', in J. Nestle (ed.) *The Persistent Desire: A Femme-Butch Reader*. Boston, Alyson.

hooks, bell (1991) *Yearning: Race, Gender, and Cultural Politics*. London: Turnaround.

hooks, bell (1992) *Black Looks: Race and Representation*. Boston: South End Press.

hooks, bell (1994) *Outlaw Culture: Resisting Representations*. London: Routledge.

Irvine, Janice M. (1990) *Disorders of Desire: Sex and Gender in Modern American Sexology*. Philadelphia: Temple University Press.

Irvine, Janice M. (1993) 'Regulated passion: The invention of inhibited sexual desire and sex addiction', in Anne McClintock (ed), *Social Text 37*. Durham, NC: Duke University Press.

Itzin, Catherine (ed.) (1992) *Pornography: Women, Violence and Civil Liberties*. Oxford: Oxford University Press.

Itzin, Catherine (1992) 'Legislating against pornography without censorship', in Catherine Itzin (ed.), *Pornography: Women, Violence and Civil Liberties*. Oxford: Oxford University Press.

Jackson, Stevi (1982) *Childhood and Sexuality: Understanding Everyday Experience*. Oxford: Basil Blackwell.

Jagose, Annamarie (1994) *Lesbian Utopics*. London: Routledge.

Jeffrey-Poulter, Stephen (1991) *Peers, Queers and Commons: The Struggle for Gay Law Reform from 1950 to the Present*. London: Routledge.

Jeffreys, Sheila (1989) 'Butch and femme: Now and then', in Lesbian History Group, *Not a Passing Phase: Reclaiming Lesbians in History 1840–1985*. London: Women's Press.

Jeffreys, Sheila (1989) 'Does it matter if they did it', in Lesbian History Group, *Not a Passing Phase: Reclaiming Lesbians in History 1840–1985*. London: Women's Press.

Jeffreys, Sheila (1990) *Anticlimax: A Feminist Perspective on the Sexual Revolution*. London: Women's Press.

Jeffreys, Sheila (1993) *The Lesbian Heresy: A Feminist Perspective on the Lesbian Sexual Revolution*. London: Women's Press.

Jones, Carol and Mahony, Pat (eds) (1989) *Learning Our Lines: Sexuality and Social Control in Education*. London: Women's Press.

Julien, Robert M. (1985) *A Primer of Drug Action*. New York: W.H. Freeman & Co.

Kaminer, Wendy (1993) *I'm Dysfunctional, You're Dysfunctional*. New York: Vintage Books.

Kasl, Charlotte D. (1989) *Women, Sex and Addiction: A Search for Love and Power*. London: Mandarin.

Kasl, Charlotte D. (1992) *Many Roads, One Journey: Moving Beyond the Twelve Steps*. New York: HarperPerennial.

Kassoff, Elizabeth (1989) 'Nonmonogamy in the lesbian community', in Esther D. Rothblum and Ellen Cole (eds), *Loving Boldly: Issues Facing Lesbians*. London: Harrington Park Press.

Katz, Johnathan Ned (1992) *Gay American History: Lesbians and Gay Men in the U.S.A.: a Documentary History*. Middlesex: Penguin Books.

Kaufman, Tara and Lincoln, Paul (1991) *High Risk Lives: Lesbian and Gay Politics After the Clause*. Dorset: Prism Press.

Kehoe, Monika (ed.) (1986) *Historical, Literary, and Erotic Aspects of Lesbianism*. London: Harrington Park Press.

Keith, Lois (ed.) (1994) *Mustn't Grumble*. London: Women's Press.

Kennedy, Elizabeth Lapovsky and Davis, Madeline D. (1994) *Boots of Leather, Slippers of Gold: The History of a Lesbian Community*. London: Penguin Books.

Kessler, Suzanne J. and McKenna, Wendy (1978) *Gender: An Ethnomethodological Approach*. London: University of Chicago Press.

King, Mary-Claire, 'Sexual orientation and the X' (1993) *Nature*, vol. 364, 22 July, pp. 288–289.

Kinsey, Alfred C., Pomeroy, Wardell B. and Martin, Clyde E. (1948) *Sexual Behaviour in the Human Male*; Philadelphia: W.B. Saunders Co.

Kinsey, Alfred C., Pomeroy, Wardell B, Martin, Clyde E. and Gebhard, Paul H. (1953) *Sexual Behaviour in the Human Female*. London: W.B. Saunders Company.

Kiss and Tell (1994) *Her Tongue on My Theory: Images, Essays and Fantasies*. Vancouver: Press Gang Publishers.

Kitzinger, Celia (1987) *The Social Construction of Lesbianism*. London: SAGE Publications.

Kitzinger, Celia (1989) 'The discursive construction of identities: Liberal humanism as an ideology of social control: The regulation of lesbian identities', in John Shotter and Kenneth J. Gergen (eds), *Texts of Identity*. London: Sage Publications.

Kitzinger, Jenny and Kitzinger, Celia (1993) ' "Doing it": Representations of lesbian sex', in Gabriele Griffin (ed.) *Outwrite: Lesbian and Popular Culture*. Colorado: Pluto Press.

Kitzinger, Celia and Perkins, Rachel (1993) *Changing Our Minds: Lesbian Feminism and Psychology*. London: Onlywomen Press.

Kominars, Sheppard B. (1989) *Accepting Ourselves: The Twelve-Step Journey of Recovery from Addiction for Gay Men and Lesbians*. London: Harper & Row.

Krestan, Jo-Ann, Bepko, Claudia S. (1980) 'The problem of fusion in the lesbian relationship', *Family Process*, vol. 19, September, pp. 277–89.

Kus, Robert J. (ed.) (1990) *Keys to Caring; Assisting Your Gay and Lesbian Clients*. Boston: Alyson Publications.

Laner, Mary Riege and Laner, Roy H. (1980) 'Sexual preference or personal style? Why lesbians are disliked', *Journal of Homosexuality*, vol. 5 (4), summer, pp. 339–54.

Langford, Wendy (1995) 'Snuglet Puglet loves to snuggle with Snuglet Piglet': Alter personalities in heterosexual love relationships', in Lynne Pearce and Jackie Stacey (eds.) *Romance Revisited*. London: Lawrence & Wishart.

Laumann, Edward O. and Gagnon, John H. (1995) 'A sociological perspective on sexual action', in Richard G. Parker and John H. Gagnon (eds) *Conceiving Sexuality: Approaches to Sex Research in the Postmodern World*. New York: Routledge.

Laumann, Edward O., Gagnon, John H., Michael, Robert T and Michaels, Stuart (1994) *The Social Organisation of Sexuality: Sexual Practices in the United States*. London: University of Chicago Press.

Lauretis, Teresa de (1994) *The Practice of Love: Lesbian Sexuality and Perverse Desire*. Bloomington: Indiana University Press.

Leonard, Zoe 'Lesbians and the AIDS crisis', in ACT UP/NY Women & AIDS Book Group, *Women, AIDS, and Activism*. Boston: South End Press.

Lerner, Harriet Goldhor (1989) *The Dance of Intimacy: A Woman's Guide to Courageous Acts of Change in Key Relationships*. London: Pandora Press.

Lesbian History Group (1989) *Not a Passing Phase: Reclaiming Lesbians in History 1840–1985*. London: Women's Press.

Lesbian London (1992) 'Life and loves of a London lesbian: Survey results', pts 1 and 2, *Lesbian London*, issue 9, September, pp. 4–5; issue 10, September/October, pp. 4–6.

Le Vay, Simon (1993) *The Sexual Brain*. London: MIT Press.

Lewis, Reina (1994) 'Dis-Graceful images: Della Grace and lesbian sado-masochism', *Feminist Review*, no. 46, spring, pp. 76–91.

Lilly, Mark (ed.) (1990) *Lesbian and Gay Writing: An Anthology of Critical Essays*. London: Macmillan.

Linden, Robin Ruth, Pagano, Darlene R., Russel, Diana E and Star, Susan Leigh (1982) *Against Sadomasochism: A Radical Feminist Analysis*. San Francisco: Frog In The Well.

Lobel, Kerry (ed.) (1986) *Naming the Violence: Speaking Out About Lesbian Battering*. Seattle: Seal Press.

Loftus, Elizabeth F. (1993) 'The reality of repressed memories', *American Psychologist*, vol. 48, no. 5, pp. 518–37.

Lorde, Audre (1980) *The Cancer Journals*. London: Sheba Feminist Publishers.

Lorde, Audre (1982) *Zami: A New Spelling of My Name*. London: Sheba Feminist Publishers.

Lorde, Audre (1984) *Sister Outsider: Essays and Speeches by Audre Lorde*. Freedom, CA.: The Crossing Press.

Lorde, Audre (1984) 'The transformation of silence into language and action', in Audre Lorde, *Sister Outsider: Essays and Speeches by Audre Lorde*. Freedom, CA.: The Crossing Press.

Lorde, Audre (1991) 'Uses of the erotic: The erotic as power', in Judith Barrington (ed.), *An Intimate Wilderness: Lesbian Writers on Sexuality*. Oregon: Eighth Mountain Press.

Loulan, JoAnn (1984) *Lesbian Sex*. San Francisco: Spinsters/Aunt Lute.

Loulan, JoAnn (1987) *Lesbian Passion: Loving Ourselves and Each Other*. San Francisco: Spinsters/Aunt Lute.

Loulan, JoAnn (1988) 'Research on the practices of 1566 lesbians and the clinical applications', in Ellen Cole and Esther D. Rothblum (eds), *Women and Sex Therapy: Closing the Circle of Sexual Knowledge*. London: Harrington Park Press.

Loulan, JoAnn (1990) *The Lesbian Erotic Dance: Butch Femme Androgyny and Other Rhythms*. San Francisco: Spinsters.

Lucy, Juicy (1987) 'If I ask you to tie me up, will you still want to love me?' in Samois (ed), *Coming to Power: Writings and Graphics on Lesbian S/M*. Boston: Alyson Publications.

Luczak, Raymond (ed.) (1993) *Eyes of Desire: A Deaf Gay and Lesbian Reader*. Boston: Alyson Publications.

Lynch, Jean M. and Reilly, Mary Ellen (1985–6) 'Role relationships: Lesbian perspectives', *Journal of Homosexuality*, vol. 12 (2), winter, pp. 53–69.

Lynch, Lee (1985) *The Swashbuckler*. Tallahassee, Fla.: Naiad Press.

Maddox, John, 'Wilful public misunderstanding of genetics' (1993) *Nature*, vol. 364, 22 July, p. 281.

Marmor, Judd (ed.) (1980) *Homosexual Behaviour: A Modern Reappraisal*. New York: Basic Books.

Marmor, Michael, Weiss, Lee R., Lyden, Margaret, Weiss, Stanley H., Saxinger, W. Carl, Spira, Thomas J. and Feorino, Paul M. (1986) 'Possible female-to-female transmission of human immunodeficiency virus', *Annals of Internal Medicine*, vol. 105, no. 6, December, p. 969.

Martin, Biddy (1992) 'Sexual practice and changing lesbian identities', in Michele Barrett and Anne Phillips (eds), *Destabilizing Theory: Contemporary Feminist Debates*. Cambridge: Polity Press.

Masica, Daniel N., Money, John and Ehrhardt, Anke A. (1971) 'Fetal feminization and female gender identity in the testicular feminizing syndrome of androgen insensitivity', *Archives of Sexual Behaviour*, vol. 1, no. 2, pp. 131–42.

Mason-John, Valerie and Khambatta, Ann (1993) *Lesbians Talk Making Black Waves*. London: Scarlet Press.

Mason-John, Valerie (ed.) (1995) *Talking Black: African and Asian Lesbians Speak Out*. London: Cassell.

Mass, Lawrence D. (1990) *Homosexuality and Sexuality: Dialogues of the Revolution: Volume 1*. London: Harrington Park Press.

Masters, William H., Johnson, Virginia E. and Kolodny, Robert C. (1986) *Masters and Johnson on Sex and Human Loving*. London: Macmillan London.

McEwen, Christian and O'Sullivan, Sue (eds) (1988) *Out the Other Side: Contemporary Lesbian Writing*. London: Virago Press.

McCauley, Elizabeth A. and Ehrhardt, Anke A, 'Role expectationis and definitions: A comparison of female transexuals and lesbians', *Journal of Homosexuality*, vol. 3, no. 2, winter 1977, pp. 137–47.

McClintock, Anne (ed.) (1993) *Social Text 37*. Durham, NC: Duke University Press.

McIntosh, Mary (1981) 'The homosexual role', in Kenneth Plummer (ed.), *The Making of the Modern Homosexual*. London: Hutchinson.

McIntosh, Mary (1993) 'Queer theory and the war of the sexes', in Joseph Bristow and Angela R. Wilson (eds), *Activating Theory: Lesbian, Gay, Bisexual Politics*. London: Lawrence & Wishart.

Mellody, Pia (1989) *Facing Codependence: What It Is, Where It Comes From, How It Sabotages Our Lives*. London: Harper & Row.

Mellody, Pia (1992) *Facing Love Addiction: Giving Yourself the Power to Change the Way You Love – The Love Connection to Codependence*. New York: HarperCollins Publishers.

Meyer, Moe (ed.) (1994) *The Politics and Poetics of Camp*. London: Routledge.

Michael, Robert T., Gagnon, John H., Laumann, Edward O. and Kolata, Gina (1994) *Sex in America: A Definitive Survey*. London: Little, Brown & Co.

Miller, Alice (1985) *Thou Shalt Not Be Aware: Society's Betrayal of the Child*. London: Pluto Press.

Miller, Neil (1995) *Out of the Past: Gay and Lesbian History From 1869 to the Present*. London: Vintage.

Millett, Kate (1977) *Sexual Politics*. London: Virago Press.

Mills, Jane (1991) *Womanwords: A Vocabulary of Culture and Patriarchal Society*. London: Virago Press.

Money, John and Dalery, Jean (1976) 'Iatrogenic homosexuality: Gender identity in seven 46, XX Chromosomal Females with Hyperadrenocortical Hermaphroditism', *Journal of Homosexuality*, vol. 1, no. 4, summer, pp. 357–71.

Monzon, Ofelia T. and Capellan, Jose M.B. (1987) 'Female-to-female transmission of HIV', *The Lancet*, 4 July, p. 47.

Moorcock, Sophie, 'Context counts' (1994) *Capital Gay*, issue 660, 2 September, p. 4.

Morin, Jack (1986) *Anal Pleasure and Health: A Guide for Men and Women*. San Francisco: Yes Press.

Morris, Jenny (1989) *Able Lives: Women's Experience of Paralysis*. London: Women's Press.

Morris, Jenny (1991) *Pride Against Prejudice: Transforming Attitudes to Disability*. London: Women's Press.

Munt, Sally (1992) *New Lesbian Criticism: Literary and Cultural Readings*. New York: Harvester Wheatsheaf.

Nestle, Joan (1987) *A Restricted Country: Essays and Short Stories*. London: Sheba Feminist Publishers.

Nestle, Joan (1989) 'The Fem Question', in C. Vance (ed.) *Pleasure and Danger: Exploring Female Sexuality*. London: Pandora.

Nestle, Joan (ed.) (1992) *The Persistent Desire: A Femme-Butch Reader*. Boston: Alyson Publications.

Newmeyer, John A., 'The sensuous hippie Part II: Gay/straight differences in regard to drugs and sexuality', *Drug Forum*, vol. 6, no. 1, 1977–78, pp. 49–55.

Newton, Esther (1979) *Mother Camp: Female Impersonators in America*. London: University of Chicago Press.

Newton, Esther (1984) 'The mythic mannish lesbian: Radclyffe Hall and the new woman', *Signs: Journal of Women in Culture and Society*, vol. 9, no. 4, pp. 557–75.

Newton, Esther and Walton, Shirley (1989) 'The Misunderstanding: Toward a more precise sexual vocabulary', in C. Vance (ed.) *Pleasure and Danger: Exploring Female Sexuality*. London: Pandora.

Nichols, Margaret (1987) 'Lesbian sexuality: Issues and developing theory', in Boston Lesbian Psychologies Collective (ed.), *Lesbian Psychologies: Explorations and Challenges*. Urbana: University of Illinois Press.

Nichols, Margaret (1987) 'Doing sex therapy with lesbians: Bending a heterosexual paradigm to fit a gay life-style', in Boston Lesbian Psychologies Collective (ed.), *Lesbian Psychologies: Explorations and Challenges*. Urbana: University of Illinois Press.

Norwood, Robin (1986) *Women Who Love Too Much*. New York: Pocket Books.

O'Connell Davidson, Julia and Layder, Derek (1994) *Methods, Sex and Madness*. London: Routledge.

O'Connor, Noreen and Ryan, Joanna (1993) *Wild Desires and Mistaken Identities: Lesbianism and Psychoanalysis*. London: Virago Press.

O'Sullivan, Sue (1990) 'Mapping: Lesbianism, AIDS and sexuality', *Feminist Review*, 34, spring, pp. 120–32.

O'Sullivan, Sue and Parmar, Pratibha (1992) *Lesbians Talk (Safer) Sex*. London: Scarlet Press.

O'Sullivan, Sue and Thomson, Kate (eds) (1992) *Positively Women: Living With AIDS*. London: Sheba Feminist Press.

Oakley, Ann, 'The facts of homosexual life' (1994) *Independent On Sunday*, 23 January, pp. 8–11.

Ogden, Gina (1990) *Everywoman's Guide to Understanding Sexual Style and Creating Intimacy*. Florida: Health Communications.

Ortner, Sherry B. and Whitehead, Harriet (eds) (1981) *Sexual Meanings: The Cultural Construction of Gender and Sexuality*. Cambridge: Cambridge University Press.

Parker, Richard G. and Gagnon, John H. (eds) (1995) *Conceiving Sexuality: Approaches to Sex Research in a Postmodern World*. London: Routledge.

Patton, Cindy (1985) *Sex and Germs: The Politics of* AIDS. Boston: South End Press.

Patton, Cindy and Kelly, Janis (1990) *Making it: A Woman's Guide to Sex in the Age of* AIDS. New York: Firebrand Books.

Paul, William, Weinrich, James D., Gonsiorek, John C. and Hotvedt, Mary E. (eds) (1982) *Homosexuality: Social, Psychological and Biological Issues*. London: Sage Publications.

Pearce, Lynne and Stacey, Jackie (eds) (1995) *Romance Revisited*. London: Lawrence & Wishart.

Penelope, Julia (1992) *Call Me Lesbian: Lesbian Lives, Lesbian Theory*. Freedom: Crossing Press.

Penelope, Julia (1992) 'Whose past are we reclaiming?', in Julia Penelope, *Call Me Lesbian: Lesbian Lives, Lesbian Theory*. Freedom: Crossing Press.

Peplau, Letitia Anne, 'What homosexuals want' (1981) *Psychology Today*, March, pp. 28–38.

Peplau, Letitia Anne (1991) 'Lesbian and gay relationships', in John C. Gonsiorek and James D. Weinrich, *Homosexuality: Research Implications for Public Policy*. Newbury Park, CA.: SAGE Publications.

Peplau, Letitia Anne and Amaro, Hortensia (1982) 'Understanding lesbian relationships', in Wiliam Paul, James D. Weinrich, John C. Gonsiorek and Mary E. Hotvedt (eds.), *Homosexuality: Social, Psychological, and Biological Issues*. London: Sage Publications.

Peplau, Letitia Anne, Padesky, Christine and Hamilton, Mykol (1982) 'Satisfaction in lesbian relationships', *Journal of Homosexuality*, vol. 8, no. 2, winter, pp. 23–35.

Perry, Kathryn (1995) 'The heart of whiteness: White subjectivity and interracial relationships', in Lynne Pearce and Jackie Stacey (eds.), *Romance Revisited*. London: Lawrence & Wishart.

Person, Ethel Spector, 'Sexuality as the mainstay of identity: Psychoanalytic perspectives', *Journal of Women in Culture and Society*, vol. 5, no. 4, 1980, pp. 605–630.

Pharr, Suzanne (1988) *Homophobia: A Weapon of Sexism*. USA: Chardon Press.

Plummer, Kenneth (ed.) (1981) *The Making of the Modern Homosexual*. London: Hutchinson.

Plummer, Kenneth (ed.) (1992) *Modern Homosexualities: Fragments of Lesbian and Gay Experience*. London: Routledge.

Plummer, Kenneth (1995) *Telling Sexual Stories: Power, Change and Social Worlds*. London: Routledge.

Polhemus, Ted and Housk, Randall (1994) *Rituals of Love: Sexual Experiments, Erotic Possibilities*. London: Picador.

Ponse, Barbara (1978) *Identities in the Lesbian World: The Social Construction of Self*. London: Greenwood Press.

Poppa, Anna (1994) 'Lesbians and HIV', *Body Positive*, no. 167, 5 April, pp. 1–3.

Powell, Vicky (1994) 'Growing pains', *Pink Paper*, issue 346, 23 September, p. 15.

Pringle, Kath, Kaufmann, Tara and Lincoln, Paul 'Clause 28 in practice', in Tara Kaufman and Paul Lincoln, *High Risk Lives: Lesbian and Gay Politics After the Clause*. Dorset: Prism Press.

Project Sigma and *City Limits* (1991) 'The final score', *City Limits*, issue 507, pp. 20–27.

Raiskin, Judith (1994) 'Invert and hybrids: Lesbian rewritings of sexual and racial identities', in Laura Doan (ed.) *The Lesbian Postmodern*. New York: Columbia University Press.

Raiteri, R., Fora, R., Gioannini, P., Lucchini, A., Terzi, M.G., Giacobbi, D. and Sinicco A. (1994) 'Zeroprevalence, risk factors and attitude to HIV-1 in a representative sample of lesbians in Turin', *Genitourinary Medicine*, vol. 70, pp. 200–05.

Raymond, Janice G. (1979) *The Transsexual Empire*. London: Women's Press.

Raymond, Janice G. (1986) *A Passion for Friends: Towards a Philosophy of Female Affection*. London: Women's Press.

Raymond, Janice (1992) 'Pornography and the politics of lesbianism', in Catherine Itzin (ed.), *Pornography: Women, Violence and Civil Liberties*. Oxford: Oxford University Press.

Reilly, Mary Ellen and Lynch, Jean M. (1990) 'Power-sharing in lesbian partnerships', *Journal of Homosexuality*, vol. 19, no. 3, pp. 1–30.

Reinisch, June M. (1990) *The Kinsey Institute New Report on Sex: What You Must Know to be Sexually Literate*. New York: St. Martin's Press.

Renvoize, Jean (1993) *Innocence Destroyed: A Study of Child Sexual Abuse*. London: Routledge.

Renzetti, Claire M. (1988) 'Violence in lesbian relationships: A preliminary analysis of causal factors', *Journal of Interpersonal Violence*, vol. 3, no. 4, December, pp. 381–99.

Reti, Irene (ed.) (1993) *Unleashing Feminism: Critiquing Lesbian Sadomasochism in the Gay Nineties*. Santa Cruz: Herbooks.

Reuben, David (1970) *Everything You Always Wanted to Know About Sex – But Were Afraid to Ask*. London: W.H. Allen.

Reuben, David (1976) *How to Get More Out of Sex: Than You Ever Thought You Could*. London: W.H. Allen & Co.

Rich, Adrienne (1993) 'Compulsory heterosexuality and lesbian existence', in H. Abelove, M.A. Barale and D.M. Halperin (eds) *The Lesbian and Gay Studies Reader*. New York: Routledge.

Richardson, Diane (1989) *Women and the AIDS Crisis*. London: Pandora Press.

Richardson, Diane (1990) *Safer Sex: The Guide for Women Today*. London: Pandora Press.

Richardson, Diane (1992) 'Constructing lesbian sexualities', in Kenneth Plummer (ed.), *Modern Homosexualities: Fragments of Lesbian and Gay Experience*. London: Routledge.

Roelofs, Sarah 'Labour and the national order: Intentionally promoting heterosexuality', in Tara Kaufman and Paul Lincoln *High Risk Lives: Lesbian and Gay Politics After the Clause*. Dorset: Prism Press.

Rofes, Eric E. (1983) *I Thought People Like That Killed Themselves: Lesbians, Gay Men and Suicide*. San Francisco: Grey Fox Press.

Rogers, Lesley and Walsh, Joan (1982) 'Shortcomings of the psychomedical research of John Money and co-workers into sex differences in behaviour: Social and political implications', *Sex Roles*, vol. 8, no. 3, pp. 269–81.

Roof, Judith (1991) *A Lure of Knowledge: Lesbian Sexuality and Theory*. New York: Columbia University Press.

Rose, Suzanna (1994) 'Sexual pride and shame in lesbians', in Beverly Greene and Gregory M. Herek (eds), *Lesbian and Gay Psychology: Theory, Research and Clinical Applications*. London: SAGE Publications.

Rosenzweig, Julie M. and Lebow, Wendy C. (1992) 'Femme on the streets, butch in the sheets? Lesbian sex-roles, dyadic adjustment, and sexual satisfaction', *Journal of Homosexuality*, vol. 23, no. 3, pp. 1–21.

Rothblum, Esther D. and Cole Ellen (eds) (1989) *Loving Boldly: Issues Facing Lesbians*. London: Harrington Park Press.

Rothblum, Esther D. (1994) 'Lesbians and physical appearance: Which model applies?', in Beverly Greene and Gregory M. Herek (eds), *Lesbian and Gay Psychology: Theory, Research and Clinical Applications*. London: SAGE Publications.

Rubin, Gayle (1987) 'The leather menace: Comments on politics and S/M', in Samois (eds), *Coming to Power: Writings and Graphics on Lesbian S/M*. Boston: Alyson Publications.

Rubin, Gayle (1989) 'Thinking sex: Notes for a radical theory of the politics of sexuality', in C. Vance (ed.) *Pleasure and Danger: Exploring Female Sexuality*. London, Pandora.

Rubin, Gayle, 'Of catamites and kings: Reflections on butch, gender and boundaries, in J. Nestle (ed.) *The Persistent Desire: A Femme-butch Reader*. Boston: Alyson Publications.

Ruehl, Sonja (1982) 'Inverts and experts: Radclyffe Hall and the lesbian identity', in Rosalind Brunt and Caroline Rowan (eds), *Feminism, Culture and Politics*. London: Lawrence & Wishart.

Ruehl, Sonja (1983) 'Sexual theory and practice: Another double standard', in Sue Cartledge and Joanna Ryan (eds), *Sex and Love: New Thoughts on Old Contradictions*. London: Women's Press.

Rusbult, Caryl E., Zembrodt, Isabella M. and Iwaniszek, John (1986) 'The impact of gender and sex-role orientation on responses to dissatisfication in close relationships', *Sex Roles*, vol. 15, nos. 1/2, pp. 1–20.

Russell, Diana (1986) *The Secret Trauma*. New York: Basic Books.

Saalfield, Catherine (1994) 'Coming to safer sex', *On Our Backs*, January/February, pp. 20–22, 38–9, 42–3.

Saghir, Marcel T. and Robins, Eli (1980) 'Clinical aspects of female homosexuality', in Judd Marmor (ed.), *Homosexual Behaviour: A Modern Reappraisal*. New York: Basic Books.

Samois (eds) (1987) *Coming to Power: Writings and Graphics on Lesbian S/M*. Boston: Alyson Publications.

Sanders, Sue and Spraggs, Gill (1989) 'Section 28 and education', in Carol Jones and Pat Mahony (eds), *Learning Our Lines: Sexuality and Social Control in Education*. London: Women's Press.

Sanford, Linda T. (1991) *Strong at the Broken Places: Overcoming the Trauma of Childhood Abuse*. London: Virago Press.

Scambler, Graham (ed.) (1991) *Sociology as Applied to Medicine*. London: Baillière Tindall.

Schaef, Anne Wilson (1987) *When Society Becomes an Addict*. Cambridge: Harper & Row.

Schaef, Anne Wilson (1992). *Co-Dependance: Misunderstood – Mistreated*. New York: HarperCollins Publishers.

Schaeffer, Brenda (1987) *Is it Love or is it Addiction?: Falling into Healthy Love*. Cambridge: Harper & Row.

Schor, Naomi and Weed, Elizabeth (1991) *Differences: A Journal of Feminist Cultural Studies: Queer Theory: Lesbian and Gay Sexualities*. Indiana: Indiana University Press.

Schramm-Evans, Zoe (1995) *Making Out: The Book of Lesbian Sex and Sexuality*. London: Pandora.

Schulman, Sarah (1994) *My American History: Lesbian and Gay Life During the Reagan/Bush Years*. London: Cassell.

Sedgwick, Eve Kosofsky (1993) 'How to bring your kids up gay', in Michael Warner (ed.) *Fear of a Queer Planet: Queer Politics and Social Theory*. London: University of Minnesota Press.

Segal, Lynne (1983) 'Sensual uncertainty, or why the clitoris is not enough', in Sue Cartledge and Joanna Ryan (eds), *Sex and Love: New Thoughts on Old Contradictions*. London: Women's Press.

Segal, Lynne (1987) *Is the Future Female?: Troubled Thoughts on Contemporary Feminism*. London: Virago Press.

Segal, Lynne (1990) *Slow Motion: Changing Masculinities, Changing Men*. London: Virago Press.

Segal, Lynne (1993) 'Does pornography cause violence? The search for evidence', in Pamela Church Gibson and Roma Gibson, *Dirty Looks: Women, Pornography, Power*. London: BFI Publishing.

Segal, Lynne (1994) *Straight Sex: The Politics of Pleasure*. London: Virago Press.

Segal, Lynne and McIntosh, Mary (eds) (1992) *Sex Exposed: Sexuality and the Pornography Debate*. London: Virago Press.

Sheba Collective (ed.) (1989) *Serious Pleasure: Lesbian Erotic Stories and Poetry*. London: Sheba Feminist Publishers.

Shotter, John and Gergen, Kenneth J. (eds) (1989) *Texts of Identity*. London: Sage Publications.

Simmonds, Felly Nkweto (1995) 'Love in black and white', in Lynne Pearce and Jackie Stacey (eds), *Romance Revisited*. London: Lawrence & Wishart.

Singer, Bennet L. and Dechamps, David (eds) (1994) *Gay and Lesbian Stats: A Pocket Guide of Facts and Figures*. New York: New Press.

Sisley, Dr. Emily L. and Harris, Bertha (1977) *The Joy of Lesbian Sex: A Tender and Liberated Guide to the Pleasures and Problems of a Lesbian Lifestyle*. New York: Pocket Books.

Smalley, Sondra (1988) 'Dependency issues in lesbian relationships', in Eli Coleman (ed.), *Integrated Identity for Gay Men and Lesbians: Psychotherapeutic Approaches for Emotional Well-Being*. London: Harrington Park Press.

Smith, Anna Marie (1992) 'Resisting the erasure of lesbian sexuality: A challenge for queer activism', in K. Plummer (ed.) *Modern Homosexualities: Fragments of Lesbian and Gay Experience*. London: Routledge.

Smyth, Cherry (1990) 'The pleasure threshold: Looking at lesbian pornography on film', *Feminist Review*, 34, Spring, pp. 152–9.

Smyth, Cherry (1992) *Lesbians Talk Queer Notions*. London: Scarlet Press.

Smyth, Cherry (1994) 'Crime and punishment', in Lily Burana, Roxxie and Linnea Due (eds) *Dagger: On Butch Women*. San Francisco: Cleis Press.

Smyth, Cherry (1995) 'What makes a man', *Attitude*, January, pp. 2–6.

Snitow, Ann Barr (1984) 'Mass market romance: Pornography for women is different', in Ann Barr Snitow et al., *Desire: The Politics of Sexuality*. London: Virago.

Snitow, Ann Barr, *et al.* (1984) *Desire: The Politics of Sexuality*. London: Virago.

Spender, Dale (1985) *Man Made Language*. London: Pandora Press.

Stanley, Liz (ed.) (1990) *Feminist Praxis: Research, Theory and Epistemology in Feminist Sociology*. London: Routledge.

Stein, Arlene (1993) 'Butch-femme and the politics of identity', in Arlene Stein (ed.), *Sisters, Sexperts, Queers: Beyond the Lesbian Nation*. London: Penguin Books.

Stein, Arlene (ed.) (1993) *Sisters, Sexperts, Queers: Beyond the Lesbian Nation*. London: Penguin Books.

Stein, Arlene (1993) 'The year of the lustful lesbian', Arlene Stein (ed.), *Sisters, Sexperts, Queers: Beyond the Lesbian Nation*. London: Penguin Books.

Stein, Edward (ed.) (1992) *Forms of Desire: Sexual Orientation and the Social Constructionist Controversy*. London: Routledge.

Stevens, Patricia E. (1994) 'HIV prevention education for lesbians and bisexual women: A cultural analysis of a community intervention', *Soc. Sci. Med.*, vol. 39, no. 11, p. 1565.

Strega, Linda and Jo, Bev (1986) 'Lesbian sex: Is it?', *Gossip: A Journal of Lesbian Feminist Ethics*, 3, pp. 65–76.

Sutherland, J.D. (ed.) (1957) *Sigmund Freud: Collected Papers: Volume II*. London: Hogarth Press and Institute of Psycho-Analysis.

Tallen, Bette S. (1990) 'Twelve step programs: A lesbian feminist critique', *National Women's Studies Association*, vol. 2, no. 3, summer, pp. 390–407.

Tatchell, Peter (1992) 'Equal rights for all: Strategies for lesbian and gay equality in Britain', in Kenneth Plummer (ed.), *Modern Homosexualities: Fragments of Lesbian and Gay Experience*. London: Routledge.

Taylor, Joelle and Chandler, Tracey (1995) *Lesbians Talk Violent Relationships*. London: Scarlet Press.

Tiefer, Leonore (1995) *Sex is Not a Natural Act and Other Essays*. Oxford: Westview Press.

Tripp, C.A. (1977) *The Homosexual Matrix*. London: Quartet Books.

Ussher, Jane M. and Baker, Christine D. (eds) (1993) *Psychological Perspectives on Sexual Problems: New Directions in Theory and Practice*. London: Routledge.

Uszkurat, Carol Anne (1993) 'Mid twentieth century lesbian romance: Reception and redress', in Gabriele Griffin (ed.) *Outwrite: Lesbian and Popular Culture*. Colorado: Pluto Press.

Vance, Carole (1989) *Pleasure and Danger: Exploring Female Sexuality*. London: Pandora.

Vance, Carole (1992) 'More Danger, More Pleasure: A Decade after the Barnard Sexuality Conference', in C. Vance (ed.) *Pleasure and Danger: Exploring Female Sexuality*. London: Pandora.

Vicinus, Martha (1989) ' "They wonder to which sex I belong": The historical roots of the modern lesbian identity', in Dennis Altman *et al.*, *Homosexuality, Which Homosexuality?: Essays from the International Scientific Conference on Lesbian and Gay Studies*. London: Gay Men's Press.

Warner, Michael (ed.) (1993) *Fear of a Queer Planet: Queer Politics and Social Theory*. London: University of Minnesota Press.

Waterman, Caroline K., Dawson Lori J. and Bologna Michael J. (1989) 'Sexual coercion in gay male and lesbian relationships: Predictors and implications for support services', *Journal of Sex Research*, vol. 26, no. 1, February, pp. 118–24.

Watney, Simon (1980) 'The ideology of GLF' in Gay Left Collective, *Homosexuality: Power and Politics*. London: Allison & Busby.

Watney, Simon (1994) 'Practices of freedom: "Citizenship" and the politics of identity in the age of AIDS', in Simon Watney, *Practices of freedom: Selected writings on HIV/AIDS*. London: Rivers Oram Press.

Watney, Simon (1994) *Practices of Freedom: Selected Writings on HIV/AIDS*. London: Rivers Oram Press.

Watney, Simon (1994) 'Queer epistemology: Activism, "outing", and the politics of sexual identities', *Critical Quarterly*, vol. 36, no. 1, spring, pp. 13–27.

Weaver, James (1992) 'The social science and psychological research evidence: Perceptual and behavioural consequences of exposure to pornography', in Catherine Itzin (ed.), *Pornography: Women, Violence and Civil Liberties*. Oxford: Oxford University Press.

Weeks, Jeffrey (1977) *Coming Out: Homosexual Politics in Britain, from the Nineteenth Century to the Present*. London: Quartet Books.

Weeks, Jeffrey (1985) *Sexuality and its Discontents: Meaning, Myths and Modern Sexualities*. London: Routledge.

Weeks, Jeffrey (1986) *Sexuality*. London: Routledge.

Weeks, Jeffrey (1991) *Against Nature: Essays on History, Sexuality and Identity*. London: Rivers Oram Press.

Weeks, Jeffrey (1995) 'History, desire, and identities', in Richard G. Parker and John H. Gagnon (ed), *Conceiving Sexuality: Approaches to Sex Research in a Postmodern World*. London: Routledge.

Wellings, Kaye, Field, Julia, Johnson, Anne and Wadsworth, Jane (1994) *Sexual Behaviour in Britain: A National Survey of Sexual Attitudes and Lifestyles*. London: Penguin Books.

West, Celeste (1989) *A Lesbian Love Advisor: The Sweet and Savory Arts of Lesbian Courtship*. Pittsburgh: Cleis Press.

Whitam, Frederick L. and Mathy, Robin M. (1991) 'Childhood cross-gender behavior of homosexual females in Brazil, Peru, the Philippines, and the United States', *Archives of Social Behaviour*, vol. 20, no. 2, pp. 151–70.

Whitehead, Harriet (1981) 'The bow and the burden strap: A new look at institutionalized homosexuality in Native North America', in Sherry B. Ortner, and Harriet Whitehead (eds), *Sexual Meanings: The Cultural Construction of Gender and Sexuality*. Cambridge: Cambridge University Press.

Wieringa, Saskia (1989) 'An Anthropological critique of constructionism: Berdaches and butches', in Dennis Altman *et al.*, *Homosexuality, Which Homosexuality?: Essays from the International Scientific Conference on Lesbian and Gay Studies*. London: Gay Men's Press.

Wilby, Peter (1994) 'Research team defends 1-in-90 gay sex claim', *Independent On Sunday*, 23 January, p. 1.

Wilby, Peter (1994) 'The survey they tried to stop: Sex and the British', *Independent On Sunday*, 16 January, pp. 4–8.

Wilkinson, Sue (ed.) (1986) *Feminist Social Psychology: Developing Theory and Practice*. Milton Keynes: Open University Press.

Wilson, Elizabeth (1983) 'I'll climb the stairway to heaven: Lesbianism in the Seventies', in Sue Cartledge and Joanna Ryan (eds), *Sex and Love: New Thoughts on Old Contradictions*. London: Women's Press.

Wilson, Barbara (1991) 'The erotic life of fictional characters', in Judith Barrington (ed.), *An Intimate Wilderness: Lesbian Writers on Sexuality*. Oregon: Eighth Mountain Press.

Wilton, Tamsin (ed.) (1995) *Immortal Invisible: Lesbians and the Moving Image*. London: Routledge.

Winks, Cathy and Semans, Anne (1994) *The Good Vibrations Guide to Sex: How to Have Safe, Fun Sex in the '90s*. San Francisco, Cleis Press.

Winnow, Jackie (1992) 'Lesbians evolving health care: Cancer and AIDS', *Feminist Review*, no. 41, summer, pp. 68–76.

Woititz, Janet Geringer (1989) *Healing Your Sexual Self*. Florida: Health Communications.

Wolf, Deborah Goleman (1979) *The Lesbian Community*. London: University of California Press.

Wolf, Michelle A. and Kielwasser, Alfred P. (eds) (1991) *Gay People, Sex, and the Media*. London: Harrington Park Press.

World Health Organization (1992) *The ICD-10 Classification of Mental and Behavioural Disorders: Clinical Description and Diagnostic Guidelines*. Geneva: World Health Organization.

index